D1741404

Feminism and Religion in the 21st Century

This anthology of brand new essays will explore the new directions of conversations occurring in relation to feminism and religion, as well as the technological modes being utilized to continue dialogue, expand borders, and create new frontiers in feminism. It is a cross-generational project bringing together the voices of foresisters with those of the 21st-century generation of feminist scholars to discuss the changing direction of feminism and religion, new methods of dialogue, and the benefits for society overall.

Gina Messina-Dysert, PhD, is Dean of the School of Graduate and Professional Studies at Ursuline College and co-founder of the blog *Feminism and Religion.*

Rosemary Radford Ruether, PhD, is Professor of Feminist Theology at Claremont Graduate University and Claremont School of Theology.

Feminism and Religion in the 21st Century

Technology, Dialogue, and Expanding Borders

Edited by Gina Messina-Dysert and Rosemary Radford Ruether

NEW YORK AND LONDON

First published 2015
by Routledge
711 Third Avenue, New York, NY 10017

and by Routledge
2 Park Square, Milton Park, Abingdon, Oxfordshire OX14 4RN

First issued in paperback 2016

*Routledge is an imprint of the Taylor & Francis Group,
an informa business*

Library of Congress Cataloging-in-Publication Data
Feminism and religion in the 21st century : technology, dialogue, and
    expanding borders / [edited by] Gina Messina-Dysert and Rosemary
Ruether. — 1 [edition].
      pages cm
    Includes bibliographical references and index.
  1. Women and religion.   2. Feminism—Religious aspects.   3. Women
in technology.   4. Feminism and science.   I. Messina-Dysert, Gina, editor.
    BL458.F454 2014
    200.82—dc23
    2014020531

ISBN 13: 978-1-138-21927-4 (pbk)
ISBN 13: 978-0-415-83193-2 (hbk)

Typeset in Times New Roman
by Apex CoVantage, LLC

Contents

Acknowledgments

Gratitude is due to many who have supported the journey of this project. First, thank you to the School of Arts and Humanities, and particularly the Women's Studies in Religion Program, at Claremont Graduate University where the ideas for both the Feminism and Religion blogging project and this anthology were birthed. It is a community that continually nurtures creativity and scholarship and supports cutting edge ideas—especially those that encourage feminist dialogue and create positive social impact.

Specifically, thank you to Tammi J. Schneider; her ongoing willingness to support students and colleagues in their endeavors represents the true spirit of feminism. Likewise, Xochitl Alvizo, who has contributed to this volume, is an incredible feminist sister and conversation partner. Her encouragement and support allowed this project to grow into its current form. Also, thank you to Steve Wiggins, who saw value in this feminist collaboration and offered the opportunity to advance an idea into an ongoing dialogue.

Every person who has contributed to the Feminism and Religion blogging project has played a significant role in the development of this anthology, particularly Grace Kao, Caroline Kline, and Cynthia Garrity-Bond. Also, much appreciation must be expressed to the founders of and contributors to the Feminism in Religion Forum, especially Kate Ott. It is wonderful to contribute to projects that collaborate rather than compete.

Finally, sincere gratitude to Chris Messina-Dysert and Herman "Herc" Ruether for ongoing feminist dialogue and partnership.

Introduction

Rosemary Radford Ruether

This collection of essays, titled *Feminism and Religion in the 21st Century: Technology, Dialogue, and Expanding Borders,* is a pioneering publication. The various writers explore the transforming effects of communication technologies, the Internet, blogs, and social media platforms, such as Twitter and Facebook, in communities of women and men involved in religion and feminism. Women are heavily involved in the digital world, dominating blogs and being a majority of those using social media. These media break boundaries, communicating globally and across many divisions, while allowing women to relate to issues from their own personal experience.

Gina Messina-Dysert, co-editor of the collection and author of the essay, "#FemReligionFuture: The New Feminist Revolution in Religion," discusses the compatibility of the digital world with feminism. Men have traditionally dominated leadership in religion, as in society generally. Education in and communication of religious issues have often taken place in venues where women were excluded, in languages in which women were not fluent. Digital media, generally carried out in English, and based in individual computers in homes, libraries, school rooms, and even in places such as cafes or parks, are much more accessible to women. There is still some limitation of access to the digital world internationally and across economic class, due to lack of ownership and training in the use of the technology, but this is becoming increasingly widespread, with even poorer children receiving iPads and computers in grade school.

Social media largely dismantles hierarchies based on gender, education, and social status. Its democratic modes of participation allow women, without regard to status, to have an equal voice to interact and express their opinion. The reliance on personal experience allows women to speak from their own story and history, without being intimidated by those who carry high educational and job qualifications. This is particularly important for religious traditions that sharply divide the ordained from the laity, and where women have not been allowed ordination or even to enter the privileged spaces reserved for men with official status. Women can create a new sense of online feminist community through interchange of views. These communities, in turn, can generate organizing and activism. Women and men concerned with changing discriminatory practices, such as failure to grant ordination to women, can generate support through online movements.

Monica Coleman, a professor at the Claremont School of Theology, and student Yvonne Augustine, write particularly about the discrimination against women in ministry in churches, in their essay, "Blogging as Religious Feminist Activism." Not only do many denominations refuse ordination to women, but even those that do ordain women often make only small and poor communities available to women's leadership. Church services enforce patriarchy, by having only male leadership or, even with some female leaders, the authoritative voices are controlled by male elites. By contrast, the blogs allow women to speak with equal authority out of their own experience. Coleman's own blog, *BeautifulMindBlog.com*, allowed her to speak of personal experiences, such as miscarriage and depression, to which religious communities are often insensitive. This sort of popular communication creates community, and gives women who lead in creating blogs a ministry in relation to such communities. It is a ministry created by mutual recognition, not by hierarchical authority. Blogger and reader create a reciprocal ministry, with the blogger also receiving ministry. This is a feminist model of ministry.

Mary Hunt, founder of the feminist movement WATER (Women's Alliance for Theology, Ethics, and Ritual) in Washington, DC, in her essay "From Typewriters to Social Networking," details how their technology has continually been transformed in the thirty-year history of their organization. Starting with electric typewriters, pens, pencils, paper, stamps, and envelopes, they have continually evolved into a movement that communicates electronically around the world. Online communication has allowed them continued expansion of their communities of relationship.

Mormon feminist Caroline Kline explores how blogs can reshape religious conversation, opening up topics that are treated in the official tradition as closed. In Mormon feminist blogs, two topics are major issues of discussion, the ordination of women to the priesthood and the meaning of Heavenly Mother. Unlike most Christian denominations, the Latter-day Saints, or Mormons, see God as dual, a Heavenly Father and a Heavenly Mother. Although this view of the divine has been a part of Mormonism from its 19th-century beginnings, since the late 20th century, the leadership of the church has rarely referenced Heavenly Mother in its God discourse and has discouraged members from praying to her. Yet her existence and meaning remains an urgent issue, especially for Mormon feminists. On Mormon feminist blogs, she is often discussed, some women having personal and deeply meaningful experiences of her which they share, while others are skeptical of the usefulness of separate gender identified concepts of deity.

Mormonism also excludes women from being ordained in the priesthood. In her essay, Mormon feminist leader Margaret Toscano discusses the Mormon "Ordain Women" movement organized online. This was initiated on March 17, 2013, and immediately generated hundreds of thousands of hits, showing the broad concern about this issue and the willingness of many Mormons to discuss this taboo subject. A much smaller group, with 711 signers, endorsed their support for women in the priesthood. Although many more support the idea, this smaller number of signed supporters shows the reluctance of Mormons to publically dispute such an idea, an idea in conflict with the official leadership. More remarkable is the role in online communication in organizing an activist movement around this question.

Roman Catholicism is another world denomination with deep conflicts over male clerical leadership, the exclusion of women from priesthood, and hierarchical ways of control and communication. Catholic writer Michele Stopera Freyhauf, in her essay "The Catholic Church and Social Media," discusses the contradictory effects of social media as used by the clerical hierarchy, in contrast to its use by nuns. The hierarchy quickly recognized the usefulness of such social media, but their dogmatic ways of communicating turned off readers and generated critical reaction against them. Evidently, social media did not lend itself to such authoritarian styles of communication and generated negative response. By contrast, nuns, who are organized as religious orders but are much more democratic and are categorized as laity by the hierarchy, were able to use social media much more effectively in the style of open-minded conversation.

Paulist priest Brett Hoover, in his essay "Faith from Nowhere: Feminist Ecclesiological Reflections on the 'Liquid Catholicism' of New Media," discussed his experience in creating the Paulist-sponsored blog *BustedHalo*. He is particularly interested in the extent to which this media created communities that could themselves be seen as church "congregations." Although many saw their communication on *BustedHalo* as extending their church involvement, most also participated in sacramental communities. The new media can also inspire activism toward social justice, which is a key element in the mission of the Church to create the "Kingdom of God." Yet he concludes that such media cannot replace sacramental communities, even though they can extend their community building and social justice work.

Jewish leader Bracha Yael discusses a similar issue of media expansion of religious congregations in the essay "From Telephone to Live Broadcast: Becoming a Brick and Mortar Synagogue Without Walls." Here, television and live broadcast were developed to expand the presence of the Los Angeles Congregation Beth Chayim Chadashim (BCC) by making their services available to those confined to their homes or hospital rooms by illness. This was also developed as a "telephone Minyan" (religious community) in which groups of people could study the Torah together by telephone. This was even used internationally, allowing a gay couple marrying in Europe to share their wedding with their religious community back in Los Angeles. Again, the media did not replace, but expanded, the synagogue as a religious community.

Islam is another religious tradition that has been expanded and democratized by social media. In her essay "Private Space, Public Forum: A Netnographic Exploration of Muslim American Women; Access and Agency in 'Islamic' Cyberspace," Kristina Benson discusses the impact of two popular

Muslim sites, Islamicity.com and SuhaibWebb.com. Muslim women traditionally were very restricted by the use of Arabic as the preferred language for the discussion of Islamic issues, and the forbidding of women to be present in the same space with unrelated men for study, prayer, and education. The Islamic sites break down these restrictions of language and space. The preferred language is English, accessible to American Muslim women. The space restrictions disappear since those who communicate are not in the same space. The Islamic sites allow women to ask questions of "an Imam" and read articles, exploring a wide range of issues of interest to women in relation to their Islamic identity.

Xochitl Alvizo discusses the enhanced effect of blogs on educational transformation in her essay "Being Undone by the Other: Feminism, Blogs and Critique." In most classrooms, the professor stands at the head of the class in a position of authority, and the students are not in a position to refute what he or she says. Scholars also publish in journals, and some other scholars may write letters of criticism to which the author might reply, but direct confrontation is limited. On blogs, however, the critical interaction between writer and reader is much more direct and immediate. The writers may face criticism that demands a deep reconsideration of their argument. Relationships are much more egalitarian, and writers must interact with critics much more directly and immediately. The relationship of writers and readers become much more interactive and transformative criticism is expanded.

Other essays in this collection explore other educational and transformative effects of online media. Elise Edwards, in her essay "Television, Social Networking, and Cultural Criticism: Alternative Methodologies for Feminist Scholarship," explores the possibilities of more-focused criticism of the gender images that appear on television, and the ability to question the way these gender images transmit certain ideas about what men and women should be and how they should behave. Kate Ott, in her essay "Creating 'Open Source' Community: Just Hospitality or Cyberspace Ivory Tower?" explores feminist theologian Letty Russell's concept of "just hospitality." For Russell, "just hospitality" was a central part of the Christian mission and the creation of redemptive community. An open table where all are welcome breaks down unjust relations in society. Ott asks whether the open, democratic participation as equals created by social media can be seen as another way to advance this redemptive process of just hospitality in our society today.

Grace Kao, professor of Ethics at the Claremont School of Theology, in her essay "Feminist Pedagogy and Technology in the Classroom," reports on how she sought to transform her way of teaching her class on Feminist Ethics by adopting feminist pedagogy and social media technology. The terms of feminist pedagogy demanded that she relinquish some of her authority and integrate the students in planning the course and grading the work. Integrating new technology resulted in two new assignments: doing interactions on the blog *Feminism and Religion*, and writing up definitions of feminist ethical terms in a school version of Wikipedia. The second proved not very inspiring for students, who mainly saw it as a dogmatic way of communicating. The blogging interactions were much more enriching in the students' views. It also became evident to Kao that, despite her commitment to feminist pedagogy, students don't always like having to co-develop the structure of a course. They prefer the professor to do that work for them.

The Internet also provides resources for finding ancestors, which many find is a spiritual quest with ethical implications. In addition to names and dates, Internet searches provide historical documents and contexts. In "Finding Ancestor Connection via the Internet," Carol P. Christ, pioneering feminist theologian, discusses the Internet resources for searching for ancestors lost in the American "melting pot," considers the good and the bad in the stories of the ancestors she discovered, and reflects on the spiritual implications of ancestor connection.

Two concluding essays explore the important topic of the role of technology in embodiment. Sara Frykenberg discusses the role of online gaming in her essay "Inter-cendent Bodies: A Study of Cyborgs, Relational Theo/alogy, and Multiple Embodiment in 21st-Century Gaming." Frykenberg discusses her involvement in the online game *Elder Scrolls IV: Oblivion*. In the context of the game, which becomes an intensive part of one's life (many spend hundreds and even thousands of hours involved in a game), she transformed her identity, became a goddess, and interacted with others with other embodiments, such as cyborgs. Online gaming thus opens up transformed bodily and inner experiences for those involved.

Rachel Wagner and Sarah Scott's essay "Broken Body, Virtual Body: Cyberfeminism and the Changing Goddess," discusses how feminist visions of transcending limited views of women, to become a goddess or a fertile earth creator, is unhelpful for those women who have "broken bodies" and are suffering because of their lack of creative and reproductive power. Wagner and Scott explore alternative feminist imaginations of creativity that might be more helpful to women who are hurting due to bodily limitations that might provide alternatives for these women.

This volume of sixteen essays opens up a great diversity of subjects. It begins to allow us to realize the transformative possibilities that are being made available to people, especially women, thanks to social media technology. This is hardly the end of this fascinating subject. It gives us only a beginning of what new possibilities are becoming available, thanks to this new technology of communication and interaction.

Part I

Expanding Borders through Social Media

1 #FemReligionFuture

The New Feminist Revolution in Religion

Gina Messina-Dysert

The digital world has expanded borders for women and has offered tools for liberation in the form of blogging and other social media platforms, such as Twitter and Facebook. In the US, 42 million women are using social media alone, with blogs being the most influential platforms.[1] While male voices have largely controlled editorial pages and opinion pieces, the blogging world has offered women the opportunity to have their thoughts and ideas heard.

Women aren't only dominating blogs, they are also 64 percent of the users on Facebook, 58 percent of users on Twitter, and 82 percent of users on Pinterest.[2] Through status updates, tweets, and pins, women become "microbloggers" and are able to articulate ideas, promote particular movements, and foster change in 140 characters or less. According to Jessica Faye Carter, "For women, social media presents abundant opportunities to lead, effect change, innovate, and build relationships across sectors, locally, nationally, and globally."[3] Globalization has made social media a valuable way for women to break through boundaries, communicate beyond various divides, and expand the scope of feminist dialogue while reflecting on viewpoints embedded in their own life experiences.

Where women's participation in religion has often been suppressed due to its patriarchal structure, the digital world has offered women a voice. Whereas men have generally dominated leadership roles in religion and society overall, various forms of social media have offered women a space to articulate ideas, claim power, and further shape their communities—religious and otherwise. In this article, I will examine the feminist nature of social media and what has become known as the "online feminist revolution." I will explore the ways that feminist scholars, students, religious leaders, activists, and community members are using social media as a powerful mode of communicating and will demonstrate how this revolution has offered a space for dialogue and expanded borders in the field of feminism and religion.

The Feminist Nature of Social Media

The development of online technology has created new methods for communicating, leading, and acting, and can be understood as feminist in nature. While social media is not always utilized in a feminist way, it is a useful tool for feminists to share their perspectives widely within a public forum and is also a medium that can be easily adapted to feminist causes. Social media embodies feminist values in a number of ways: it eliminates hierarchies, is based largely on personal experience, and provides women with the ability to connect with other women, regardless of geographical and situational boundaries.

A democratic participation process is characteristic of blogs and social media platforms; persons are able to share their views on topics that they find important and others can respond with their own perspectives. Both instances allow for reflection on personal experience and result in hierarchy being broken. In addition, the focus on personal experience and sharing one's own story eliminates an authoritative tone. "Women are claiming their experience and voicing what is often not said within the confines of a patriarchal culture. In doing so, women are empowered and empower other women to claim their voice and speak their own truth."[4]

Social media also addresses accessibility issues for women. Geography and other life circumstances often keep women from meeting in physical locations. However, blogs and other social media platforms allow women to "gather" in a space where they can dialogue about issues that are important to them while participating in relationship building. Through these platforms, women are able to engage in conversations that are otherwise not accessible. In addition, as Gwendolyn Beetham and Jessica Valenti state, "contemporary globalization has made the Internet—and blogs in particular—a valuable way for feminists to communicate through and beyond various divides."[5]

There has been much debate about whether social media and the web offer tools and opportunities for new models of leadership. The Internet can be used to support and reinforce patriarchy and other forms of structural violence; certainly this is true. However, feminist movements online have demonstrated that development of leadership in such spaces can "provide a means of resisting the hierarchical, insular, monocultural structure of traditional institutions."[6]

Feminists who use online technology are continually creating new ways to act, while sparking new conversations that urge feminism in the 21st century onward. Recognizing social media as a powerful resource, feminists use it to propel movements forward, amplify their voices, and create change. Because the web allows for decentralized movements that uplift numerous voices, anyone with the ability to use online tools can share their ideas widely and become a leader in the feminist movement.

Online Feminism

Feminist work within online spaces has become a significant implementation of contemporary feminism. Technology allows feminists to harness the power of social media to create dialogue and encourage activism around issues related to gender equality and social justice. As Courtney Martin and Vanessa Valenti argue, "No other form of activism in history has empowered one individual to prompt tens of thousands to take action on a singular issue—within minutes."[7] Thus, online feminism, also known as the "new feminist revolution," has a widespread impact with endless potential.

The need for a public platform where women could voice their thoughts and opinions led to the rise of online feminism. Online forums, newsgroups, and blogs that surfaced early on provided a powerful space for feminist voices and propelled the next phase of the feminist movement forward. Beginning as simple sites, these spaces quickly grew into communities of hundreds of thousands. Those in search of platforms that allowed self-expression found them online through blogs and other social media platforms.

Online feminism brings new energy to the table and allows the personal to become political. The capacity for sharing experience and building community offers women a voice and eliminates feelings of isolation. This is particularly powerful for young women who look to online blogs and forums to find feminism, and the result can be life-saving connectivity. Today, women lead as social media users. The Pew Research Center's Internet and American Life Project completed in 2011 found that the "power users of social networking" are young adult women between the ages of 18 to 29 years old.[8]

Because of this trend, many have come to identify "feminist blogs as the consciousness-raising group of the 21st century."[9] As Martin and Valenti explain,

> The very functionality of blogs—the self-publishing platforms and commenting community—allow people to connect with each other, creating an intentional space to share personal opinions, experiences of injustice, and ideas, all with a feminist lens. Consciousness-raising groups were said to be the "backbone" of second-wave feminism; now, instead of a living room of 8–10 women, it's an online network of thousands.[10]

The development of social technologies has resulted in a wide range of web-based tools that have produced online feminism as we know it today.

Online feminism also offers a new channel for activism. In the past, women's suffrage and the second-wave movement took to the streets using protest signs and chants to advance the cause. Today, in the 21st century, feminists are using social media to promote feminist movements, raise awareness, and call for justice—all while organizing tens of thousands in minutes. As Martin and Valenti explain, "The rapid innovation and creativity that characterize online activist work are game-changers in the contemporary art of making change."[11]

Social media offers a new entry point for feminist activism and promotes citizen-produced media. For instance, online communities such as Feministing[12] and Feministe[13] offer platforms where bloggers are commenting on current events using a feminist lens. In doing so, social justice issues that are ignored by mainstream media are highlighted and brought to the forefront while engaging gender dynamics.

In addition to raising awareness, online feminism often offers paths for action that create a collective effort for change. Organizations such as Move

On[14] and Hollaback![15] have successfully utilized technology to build communities, share information, advance petitions and pledges, and utilize other social media tools to mobilize feminist action online and on the ground.

While online organizations and communities are making an incredible impact in the feminist movement, offline organizing continues to be an important tactic to "galvanize the masses." As Martin and Valenti point out, "Waves of protests across South Asia [in 2013] following the death of a 23-year-old gang rape victim in Delhi are just one powerful reminder of the impact that a collective group of people can make on the ground."[16]

This said, these protests are also a terrific example of how offline movements are participating in online feminism and how feminist activism has spread to the online world. Those who marched in Delhi's streets did so with technology in hand and were actively tweeting while protesting. The hashtag[17] #Delhibraveheart was added to tweets and other social media posts, which allowed persons from around the world to participate in the movement. Those who were not in Delhi but also passionate about the movement were able to keep up with the protest while sharing their own thoughts through social media using the same hashtag. Although the initial reaction to the protests by government officials was weak, the combination of both street and online activism compelled a response.

Online activist work has become understood as a game changer in contemporary movements for social justice. Rallies and marches on the ground demand weeks and often months to prepare and organize people in a particular location. However, thousands can be mobilized in a matter of minutes via online feminism. "Whether you're signing an online petition, participating in a Twitter campaign against harmful legislation, or blogging about a news article, technological tools have made it infinitely easier for people invested in social justice to play their part."[18]

It must also be noted that online feminism has created a space for radical learning and accountability. There is no one single feminist movement; rather, numerous intersectional movements are working in tandem and learning from one another, resulting in an inevitable and thriving multiplicity. While the feminist movement has a complicated history and continues to battle various "isms"—including racism, classism, homophobia, and other forms of oppression—online technology has "allowed for a more open space of accountability and learning, helping to push mainstream feminism to be less monolithic."[19]

Intersectionality, a theory of practice widely recognized within the world of online feminism, focuses on the "intersecting" identities that women hold and how they contribute to their overall experience of oppression.[20] Understanding privilege and the ways it impacts our work and positions within community is a major focus for online feminist dialogue. The trending hashtag #SolidarityIsForWhiteWomen is an important example of how social media platforms have functioned to move the conversation forward and continue the struggle against "isms."

Launched by Mikki Kendall, the hashtag "was intended to be Twitter shorthand for how often feminists of color are told that the racism they experience 'isn't a feminist issue.'"[21] #SolidarityIsForWhiteWomen quickly spread across Twitter, and persons from various backgrounds were chiming in to share their experiences and frustrations. The hashtag was then picked up by bloggers and across other social media platforms. Dirk von der Horst and Marian Williams both weighed in on the issue on the blog *Feminism and Religion*.[22] NPR and *The Huffington Post*[23] were also among major news sources that shared stories examining #SolidarityIs-ForWhiteWomen and the need for dialogue. The result was—and is—an ongoing conversation "between feminists about feminism and its future."[24]

The New Feminist Revolution in Religion

The intersecting of online feminism and religion has led to a new feminist revolution in religion that is expanding borders and building new frontiers. Recognizing the benefits and the potential of the online feminist movement, theologians and activists have collaborated to create new spaces for feminist thought in religion. Whereas women continue to be discriminated against within the confines of patriarchal religious traditions, the creation of feminist online platforms offer a space where women can participate in the benefits of the new feminist revolution—they can articulate thoughts, share experience, claim power, become leaders, and work for change. Websites and blogging communities allow women and men to come together, across borders, to discuss various issues related to religion and social justice from a feminist perspective. Online movements are creating new paths for activism related to women's issues in religion. The result is that social media and online spaces are reanimating the feminist movement in religion. Women's experiences and voices are being uplifted, they are claiming leadership roles, and continuing activism through new channels.

Experience

Martin and Valenti discuss the importance of personal experience, storytelling, and building relationships that takes place online, a critical element for women who are in search of dialogue related to religion. As Carol Christ states, the "voices of women are a lifeline."[25]

> Without stories a woman is lost when she comes to make the important decisions of her life. She does not learn to value her struggles, to celebrate her strengths, to comprehend her pain. Without stories she cannot understand herself. Without stories she is alienated from those experiences of self and world that have been called spiritual or religious. She is closed in silence. The expression of women's spiritual quest is integrally related to the telling of women's stories. If women's stories are not told, the depth of women's souls will not be known.[26]

The web world provides access to women's stories and allows women to connect regardless of geographical or other situational factors. It permits the sharing of experience and community building, something quite significant, given the level of isolation some women experience, particularly in relation to their religious traditions.

According to Christ,

> the most meaningful mode of writing feminist thealogy is to tell our stories in such a way that we confront the sources of our despair and name anew the great powers that give shape and meaning to our lives . . . there is no other way for us to express the new visions of the sacred that emerge as we heal the trauma of having been closed in silence for so long.[27]

Thus, theological discourses are also transformative narratives; they have the ability to change the way we think. Women who utilize social media are "breaking their silence, naming their own experiences and participating in discourses that have transformative powers."[28]

Feminist Leadership and Spaces in Religion

Although women are accepted as members and participants within patriarchal religious traditions, gender dynamics continue to be a serious issue. Women in both Catholic and Mormon traditions are refused ordination. Muslim women cannot lead prayer within congregations that include both genders, and Jewish women are limited in prayer at the Western Wall in Jerusalem. Scriptural interpretations are often misogynistic, and violence against women continues to be linked to theological misunderstandings. Thus, women within patriarchal religious traditions have responded with a call for justice and continue to do so today using online technology.

Where their traditions have denied women leadership roles, the capabilities of online technology turns the tables. The power of social media allows women to circumnavigate patriarchal systems to become leaders that can effect real change. For example, Mary Hunt is a foresister of the feminist movement in religion who embraced technology as a powerful resource early on.[29] She co-founded (with Diann Neu) the Women's Alliance for Theology, Ethics and Ritual (WATER) in 1983, "in response to the need for theological, ethical, and liturgical development for and by women."[30] Since its inception, the organization has grown and now offers resources and services to women around the world who are passionate about feminist issues in religion. Through teleconferences, blogs, and continued work using various social media outlets, Hunt has changed the conversation. She has paved the way for the next generation of feminist scholars and activists in the field, while demonstrating the incredible impact one voice can make in the movement.

Today, feminist scholars and activists in religion continue to utilize technology as a means of "taking the microphone" and making their voices heard.

Monica Coleman has established herself as a leader in feminist and womanist theology through traditional scholarship[31] and also with her website,[32] *BeautifulMindBlog.com*,[33] Facebook,[34] Twitter,[35] and YouTube.[36] In addition, she blogs on a regular basis with other sites, including *Feminism and Religion,*[37] *Patheos,*[38] and *The Huffington Post.*[39] Likewise, Najeeba Syeed utilizes her website,[40] Tumblr,[41] Twitter,[42] and Facebook[43] as a means of continuing her scholarship within the online world and encouraging dialogue in relation to feminist issues for Islamic women.

Caroline Kline has been instrumental in leading the Mormon feminist movement forward as a result of her co-founding the Mormon feminist blog, *The Exponent.*[44] The site brings together an array of women's voices from around the world to examine gendered issues that challenge women in the Mormon Church. On average, the site receives about 60,000 hits per month and hosts an ongoing dialogue on Mormon feminist issues. The opportunities to share experience, build relationships, and work for change have made *The Exponent* a key resource among Mormon women.

Kline also collaborated with me, Xochitl Alvizo, and Cynthia Garrity Bond to co-found *Feminism and Religion,* a blogging site dedicated to exploring feminism in relation to religion and social justice while bringing academics, activists, and the greater community together to engage in dialogue. Since its inception in 2011, the site has grown to a community that extends to 181 countries and on every continent around the world, a testament to the need for such platforms and their abilities to create change. Foresisters of the feminist movement in religion and theo/alogy—including Amina Wadud, Carol Christ, Kelly Brown Douglas, Rita Gross, and Rosemary Radford Ruether—embrace technological opportunities and participate in ongoing conversations. They take part in the building of new frontiers while encouraging the next generation of feminist scholars and activists to carry the movement forward.

Furthermore, with the goal of "generat[ing] new feminist scholarship in religion and to create spaces for such scholarship to emerge,"[45] Kate Ott has been a key leader behind reshaping the non-profit organization Feminist Studies in Religion, Inc., or FSR, Inc.[46] She serves on the board, and manages and regularly contributes to the companion website *Feminist Studies in Religion*[47] that includes both the journal and the *Feminist Studies in Religion Forum.*[48] The site brings together both academia and grassroots movements to further dialogue and is well recognized for its history in the feminist movement in religion.

Each of these women and these spaces are making an incredible impact in the field of feminism and religion through online technology. Their voices are no longer confined to the walls of academia or small gatherings in libraries or coffee shops; instead a global conversation is ensuing that includes new perspectives and experiences. Utilizing blogs and other social media platforms, they are able to engage a larger audience, dialogue with diverse voices, and continue their own learning in the process. In doing so, borders are being expanded, and new frontiers in feminism are being built.

Activism

The intersection of online feminism and religion has also created a new space to work for change. Feminist leadership coupled with the powerful resource of social media has created a new entry point for activism focused on women's issues and social justice. With continued conversations about the need for women's leadership within patriarchal religious traditions, movements have been developed utilizing online resources to work toward reducing gender inequalities.

WATER, *The Exponent, Feminism and Religion,* and *Feminist Studies in Religion,* all participate in activism through their webwork. Feminist theologians and activists engage in multiple women-focused causes through online platforms, including reproductive justice and violence against women. This said, the issue of women's ordination is one that has received major attention in social media campaigns.

The Women's Ordination Conference (WOC),[49] a Catholic movement to ordain women, has been operating on the ground since 1974. Now with a full online campaign, WOC hosts a regular blog, connects with others via Facebook[50] and Twitter,[51] and organizes on-the-ground rallies using social media. Thanks to the brilliant mind of Assistant Director Kate Conmy, WOC increased the profile of its campaign with over 160,000 hits on its YouTube video "Ordain a Lady."[52] Likewise, *Roman Catholic Women Priests*[53] utilizes social media to organize, share information about upcoming ordinations, and call for women priests in the Catholic Church.

Ordain Women[54] is the newest online campaign focused on Mormon women's ordination and launched in March 2013. With the belief that "women must be ordained in order for our faith to reflect the equity and expansiveness of these teachings," Ordain Women has set out to draw attention to the gender inequalities and work for women's ordination in the Mormon Church. The site began by showcasing twenty-eight profiles—a purposeful mirror of the "I am a Mormon" LDS campaign—of mostly Mormon individuals who support women's ordination. This was and is an incredible act of courage, considering the potential threat of excommunication for publicly taking a stand against Church teaching. Since its launch, there are now hundreds of profiles online, with new supporters joining the campaign daily.

The campaign organized an on the ground "gathering" of women on October 5, 2013, in Salt Lake City, Utah, in Temple Square who requested entrance into an all-male priesthood meeting.[55] While they were denied admission, Ordain Women achieved huge successes. Utilizing technology, the online campaign brought together women from around the country to participate in the gathering. In addition, the all-male priesthood was forced to take a serious look at the situation and develop a response. While women were not admitted to the meeting, the Church decided to televise the meeting for the first time in history, a major victory for Ordain Women. Finally, following the on-the-ground movement coupled with the online campaign, Ordain Women received major media attention and its site had nearly 50,000 hits on the first day following the gathering outside the priesthood meeting. Their cause was moved into the spotlight and is now getting the attention it deserves.

Conclusion

Whereas women have been silenced by traditional forms of media, online spaces have given women a voice. In doing so, the digital world has offered liberative tools that expand borders and create new frontiers. Online feminism has changed the way that contemporary feminism is celebrated and enacted. With the significant opportunities presented via social media platforms, women are able to claim leadership roles, effect change, and build global communities while reflecting on their personal experiences.

The intersection of religion and online feminism has created a new feminist revolution in religion. Harnessing the power of social media to create dialogue and encourage activism related to gender-based issues is a game changer. Feminist scholars, theologians, and activists no longer experience some of the major limitations that existed in the past. Rather than being confined to the walls of academia, they are able to engage in global dialogue, resulting in evolving conversations that examine multiple perspectives and experiences.

Through blogging communities and other social media platforms, women are able to share and learn from other women's experiences in religion. They are breaking silence, telling stories, and building relationships while honoring the roles women play in their traditions. In doing so, women are amplifying their voices and claiming leadership roles. Furthermore, with the power of online spaces, feminist activist movements have the potential to engage the energy of persons from around the world to make change. Thus, online technology has changed the way the feminist movement functions and online feminism has intersected with religion to expand borders, build new frontiers, and uplift women's roles within their traditions.

Notes

1. Anita Campbell, "42 Million U.S. Women Use Social Media: Blogs Most Influential," *Small Business Trends,* http://smallbiztrends.com/2009/05/42-million-women-use-social-media-blogs.html, cited in Gina Messina-Dysert, "Women and Blogging: An Exercise in the Thealogy of Carol Christ," in *Journal of Religion and Popular Culture* 23, no. 2 (July 2011): 155–165.
2. See Britney Fitzgerald, "More Women on Facebook, Twitter, and Pinterest Than Men," *The Huffington Post,* July 9, 2012, www.huffingtonpost.com/2012/07/09/women-facebook-twitter-pinterest_n_1655164.html.
3. Jessica Faye Carter, "Why Social Media Means Big Opportunities for Women," *Mashable,* Feburary 15, 2010, http://mashable.com/2010/02/15/social-media-women/
4. Gina Messina-Dysert, "Women and Blogging: An Exercise in the Thealogy of Carol Christ," in *Journal of Religion and Popular Culture* 23, no. 2 (July 2011): 158.
5. Gwendolyn Beetham and Jessica Valenti, "Blogging Feminism: (Web)Sites of Resistance," *The Scholar and Feminist Online* 5, no. 2 (Spring 2007), www.barnard.edu/sfonline/reprotech/index.htm.

6. Martin and Valenti, 11.
7. Courtney E. Martin and Vanessa Valenti, "What Is Online Feminism?" *#FemFuture: Online Revolution.* New Feminist Solutions Series, Vol. 8. (2013): 6, http://bcrw.barnard.edu/wp-content/nfs/reports/NFS8-FemFuture-Online-Revolution-Report-April-15-2013.pdf.
8. Mary Madden and Kathryn Zickuhr, "65% of Online Adults Use Social Networking Sites," Pew Internet and American Life Project, 2011, http://pewinternet.org/Reports/2011/Social-Networking-Sites.aspx.
9. Ibid.
10. Ibid.
11. Martin and Valenti, 8.
12. See www.feministing.com.
13. See www.feministe.com.
14. Move On is a community of 8 million people using technology to work for progressive change: http://front.moveon.org/.
15. Hollaback! is a non-profit organization and movement to end street harassment: www.ihollaback.org/.
16. Martin and Valenti, 7.
17. A hashtag is represented by the # and functions as a filter for a particular theme or meme. A meme is an idea or action that spreads online from person to person using mimicry and can take various forms (i.e., image, hyperlink, video, website, or hashtag). For instance, #DelhiBraveheart is a meme.
18. Martin and Valenti, 8.
19. Ibid., 17.
20. See Leslie McCall, "The Complexity of Intersectionality," *Journal of Women in Culture and Society* 30, no. 3 (Spring 2005): 1771–1800.
21. Mikki Kendall, "#SolidarityisforWhiteWomen: Women of Color's Issue with Digital Feminism," *The Guardian,* August 14, 2013, www.theguardian.com/commentisfree/2013/aug/14/solidarityisforwhitewomen-hashtag-feminism.
22. See Dirk von der Horst, "#SolidarityIsForWhiteWomen and the Power of Micropolitics," *Feminism and Religion* (blog), September 18, 2013, http://feminismandreligion.com/2013/09/18/solidarityisforwhitewomen-and-the-power-of-micropolitics-by-dirk-von-der-horst/; and Marian Williams, "Feminism vs. Humanism: A Response to an Idealized Feminist Identity," *Feminism and Religion* (blog), September 30, 2013, http://feminismandreligion.com/2013/09/30/feminism-vs-humanism-a-response-to-an-idealized-feminist-identity-by-mariam-williams/.
23. See "Twitter Sparks a Serious Discussion about Race and Feminism," NPR, August 23, 2013, www.npr.org/blogs/codeswitch/2013/08/22/214525023/twitter-sparks-a-serious-discussion-about-race-and-feminism; and Sarah Milstein, "5 Ways White Feminists Can Address Our Racism," *The Huffington Post,* September 24, 2013, www.huffingtonpost.com/sarah-milstein/5-ways-white-feminists-can-address-our-own-racism_b_3955065.html.
24. Ibid.
25. Carol Christ, *Rebirth of the Goddess: Finding Meaning in Feminist Spirituality* (New York: Addison Wesley Publishing, 1997), 41.
26. Carol Christ, *Diving Deep and Surfacing: Women Writers on Spiritual Quest* (Boston, MA: Beacon Press, 1980), 1.
27. Christ, *Diving Deep and Surfacing,* 138.
28. Messina-Dysert, 158.
29. See Mary Hunt, "From Typewriters to Social Networking: A Feminist Organization's Techno History," in *Feminism and Religion in the 21st Century: Technology, Dialogue, and Expanding Borders,* ed. Gina Messina-Dysert and Rosemary Radford Ruether (New York: Routlege, 2014), 69–76.
30. "About Us," WATER, www.waterwomensalliance.org/about-us/.

31. Note that I use "traditional scholarship" to refer to publishing in print, scholarly journals, and books. Use of technology to continue dialogue through blogging, podcasting, tweeting, and other social media platforms must also be understood as scholarship and is often referred to as engaged or public scholarship.
32. See http://monicaacoleman.com.
33. See http://monicaacoleman.com/blog/.
34. Access Monica Coleman's public Facebook page at www.facebook.com/revdrmon ica?v=app_4949752878&ref=ts.
35. Access Coleman's Twitter feed at https://twitter.com/monicaacoleman.
36. Coleman's Youtube channel can be accessed at www.youtube.com/user/ revdrmonica?feature=watch.
37. Coleman's blogs on *Feminism and Religion* can be accessed at http://feminisman dreligion.com/author/mcolemancst/.
38. Coleman's blogs on *Patheos* can be accessed at www.patheos.com/About-Patheos/ Monica-Coleman.html.
39. Coleman's blogs on *The Huffington Post* can be accessed at www.huffingtonpost. com/monica-a-coleman/.
40. Najeeba Syeed's website can be accessed at http://najeeba.com/.
41. Syeed's blog *Najeeba's Peace* on Tumblr can be accessed at http://najee basyeedmiller.tumblr.com/.
42. Syeed's Twitter feed can be accessed at https://twitter.com/NajeebaSyeed.
43. Syeed's public Facebook page can be accessed at www.facebook.com/pages/ Najeeba-Syeed-miller/138101682881264.
44. See *The Exponent,* www.the-exponent.com/.
45. See "About FSR," *Feminist Studies in Religion,* www.fsrinc.org/fsr/about-fsr.
46. *The Journal of Feminist Studies in Religion* can be accessed at www.fsrinc.org/jfsr.
47. See *Feminist Studies in Religion,* www.fsrinc.org/.
48. See *The Feminist Studies in Religion Forum,* www.fsrinc.org/blog.
49. For more on the Women's Ordination Conference see www.womensordination. org/.
50. WOC's Facebook page can be accessed at www.facebook.com/OrdainWomen? ref=br_tf.
51. WOC's Twitter feed can be accessed at https://twitter.com/OrdainWomen.
52. See "Ordain A Lady," www.youtube.com/watch?feature=player_detailpage& v=Y0S2WlvNTU8.
53. For more on Roman Catholic Women Priests, see http://romancatholicwomen- priests.org/.
54. For more on Ordain Women, see http://ordainwomen.org. Also see Caroline Kline, "Mormons Who Advocate Women's Ordination," *Feminism and Religion* (blog), March 26, 2013, http://feminismandreligion.com/2013/03/26/mormons-advocate- for-womens-ordination-by-caroline-klline/; Margaret Toscano, "Women's Ordina- tion and the Mormon Church," *Feminism and Religion* (blog), April 5, 2013, http:// feminismandreligion.com/2013/04/05/womens-ordination-and-the-mormon- church-by-margaret-toscano/ ; and Toscano, "The Mormon" Ordain Women "Move- ment: The Virtue of Virtual Activism," in *Feminism and Religion in the 21st Century: Technology, Dialogue, and Expanding Borders,* ed. Gina Messina-Dysert and Rosemary Radford Ruether (New York: Routledge, 2014), 153–166.
55. See Aimee Hickman, "Making Inequality Visible: Mormons Seeking Women's Ordination Are Turned Away from Priesthood Conference," *Feminism and Religion* (blog), October 22, 2013, http://feminismandreligion.com/2013/10/22/making- inequality-visible-mormons-seeking-womens-ordination-are-turned-away-from- priesthood-conference-by-aimee-hickman/.

2 Blogging as Religious Feminist Activism

Ministry To, Through, With, and From

Monica A. Coleman with
C. Yvonne Augustine

Although women increasingly are represented in ordained Christian ministry, they still rarely receive proportionate or equal treatment with their male clergy counterparts. The last fifteen years have seen the creation and rise of online journaling, commonly known as blogging. Blogging can facilitate activist activity around issues that religious feminists have long advocated: breaking silence and raising consciousness, cultivating a hermeneutic of suspicion, and creating community. Unlike traditional forms of church leadership, blogging can facilitate forms of ministry with rhizomatic networking, as women find healing for their wounds.

Women are often outside of the power structures of Christian communities. That is, church can be a particularly patriarchal setting. In her introduction to feminist theology, Anne M. Clifford notes that most people experience "being church" at Sunday services. Yet in those worship services, the "secondary status of women is symbolically reinforced."[1] Sunday services usually includes preaching and scriptures that rarely focus on women, and invoke language in prayers, songs, and liturgies that suggest that men represent the whole of humanity before God (i.e., "faith of our fathers," "brotherhood of believers").

While women have long been accepted as members of Christian congregations, they are not equally represented in church leadership. In 1853, Antoinette Brown (a Unitarian) became the first woman ordained into ministry in the United States. A 2010 study shows that only 12 percent of American Christian congregations have female pastors.[2] In some mainline Protestant denominations, statistics reveal that up to 40 percent of clergy are women. The numbers are as low as 2–8 percent in evangelical and Pentecostal traditions. Ordination of women has not led to equal treatment in ministry. Female clergy are more likely to be associate or assistant clergy or employed as chaplains in hospitals, prisons, or colleges than to serve as a lead pastor of a local church.[3] Clifford concludes that "ordained women constitute a type of 'second-class' status among the ordained."[4] Catholicism and several Protestant Christian denominations still disallow women from ordained ministry.

In the denominations where women are ordained as clergy, they often report discrimination in both church assignment and treatment by parishioners and other officers within the church structure. Ordained African Methodist

Episcopal minister Renita Weems writes of her decision not to pursue full-time parish ministry, noting how female pastors are treated: "Women who entered the ministry [in the late 1970s], when I was ordained, endured the mocks and jeers of family, friends, and male ministers in order to be ordained and had nothing to look forward to but assignments to a string of some of the smallest, poorest, and most difficult charges in the conference."[5] While things have improved since then, there is still a lack of equity in the pastoral experience for women and men—whether the discrimination comes from church authoritative structures, or from parishioners in the congregation.

This discussion of female clergy assumes traditional concepts of ministry wherein a minister is one who has the authority (usually through ordination from a hierarchical or congregational authority) to teach, proclaim, and perform religious services, most notably sacraments. Having worked outside of ordained ministry for so long, many women have assumed leadership and service roles in church auxiliaries, missionary activity, working with youth, and as lay preachers. Unless preaching, however, women rarely name their church activism as "ministry."

The blogosphere presents new opportunities for women in ministry. Some women are able to explicitly discuss the role of feminism in religion through their blogs. In other blogs, women discuss the intersection of faith and women's issues. An examination of selected blogs reveals that blogging can embrace the values of religious feminism, and re-form ministry in non-hierarchical manners.

Blogging

The modern blog has roots in 1994 when a couple of individuals kept online diaries. In 1997, Jorn Barger coined the term "weblog."[6] The short form "blog" is widely credited to Peter Merholz, who contracted the term into "we blog" on his own weblog.[7] With the advent of free and inexpensive blogging software and programs, blogging is, in the words of media pundit and author Jeff Jarvis, "the easiest, cheapest, fastest publishing tool ever invented."[8] More than a regularly updated website, a blog has particular genre characteristics. In their discussion of blogging as social action, Carolyn R. Miller and Dawn Shepherd note that blogs are known by "their reverse chronology, frequent updating, and combination of links with personal commentary."[9]

While the format of the blog is part of what makes blogs so effective, the content as per the blogger is the reason for the popularity of most blogs. Blogging in reverse chronological order "provides a sense of immediacy . . . that reinforces the impression that the content is true."[10] Readers expect a level of authenticity in blogs. (This is most revealed in the controversies that arise when readers find that a blog persona has been fictionalized.) The co-founder of Pyra (the company that created Blogger blogging software) Evan Williams lists "personality" as one of the three characteristics that create a blog's popularity.[11] Shepherd and Miller connect this "personality" to the content of the blog. That is, the blog's content is meant to be revelatory of the blogger's self. Even as the blogger constructs a self through the blog (as one would in any public medium), the blogger selects and presents herself or himself in a way that is "genuinely personal." Thus, the format of blogging becomes a revolutionary act of claiming self and voice. Jarvis applauds blogging for exactly this reason when he says, "The people have a voice they didn't have before."

Religious Feminism

As an offering of self and voice, blogs are poised to reflect the values of religious feminism. In their introduction to feminist theology, Lisa Isherwood and Dorothea McEwan note that various feminist interpretations of Christianity stress "the importance of relationships, of justice making, of locating truths in the lived experience [and] of the need for solidarity."[12] Three themes frequently arise in religious women's blogging: (1) breaking silence and raising consciousness, (2) cultivating a hermeneutic of suspicion, and (3) creating community.

Breaking Silence/Raising Consciousness

In her well-known essay "The Transformation of Silence into Language and Action," black feminist Audre Lorde describes the importance of breaking silence for feminist activism. She begins by stating that it is important to overcome fear and judgment in order to give voice to personal experience. She writes, "I have come to believe over and over again that what is most important to me must be spoken, made verbal and shared, even at the risk of having it bruised or misunderstood."[13] Breaking silence is not just for the purposes of self-revelation. It is also important to share the stories and experiences of other women. Lorde writes, "And where the words of women are crying to be heard, we must each of us recognize our responsibility to seek those words out, to read them and share them and examine them in their pertinence to our lives."[14]

Breaking silences is helpful in forming feminist community. Lorde writes,

> But for every real word spoken, for every attempt I had ever made to speak those truths for which I am still seeking, I had made contact with other women while we examined the words to fit a world in which we all believed, bridging our differences.[15]

Lorde implies that the contact with other women helped to bridge differences as they sought words for their experiences.

Thus, it is feminist activity when women write and speak about issues where there is often silence and shame. This becomes most powerful when linking one's personal experience with the experiences of other women and political action. The feminist movement of the 1960s and 1970s referred to this as "consciousness-raising." Borrowing the technique from the United States civil rights movement, Kathie Sarachild outlined a program for "Radical Feminist Consciousness-Raising" used by the New York Radical Women wherein women gathered in small groups to share their personal experiences of an issue (usually related to the oppression of women). Sharing the personal stories enabled connections to larger political realities.[16] Sarachild concludes, "Consciousness-raising was seen as both a method for arriving at the truth and a means for action and organizing."[17] It was a process by which one comes to see that "the personal is political."[18] Mujerista and Latina theologians often call this "conscientization," wherein the goal is to encourage people to listen to and validate their experiences—especially experiences of subjugation.[19]

Blogger Renita Weems is explicit about her intent in breaking silences through her blog. Weems blogged on BeliefNet.com and her own blog at SomethingWithin.com. *Something Within* carries the tagline: "for thinking women of faith." Weems notes that she blogs at *Something Within* for public impact as a woman,

> It was time for me as a woman in ministry, a [Hebrew Bible] scholar who's written about religion, gender, and pop culture, and as someone who's written books on inner healing that it's important that I add my voice to those trying to make sense of the things taking place in our broader society.[20]

As Weems notes that she will comment on public events, she is also clear that silence is a form of religious transgression. Weems writes, "What does it matter if I'm a woman of faith if I'm silent about what I see and perceive are those luminous moments when things are more than they seem?"[21]

In one post, Weems writes about how she is wearing red in solidarity with those who stand up against violence against women, especially sexual and domestic violence. Weems describes the intimate violence experienced by her grandmother and stories current in the news headlines. This personal sharing leads to sharing by others. In the comments of this post, other women indicate that they, too, are wearing red to honor the experiences of their great grandmother or mother or daughter or self who has survived (or sometimes died from) domestic violence or rape.[22] As Weems breaks her own family's silence, other women share their stories and lament about the news headlines. They then take political action—most by wearing red, others by indicating that they are planning to attend the rally about the recent victim in the news.

FeminismAndReligion.com is a blog started by female graduate students in Women's Studies in Religion at Claremont Graduate University. With more than thirty regular contributors and additional guest contributors, *Feminism and Religion (FAR)* explicitly strives to share the learnings from the academy with a wider public. They note that the blog's hope is that "feminist scholars of religion—and all who are interested in these issues—will use this forum to share their ideas, insights, and experiences, so that this community of thinkers will be nurtured as we explore diverse and new directions."[23] This blog transgresses gender and religious boundaries with male and female contributors covering Christianity, goddess traditions, Islam, Hinduism, atheism, etc.

FAR co-founder Gina Messina-Dysert stresses that giving voice to challenges has been an important function of *Feminism and Religion*. She says, "The shared experience and feeling of being validated is so important. Being able to speak your pain—to publicly acknowledge your struggles, the ways you've been oppressed is crucial in the healing process and that certainly takes place on *FAR*."[24] Like the aforementioned post on *Something Within*, Messina-Dysert also experiences camaraderie with those who respond to her blog posts. She specifically mentions the response to writing about her struggle with infertility and Catholic expectations of women and biological motherhood: "My post about struggling with infertility was an incredibly healing moment as it made me realize I was not alone. So many [people] signed on to comment and share their own stories and grief. It was really amazing."[25] Messina-Dysert is clear that part of the power of breaking silences is to raise consciousness about ways that women experience oppression.

Cultivating a Hermeneutic of Suspicion

Another important theme of religious feminism involves using particular interpretive lenses that reveal oppression against women. Anne Clifford connects sin and patriarchal interpretation of texts and culture: "Reconstructionist feminist theology not only brings to consciousness the experiences of discrimination and subordination that patriarchy and androcentrism promote, but also unmasks them as not of God and therefore sinful."[26] Clifford's description implies that consciousness-raising may lead to a process of un-masking patriarchy. This un-masking of patriarchy is a key component of cultivating a hermeneutic of suspicion.

In religious feminism, New Testament scholar Elisabeth Schussler Fiorenza is best known for her adaptation of Paul Ricoeur's terminology of having a "hermeneutic of suspicion." Schussler Fiorenza notes that feminists should have a "hermeneutics of suspicion" rather than a hermeneutics of consent and affirmation.[27] A hermeneutics of suspicion raises consciousness in accounting for the culturally determined gender roles and patriarchy in biblical texts. "A hermeneutics of suspicion seeks to explore the liberating or oppressive values and visions inscribed in the text by identifying the androcentric-patriarchal character and dynamics of the text and its interpretations."[28] It is as important to note what is being said and done to women, as it is to note the places where there are silences.

Fiorenza balances this concept with a "hermeneutics of remembrance" that "seeks to uncover both the values inscribed in the text and the patriarchal or emancipatory interests of its historical contextualization."[29] In this move, interpreters can reclaim the value for women in the past and engage in modes of solidarity with women (in the past and present) who struggle for justice and dignity. This is followed by a hermeneutics of creative actualization where feminist interpreters actively engage women in the ongoing biblical story of liberation. Schussler Fiorenza writes that this hermeneutics "allows women to enter the biblical story with the help of historical imagination, artistic representation, and liturgical ritualization."[30] The hermeneutics of creative actualization is a constructive move that is oriented toward the future of women in churches.

I often invoke these feminist hermeneutics in my own experiences as blogger. I write on the intersection of depression and faith on my blog at BeautifulMindBlog.com. In a series I wrote after the miscarriage of twins, I critique how the Bible relays stories about barren women. In the biblical accounting of women's barrenness, infertility is always the woman's fault. In each scenario, the woman cries out to God, God "opens her womb," and the woman bears a male child who becomes an important religious leader. I directly connect this to patriarchy by opening the post, "I know that men wrote the Bible." I write about the complexity of miscarriage and infertility in today's world and about the women who supported me in the weeks after I miscarried. I then imagine what might occur if women wrote the Bible,

> If women wrote the Bible, it might mention how messy the enterprise of not having children really is. It might mention the girl children the women loved. It might talk about how the men were in the temple, while the bleeding women gathered somewhere else . . . If [I] wrote the Bible, I'd write about barren women and the women who support them.[31]

I combined my critique of biblical texts that give one-sided patriarchal views of barren women with an imaginative reconstruction that connected my experience and those of other contemporary women with the biblical women.

These hermeneutics of suspicion, remembrance, and creative actualization are common features of religious feminist blogging, although the "text" need not always be the Christian Bible. The *Feminist Studies in Religion* forum is one project of feminist religious scholarly activity connected to the *Journal of Feminist Studies in Religion*. Featuring several feminist and womanist scholars of religion, *FSR Inc.*'s blog offers feminist religious commentary on teaching, culture, world events, and academic news. In her blog on the 2013 Boston Marathon Bombing, Hebrew Bible scholar Susanne Scholz applies a hermeneutics of suspicion to the news coverage of the men accused of placing the bombs at the marathon. She notes the way the media refers to them as "disaffected young men," and asks why women tend to turn their disaffection inwardly, causing self-harm, while men turn to violent acts. Scholz juxtaposes her reading with remarks by governor of North Carolina Pat McCrory, who singles out gender studies as a focus of concentration that should not be supported by public universities because it does not "get someone a job."[32] Scholz interrogates the descriptions of the accused bombers by suggesting that a feminist reading offers more complex analysis: "Does the disaffection [of the accused bombers] indeed go back to the patriarchal order and images of masculinity? . . . At least, gender studies can point to the intersectionality of masculinity, ethnicity, class, geopolitics, and religion."[33] Scholz concludes by hoping that Governor McCrory will take a gender studies class at a local college so he can understand the value of feminist hermeneutics. Using the text of current events, Scholz also brings feminist hermeneutics to feminist religious blogging.

Creating Community

Creating non-hierarchical community is a value and goal of women's liberation and feminist religious scholarships. Like the consciousness-raising groups in women's homes, feminist communities are grounded in women's experience and understand the formation of women's communities as a political act. On the one hand, women's communities are political, as they connect personal individual experiences to larger political and policy issues. On the other hand, women's communities are political acts because they can serve as a source of empowerment, in contradistinction from communities where oppression is experienced. Isherwood and McEwan affirm the ways that many feminist theologies understand the connection between individual and community: "Feminist theologies are attempts to start with the individual and to stay with individual experience while also creating networks and communities of mutual empowerment."[34] Thus, the creation of community is often an explicit for feminist religious activism.

Speaking of *FAR*, Messina-Dysert states that she always intended for the blog to create community. For Messina-Dysert, the formation of community is closely tied to diversity and transgressing traditional boundaries,

> Too often we keep these conversations [about feminism and religion] within the walls of academia or within the structure of the Church and *FAR* offer[s] an opportunity to bring voices together from different backgrounds, perspectives, and experiences to acknowledge the many issues women face in their traditions.[35]

Messina-Dysert's view of blog community comes from the varied perspectives represented in *FAR*.

Unlike the feminist consciousness-raising groups of the 1960s and 1970s, individuals are not gathering in small groups in someone's home. One must assess community formation differently for a blog. In an early article about the social networking that emerges from blogging, Torill Mortensen and Jill Walker state that blogs create networking as individuals link from one site to another,

> Weblogs tend to come together in clusters as they link to each other. A reader of your site may link to you; you see the link in your referral stats and start reading their blog. You find it interesting, and link back to it. The readers of your blog, some of who keep their own blogs, start reading the other blog, and some of them also link to it.[36]

As blogging has evolved with Web 2.0 technology that allows readers to contribute to the sites that they read, blogs often create community in the comments section. Messina-Dysert evaluates *FAR*'s community by the responses she receives: "Every time someone says 'Yes, that is my experience too,' it is incredibly validating."[37]

Therese Borchard also notes the ways that responses to her blog create community. Borchard is a mental health writer who blogged at *Beyond Blue* on BeliefNet.com. Started in 2006, *Beyond Blue* was named a top depression blog various times between 2007 and 2013 by entities such as the Depression Treatment Center, PsychCentral.com, and Healthline.com. Although depression affects men and women, the National Institute of Mental Health notes that women are 70 percent more likely than men to experience depression during their lifetime.[38] In many ways, depression is a "feminized" issue. Borchard notes that *Beyond Blue* creates community through a discussion board that was an extension of the blog. "There were very real friendships that formed there, as persons said it had become an important support group for them."[39] In fact, Borchard adds, two readers who met on the discussion board ended up getting married.

FSR Inc.'s blog realizes community in a different way. The primary audience is akin to the bloggers—other religious studies scholars and activists. The blog's goal is, according to contributing blogger and feminist ethicist Kate M. Ott, "to have more timely and critical views available from a feminist perspective."[40] Ott notes that there are two communities created by the blog. As with other blogs, there is the readership as community. Yet as a blog with multiple contributors, *FSR Inc.*'s blog also experiences the community of blogger and board members. This community is brought together and held together by a "similar vision for the world" and the desire to "promote that vision through thoughtful critique and scholarship."[41]

In December 2009, Renita Weems explicitly posed the question about whether or not friendships and community created online are on par with flesh-and-blood friendships: "Are our virtual friends with whom we engage in long, heated, but friendly banter with for days, weeks, months, perhaps years on end—are these people real friends?"[42] Weems gives an emphatic "no" to this question, with agreement from many blog readers in the comments section. Other readers disagree, however. One reader finds that there is a communal experience being formed in places like blog readership. This reader likens blog community to dancing at a party to "your song," while others do the dance to the same song as "their song." Without affirming that friendships are formed through this common experience, the reader is adamant that something communal happens in the sharing. This reader concludes that online communities serve as "a clearing house of sorts, where you can identify kindred spirits."[43] Another reader notes learning about rhetoric and skills of debate, while also feeling "mothered" in online forums. This same reader concludes, "Perhaps if someone comes from a situation where face to face contact is dangerous or unhealthy, these online relationships can be a ray of hope and have a permanent positive impact."[44] This reader's comment supports the thesis that the blogosphere may form a kind of creative community, another kind of ministry, if you will, for women who have not experienced justice or equity in ordained ministry settings. Yet Weems's query also illustrates that the community formed in blogging is different from face-to-face relationships.

Rhizomatic Networking

During the early development of blogs, Evan Williams notes that personality is a key component for the popularity of a blog. The personality of the blogger shapes the content since blogs usually involve personal reflection. In addition, many people follow blogs because of their affinity for the blogger. One response to *Something Within* indicated that the blogger was particularly interested in the blog because Weems was writing it. The responder says: "I have been following your ministry . . . I know that you are [a] voice, crying out in the wilderness, a catalyst for change in womanness [sic] issues."[45] As individuals share blog postings with their personal and social networks, it's hard to deny that a blog's reception is not related in part to "following" the work of an individual.

Nevertheless, as some kind of community is created on a blog and as a blogger has the opportunity to dialogue with readers in the comments of a particular posting, community may be formed in non-hierarchical ways. Isherwood and McEwan argue that non-hierarchical networks are a goal for feminist theologians: "They conceptualize a framework that builds up and not one that limits or eliminates experiences. Thus feminist thinkers have stressed that they do not build systems, structures or hierarchies; instead they have emphasized the values of networking."[46]

The concept of a rhizome is helpful for thinking about how networking occurs in religious feminist blogging. Postmodern philosophers Giles Deleuze and Felix Guattari bring this botanical concept to theories of sociality. A rhizome is a plant structure that grows by expansion rather than through seed dispersion. This is non-linear growth: "Unlike trees or their roots, the rhizome connects any point to any other point, and its traits are not necessarily linked to traits of the same nature . . . and has multiple entranceways and exits and its own lines of flight."[47] Feminist theologian Laurel Schneider expounds on the idea of a rhizome when explaining divine multiplicity. For Schneider, multiplicity is not only a characteristic of divinity, but also a pattern for a-centered relationality. Linking Barbara Holmes's discussion of the universe as "omnicentric," and Deleuze's discussion of "rhizome," Schneider states that it is important to think of community as containing a multiplicity of a-centered relations.[48]

One characteristic of a rhizomatic structure is "leaking." Societies that are alive are always "leaking," and can be understood in terms of how they deal with these leaks. Schneider notes that this "leaking" provides an opening for liberation: "Because of the rhizomatic omnicentricity, the most malignant forces of domination . . . cannot plug all of the leaks, no matter how brutally or systematically they may succeed at doing for a time."[49] Blogs, and specifically the blogosphere of religious feminists and the women who build community with them, resemble a rhizomatic structure in many ways.

As women's voices are silenced or muted in traditional church structures, they began to "leak" in the blogosphere.

There is no systematized hierarchy in the blogosphere. Among the many blogs out there, there is no "lead" female blogger; rather there are many bloggers with different interests writing for various audiences. Within blogs that feature many contributing authors (like *FSR Inc.* or *FAR*), there is, likewise, no lead blogger. As noted above, women are creating community by interacting with readers, and with writers of other blogs. While not every occurrence is adventitious, the majority of instances of the community of blogging seem to be serendipitous, rather than by design or some type of inherent nature. That is, a reader might discover a blog from an Internet search or links from other sites, and then become a regular or occasional reader of said blog. It's difficult to ascertain the size of the blogosphere (as it changes daily) or note any one source controlling its evolution, norms, or standards.

In this way, blogging is extremely conducive in creating community where there is none, or, as the reader of *Something Within* intimated, where community has been deeply damaged. In this dynamic environment, there is no one source or voice, participation is open ended, and growth is unmonitored and uninhibited. Voices are not muted, because expression and growth can take place at any and every point of the community. It is freely dynamic, and can change at any time, not only based on the volition of those in community, but also based on the changes in technology by which these communities are formed. At any point and time community can shift, "break," re-form, change direction, and re-create. As such, it cannot be controlled by hierarchical structures, and thus is attractive to those who have been left out of decision-making participation in the more linear structures.

Ministry To, Through, With, and From

The rhizomatic networking of religious feminists allows women to experience ministry in new ways. Ministry is not about the authorization to perform certain rites. It requires no formal church structure. Rather, religious feminist bloggers may experience themselves as ministers through their blogs. They may also receive ministry through their blogging. Blogging as ministry may be particularly noteworthy for women in traditions that bar women from ordained ministry.

Messina-Dysert, Ott, and Borchard have Catholic roots and commitments, and variously describe how ministry occurs in their blogging. Messina-Dysert indicates that she experiences the blogging at *FAR* as ministry because she and the other contributing bloggers "are acting as leaders in [their] traditions by joining the conversation in a public way."[50] Yet ministering *to* others is about more than being a leader. Messina-Dysert continues: "We are also creating opportunities for dialogue—not to mention validating the experiences of others." By drawing the circle of conversation wider and with validation, ministry occurs.

Borchard describes ministry *with* the people who read her blog. Using theological language, she states, "I do feel like a minister in that I feel the presence of the Holy Spirit in the exchanges between my readers and me. I take just as much from them as they do from me, and the interaction reminds me of the passage 'where there are two or three gathered, I [God] am in their presence.'"[51] For Borchard, the creation of community in dialogue is pneumatological work and presence. Borchard is a minister because of divine presence active in the relationship with her readers. Ott says something similar, although she grounds her understanding of ministry in ethics: "For me, ministry is a calling to social justice action . . . as readers share posts of respond/engage the subject matter, I feel that together we are promoting consciousness-raising toward a shared ministry."[52] For Ott, ministry occurs in blogging precisely because of the interaction that Web 2.0 technology allows. Without the reader comments and responses and exchanges that a blogger can have with her reader, ministry would not occur. In these examples, ministry occurs *with* readers. The blog opens the space for Spirit to work. There are many ways that Catholic women exercise leadership and ministry. These testimonies suggest that blogging may be one of those paths, and a non-hierarchical path at that.

In my work with blogging about depression and faith, I experience ministry *from* the responses I receive to my blogs. Since I blog about topics about which there is still significant stigma, most responses I receive are not in the comments section of the blog. Rather, I receive many individual emails from readers who share how meaningful particular posts and topics are experienced. One email I received from a woman who was receiving inpatient treatment for depression included the following words (used with permission): "I am currently in an inpatient psychiatric program for severe depression. I'm learning a lot about what it means to live with this illness and I am frequently scared. Your posts make it seem like I am not alone."[53] With this missive, I felt ministry *from* the reader of my blog. Not only did she affirm my ministry of breaking silence, but knowing that sharing my words and experiences could creatively transform the life of another woman ministered to my soul as well. Because, like her, I am still learning to live with my condition and I experience fear and loneliness. Her words create community and camaraderie for me, as well.

Ministry also occurs in the healing work of religious feminist blogs. The blog topics alone break silence and create spaces of healing for women. The topics mentioned in this essay thus far include infertility, miscarriage, domestic violence, and depression. Exploring the intersection of faith and these "women's issues" is an important component of how blogging offers ministry. For Weems, this is an intentional dynamic of her blogging. In her first post on *Something Within*, she writes,

> I've spent a life time writing about women's inner healing, and I will continue to touch upon that topic because there remains lots of healing that

needs to be done. With this new blog I have the chance now to comment on a wider array of interests. I get to talk about some of the issues and events in our culture that contribute to our hurt as women, and our continued struggle for selfhood as people of color.[54]

Weems is clear that she is expanding her blog to include the ways that society and culture contribute to the pain and dehumanization of minorities. Thus, her healing work moves from personal experiences to political activity.

Thus, religious feminist blogging not only offers space for discussion about women's issues that rarely receive attention in mainstream churches, but it can also work alongside church ministry to meet the needs of a wider faithful public. Borchard believes that *Beyond Blue* is a complement to church,

> Many of my readers are devout Christians and attend services. The blog helps them fill in the gaps that the church service can't. For example, every service can't be about the tools needed to make it through a depressive episode . . . for specific tools, the blog is helpful.[55]

Borchard's blog can be seen as a kind of para-ecclesial ministry. Messina-Dysert, on the other hand, is reformational in her understanding of *FAR*. She states that she hopes that blogging will improve the church: "My hope is that FAR is leading us on a journey that will help to improve things in the churches and in the meantime, I think it allows women and men to have a voice that is otherwise silenced."[56]

These concepts of ministry for women are expanded *in and through* the medium of blogging. As religious feminists blog about women's issues, current events, spirituality, sources of pain and contemporary scholarship, they redefine ministry for women. Working outside of hierarchical structures of authority, blogging can be religious feminist activism as women bloggers and their readers break silences, raise consciousnesses, critically analyze, and create communities. Isherwood and McEwan write about how feminist theology makes important critiques about the power and use of language: "The strength women find in networks is found precisely because they can break many silences within themselves by speaking with other. *We must do this or our empowerment will be lost*" [emphasis mine].[57] As blogging empowers both blogger and reader, it is feminist ministry. Bloggers not only function as ministers, but they may also minister with and receive ministry from the readers of their blogs. In this way, they create organic networks that offer room for healing and liberation.

Notes

1. Anne M. Clifford, *Introducing Feminist Theology* (Maryknoll, NY: Orbis, 2001), 31.
2. "A Quick Question: What Percentage of Pastors Are Female?" *Hartford Institute for Religion Research*, http://hirr.hartsem.edu/research/quick_question3.html.
3. Clifford, 155.
4. Ibid.

5. Renita Weems, *Listening for God: A Minister's Journey through Silence and Doubt* (New York: Simon and Schuster, 1999), 120.
6. Jenna Wortham, "After 10 Years of Blogs, the Future's Brighter Than Ever," *Wired*, December 17, 2007, www.wired.com/entertainment/theweb/news/2007/12/blog_anniversary.
7. "Origins of 'Blog' and 'Blogger,'" *American Dialect Society Mailing List*, April 20, 2008, http://listserv.linguistlist.org/cgi-bin/wa?A2=ind0804C&L=ADS-L&P=R16795&I=-3.
8. Quoted in Wortham.
9. Carolyn R. Miller and Dawn Shepherd, "Blogging as Social Action: A Genre Analysis of the Weblog," *Into the Blogosphere: Rhetoric, Community and Culture of Weblogs,* http://blog.lib.umn.edu/blogosphere/blogging_as_social_action_a_genre_analysis_of_the_weblog.html.
10. Ibid.
11. Ibid. The other characteristics are "frequency of posting" and "brevity."
12. Lisa Isherwood and Dorothea McEwan, *Introducing Feminist Theology*, 2nd edition (New York: T & T Clark, 2001), 13.
13. Audre Lorde, *Sister Outsider: Essays and Speeches by Audre Lorde* (Trumansburg, NY: The Crossing Press, 1984), 40.
14. Ibid., 43.
15. Ibid., 41.
16. Kathie Sarachild, "Consciousness-Raising: A Radical Weapon," in *Feminist Revolution* (New York: Random House, 1978), 144–150. http://library.duke.edu/rubenstein/scriptorium/wlm/fem/sarachild.html.
17. Sarachild.
18. "The personal is political" is a slogan of the women's liberation movement of the 1960s and 1970s.
19. Clifford, 36.
20. Renita Weems, "Welcome to My Blog," *Something Within* (blog), April 18, 2007, www.somethingwithin.com/blog/?p=6.
21. Ibid.
22. "11 Responses to 'I'm Wearing Red Today'" *Something Within* (blog), October 31–November 5, 2007, www.somethingwithin.com/blog/?p=81#comments.
23. "About," *Feminism and Religion* (blog), http://feminismandreligion.com/about/.
24. Gina Messina-Dysert, e-mail message to author, September 22, 2013.
25. Ibid.
26. Clifford, 36.
27. Elisabeth Schussler Fiorenza, *Bread Not Stone: The Challenge of Feminist Biblical Interpretation* (Boston, MA: Beacon, 1995), 15.
28. Elisabeth Schussler Fiorenza, *But She Said: Feminist Practices of Biblical Interpretation* (Boston, MA: Beacon, 1993), 57.
29. Ibid., 62.
30. Schussler Fiorenza, *Bread Not Stone*, 20.
31. Monica A. Coleman, "The Barren Woman Bible," Women in Spirit and Flesh, *Patheos* (column), October 3, 2011, www.patheos.com/Resources/Additional-Resources/Barren-Woman-Bible-Monica-Coleman-10-04-2011.html.
32. Frank Bruni, "Questioning the Mission of College," *The New York Times*, April 20, 2013, www.nytimes.com/2013/04/21/opinion/sunday/bruni-questioning-the-missionof-college.html.
33. Susanne Scholz, "The Boston Marathon Bombing, Gender Studies, and Disaffected Young Men," *FSR Inc.* (blog), April 21, 2013, www.fsrinc.org/blog/boston-marathon-bombing-gender-studies-and-disaffected-young-women-and-men.
34. Isherwood and McEwan, 14.
35. Messina-Dysert.

36. Torill Mortensen and Jill Walker, "Blogging Thoughts: Personal Publication as an Online Research Tool," in Andrew Morrison, ed. *Researching ICTs in Context* (Oslo, Norway: Intermedia, 2002), 271.
37. Ibid.
38. "Major Depressive Disorder Among Adults," *National Institute of Mental Health*, www.nimh.nih.gov/statistics/1mdd_adult.shtml.
39. Therese Borchard, e-mail to author, September 22, 2013.
40. Kate Ott, e-mail to author, September 23, 2013.
41. Ibid.
42. Renita Weems, "Relationships 2.0: Virtual vs. Real Flesh-and-Blood Friendships," *Something Within* (blog), December 2, 2009, www.somethingwithin.com/blog/?p=334.
43. Nick Peterson, December 3, 2009 (9:14 am), comment on Weems "Relationships 2.0." www.somethingwithin.com/blog/?p=334#comments.
44. Derrick, December 2, 2009 (10:38 pm), comment on Weems "Relationships 2.0." www.somethingwithin.com/blog/?p=334#comments.
45. Weems, "Welcome to My Blog."
46. Isherwood and McEwan, 14.
47. Gilles Deleuze and Felix Guattari, *A Thousand Plateaus*, trans. Brian Massumi (New York: Continuum, 1987), 23.
48. Laurel Schneider, *Beyond Monothesim: A Theology of Multiplicity* (New York: Routledge, 2007), 176–179.
49. Schneider, 177.
50. Messina-Dysert.
51. Borchard.
52. Ott.
53. Name withheld, e-mail to author, August 4, 2011.
54. Weems, "Welcome to My Blog."
55. Borchard.
56. Messina-Dysert.
57. Isherwood and McEwan, 119.

3 Mormon Feminist Blogs and Heavenly Mother

Spaces for Ambivalence and Innovation in Practice and Theology

Caroline Kline

Over the last decade, Mormon women's blogs have blossomed over the Internet. An important subset of Mormon women's blogs is Mormon feminist blogs. Like other Mormon women's blogs, Mormon feminist blogs often discuss the triumphs and challenges of motherhood, but they also produce innovative ideas regarding Mormon practice and theology, as feminist Mormons work to resolve the sometimes-conflicting ideals that feminism and Mormonism present.

I found the world of Mormon feminist blogs in 2005 at a time when I was struggling to navigate my feminist path within Mormonism. These blogs proved to be a lifeline—here I found and befriended innovative and insightful women striving to live authentic and progressive Mormon lives. As I became more deeply entrenched in this world of Mormon feminist blogs, I saw this new blogging forum opening space for a religious ambivalence that leads to innovative and creative approaches to living and thinking about the Mormon faith. In this chapter, I focus particularly on feminist Mormon ambivalence toward the unique Mormon doctrine of Heavenly Mother.

Religious Ambivalence and Mormon Feminist Blogs

In *The Religious Imagination of the American Woman*, Mary Bednarowksi discusses how scholars have historically tied women's religious thought in America to dissent (Anne Hutchinson, Mary Baker Eddy, etc.).[1] Bednarowski, however, is interested in another phenomenon that she sees women experiencing within various faith traditions: religious ambivalence. According to her definition, religious ambivalence is the feeling of being simultaneously an insider and an outsider in a tradition—an insider because a woman often uses the tradition's ideas, language, and framework to shape her world view, but an outsider because as a woman, she sees her full personhood denied in sacred texts and by leaders who may exclude women from leadership roles. Bednarowski describes ambivalence as feelings of being nurtured by a tradition, but at the same time constrained by it. This tension can lead, Bednarowski argues, to creativity and innovation as women attempt to find ways to resolve this conflict. She writes,

Ambivalence emerges as a virtue to be cultivated . . . there is a *vitalizing quality* to its manifestations. It is a willed ambivalence, a sustained and cultivated ambivalence, an aware ambivalence. This is an ambivalence that requires women always to be vigilant, always *to be critical* of their communities' inclinations toward exclusion and distortion and at the same time *be open to new possibilities to hold up or reform or transform or dig up*, from wherever they have been hiding, their traditions' most liberating and healing insights. It is an ambivalence that demands wariness that does not lapse into cynicism, loyalty that does not succumb to docility or resignation, *creativity* that flourishes on the margins without losing sight of the center.[2] (Emphasis mine)

In this paper, I examine Mormon feminist blog posts on Heavenly Mother for evidence not only of religious ambivalence, but also of the "vitalizing quality"—innovation, creativity, new possibilities, and criticism—that emerges from these feelings of being simultaneously nurtured and constrained by a tradition. I focus on ambivalence regarding the Mormon doctrine of Heavenly Mother because she is one of the two main topics to which Mormon feminists continually return (women's relationship to male priesthood authority being the other), and because the doctrine has become increasingly taboo to discuss in official Mormon Church forums over the last two decades. While this paper seeks to examine the ways that Heavenly Mother is discussed in innovative ways on blogs, it is not an exhaustive examination. I examine a small selection of posts that represent the various kinds of conversations Mormon feminist bloggers regularly have about Heavenly Mother.

Blogs are a particularly good forum for Mormon religious ambivalence for a number of reasons. First, blogs are not sponsored by the Church, which has no control over their content. The material has not been "correlated," that is filtered through the centralized bureaucratic structure that approves all materials (books, lesson manuals, pamphlets) used in local Mormon congregations.[3] Because this is a forum outside the official LDS Church boundaries, writers are free to speculate theologically or discuss unconventional practices or rituals they have privately created.[4] Second, because blogs are online, there are no geographical constraints. People from various parts of the world come together to discuss topics that they might not be able to pursue in their local communities. Third, blogs are a particularly good forum for Mormon women's religious ambivalence, because Mormon feminist blogs are controlled, written, and often designed by women. Women direct the conversation, shape and lead the discussion, and even delete off-topic or insulting comments. Women are free to discuss gender issues, distance themselves from Church norms, or express criticism of Church doctrine and policies, all of which could bring social or ecclesiastical repercussions if brought up in church. Fourth, unlike print materials, blogging fosters real relationships between writers and readers. Mormon feminists for decades have been publishing articles, books, and periodicals that document religious ambivalence.[5] Blogging, however, forms an immediate community as commenters share ideas with the blog post writers, and writers respond back to commenters. With this sense of solidarity and support from online friends, creativity flourishes as bloggers are emboldened to tread into difficult new territory. Fifth, the very nature of blogging, with its somewhat ephemeral content—visible one day, buried in archives the next—gives bloggers a degree of protection from LDS Church discipline as they criticize, speculate, or innovate.[6] The amount of content produced on blogs is so large that it is nearly impossible for interested Church leaders to constantly monitor these sites. The possibility of anonymity for blog writers and commenters likewise fosters that sense of protection.

The Doctrine of Mother in Heaven

While other Judeo-Christian faith traditions embrace an amorphous, technically sexless God, Mormonism's Heavenly Father is literally anatomically male. He is the god Mormons pray to, worship, and reference. And yet within the Mormon tradition are teachings about Heavenly Mother, an embodied perfect goddess, the wife of Heavenly Father and mother to all the spirits who are eventually born into bodies on earth. Heavenly Mother occupies a nebulous place in Mormon doctrine. Canonized scripture does not acknowledge her existence, yet Mormon Church founder Joseph Smith is reported by others as having had visions of her,[7] and his plural wife, Eliza R. Snow, wrote the text of a beloved hymn mentioning God the Mother, a hymn that Mormon congregations still sing today.[8]

This idea of a Mother God gained traction during the latter part of the 19th century among several Mormon leaders and prophets, yet in the 20th and 21st centuries, she is seldom mentioned in sermons from Church leaders and members. Moreover, Mormons are instructed by their leaders to not pray to her.[9] The topic came to a head in the 1990s and early 2000s when a handful of Mormon feminists were disfellowshipped or excommunicated, at least in part because of their refusal to stop writing and talking about God the Mother.[10] Today, Mormon leaders encourage their members to refer to God as "Heavenly Father." Thus, Heavenly Mother—a divine, embodied female, equal in glory and goodness to Heavenly Father—is puzzlingly absent from official Mormon worship and rhetoric.[11]

Heavenly Mother's status, identity, and relationship with her mortal children are of enormous importance to Mormon feminists because these have implications for the eternal destiny of her daughters here on earth. Mormons believe that their divine destinies are to progress to the status of God the Mother and Father, and ultimately become gods themselves.[12] Because gender is eternal in the Mormon framework, Mormon women look to teachings about Heavenly Mother for indications of what their eternal future holds. However, with the disappearance of Heavenly Mother from official Church rhetoric, Mormon feminists are often left wondering if their divine destiny is invisibility and silence, which stands in stark contrast to the involved loving Father God Mormon men have as their divine model.

Ambivalence and Innovative Worship

Despite the slow marginalization and disappearance of this unique Mormon belief from official Mormon discourse, Mormon feminist blogs have opened up a space in which Mormon women share their ideas about and experiences with her, express their pain at her absence from official Mormon discourse, and analyze the implications of the Heavenly Mother doctrine on their own senses of eternal identity and selfhood.[13] These blogs are windows into the inner worlds of Mormon women, intimate in their details and frank in their discussions, as they tread into doctrinal territory and religious practice considered nearly taboo in contemporary Mormonism.

The preeminent Mormon feminist blog is *Feminist Mormon Housewives*, which displays Mormon women's religious ambivalence on many topics. Because of the tension between its feminism and its Mormonism, and because of the divided identities these women are negotiating, the blog is a highly creative outlet. One post on *Feminist Mormon Housewives*, written by an anonymous author and entitled "On Praying to Heavenly Mother," is a particularly rich example of religious ambivalence. The entry displays a number of recurring themes and ideas in posts about Heavenly Mother on Mormon blogs. The author begins her post with statements about her fear of repercussions. She states, "I write this anonymously, honestly worried about repercussions . . . from friends and family who know me . . . I don't want to be shunned in my ward [congregation]," illustrating why blogs are such an important forum for Mormon women's religious ambivalence—it is here, in the blogging world, that she can tell her story honestly and feel some degree of safety in doing so.[14] This fear of repercussions is a theme that recurs in many posts and comments about Heavenly Mother.

The same post illustrates another common theme: speculation about Heavenly Mother's near invisibility. This author says that she has wondered "what the big brouhaha is about doing it [praying to Heavenly Mother]" and guesses that the prohibition "goes back . . . to the time of fertility cults and female goddesses that are seen as less desirable to the ideals of both chaste womanhood and Mormon womanhood."[15] Thus, the author weaves her personal experience with and yearning for Heavenly Mother with a possible explanation of the current policy of not praying to her. The ambivalence is apparent—she wants to believe that her leaders have good reason for discouraging Mormons from having a relationship with Heavenly Mother, but she personally feels that praying to her should not be a problem.

The author then points to the double bind so often mentioned by women on the blogs:

> As daughters of Heavenly Parents, we are taught that our gender is no accident, that in fact it is eternal in nature. Further we are taught that as women we inherit divine qualities inherent to being female. So surely if we are taught about the divine qualities of one of our Heavenly Parents,

our Father-the-male part, then we are losing out on imitating the divine qualities of our Mother-the-female part, ironically the counterpart we are indeed striving to become.[16]

Thus, the author, as a believer in eternal gender, questions where her divine role model is. She manifests both conflicting feelings of loyalty to her leaders and dissatisfaction with the current policy.

She then shares her personal story of communing with the divine feminine. She states, "Through personal revelation I know that my Mother in Heaven lives," and continues,

> I knelt down by my bed in the middle of the day pleading to my Father in Heaven for help as a wife and mother, feeling much overwhelmed and unsure of myself. This time I felt the love of not only my Father in Heaven, [but also] of a Mother in Heaven. I felt her love, support, wisdom and understanding as a mother who desired to give her daughter, me, all that she had to assist me with my own earthly family. I felt at that time that I could address her and discuss with her the things pertinent to earthly womanhood that only a woman herself would understand . . . I was not seeking her, but thankfully, I discovered her.[17]

The author's language is carefully selected. She never actually says that she has prayed to Heavenly Mother. Rather, she has "addressed," "discussed," and "discovered" her. In her fear of repercussions from her Mormon community, her knowledge that her experience is highly unconventional, and her undeniably positive experience communing with Heavenly Mother, this author negotiates her way between tradition and innovation. This post is filled with ambivalence and internal conflict that manifest themselves in the innovative and nontraditional private practice of communing with Heavenly Mother.

Not only does this post illustrate Bednarowski's theory of the vitality and innovation that can arise from women's religious ambivalence, but the 156 comments that respond to this post do as well. These comments tend to reflect one or more of the themes in the post itself—fear of repercussions, theological speculations for Heavenly Mother's absence, personal stories of unique experiences with Heavenly Mother, etc. A few of these comments are particularly good illustrations of ambivalence leading to creativity. For example, some commenters, in their efforts to follow the guidelines of Church leaders, do not pray to her, but they do search for her in sacred texts, by assigning the concepts or figures of wisdom, Elohim and Asherah, to her. Thus, they engage in creative scripture reading and interpretation. Others recount personal experiences of non-conventional practice in attempts to reach out to Heavenly Mother. One woman comments that she has composed a new verse to the LDS hymn "Love One Another" that centers on Heavenly Mother. She writes, "Love Heavenly Mother/ Feel Her within you/ She's always with you/ Love Heavenly Mother/ With all your heart, soul, mind, and your strength/ She'll feed your soul/ If you love Her." This new hymn verse is a striking example of ambivalence, as the commenter takes this beloved LDS hymn as her anchor and constructs a new vision of inclusion toward Heavenly Mother with it. The verse writer comments on her motivation for this project:

> I included the verse about Heavenly Mother because it is powerful to me to envision the Divine Feminine nourishing my soul. Metaphorically I am a developing fetus in Her womb, an infant at Her breast, and a babe in Her arms. Metaphorically I have Father's Seed in my heart and Mother's Living Water pouring through me, both essential to my spiritual rebirth and the enlargement of my soul.[18]

This commenter poetically echoes the anonymous post author's belief of the importance of both Heavenly Parents to her spiritual development. In the end, religious ambivalence is manifest in both post and comments, as women yearn to reach out to their Mother and ultimately develop innovative practices to do so.

Ambivalence and Critical Readings

The anonymous author's post and the subsequent comments are largely positive toward the Heavenly Mother doctrine, since these women found the idea of Heavenly Mother empowering and were trying to seek her out. Other posts take a more negative view of the Heavenly Mother doctrine, finding its implications problematic. This approach is an important creative theological act: to point out logical problems with certain doctrines is to open space for imagining alternatives.

The next post, which is from another of the three most important feminist Mormon blogs, *Zelophehad's Daughters*, highlights a critical reading of the Mother in Heaven doctrine. Whereas the previous post was personal and experiential, this one is analytic and logical. As in the *Feminist Mormon Housewives* post, Lynnette begins with justifications for Heavenly Mother's absence from our lives, but unlike the first poster, Lynnette roundly rejects them. She states, "Heavenly Mother was too special to talk to? Heavenly Father was protecting her from her children? Worshipping a woman would lead you in the direction of pagan fertility rites? That's just the way things had always been done (this, in a church which claimed continuing revelation)? Each argument seemed sillier than the last."[19] Thus, in just a few sentences, Lynnette questions the reasoning behind many popular Mormon rationalizations for Heavenly Mother's invisibility in mortal lives.

She then enumerates two of her main concerns with the doctrine of Heavenly Mother: that it infers male subsumption of the female, and that it infers eternal gender roles. She states her reservations about the doctrine, saying, "If Heavenly Mother exists, what we have is a divine role model for women which may be more disturbing than no role model at all—one in which women are silenced to the point of invisibility, in which they seem to disappear altogether into the identity of their husbands."[20] For Lynnette, a universe without a Heavenly Mother, even with the challenge of not having a female divine role model, may be more palatable than one in which the female divine role model is subsumed into the male and silenced. She elaborates further on this problem, questioning whether this doctrine implies that women (but not men) have to sacrifice their individual identity "to the point where we can only guess as to whether a female is even present in the relationship."[21] Lynnette demonstrates another facet of ambivalence—a willingness "to be critical of [her] communit[y's] inclinations toward exclusion."[22] This ambivalence is rooted in her devout Mormon belief in the worth of all souls and God being no respecter of persons, a belief that she feels conflicts with the current LDS model of the divine fate of females.

Lynnette's next major criticism of the Heavenly Mother doctrine centers around its implications of gender roles being eternal. She finds it less limiting and more inspiring to think that gender roles are not eternal, that everyone, male or female, can someday be like God. She states,

> If there is no Heavenly Mother, women as well as men can confidently aspire to be like their Father, to somehow share in the life of God and all that goes along with that—but the existence of Heavenly Mother indicates that females are on an alternate path. Women, like men, might lay claim to some spark of the divine; but when one talks of women becoming god-like there is always an asterisk, because we do not know what female divinity entails.[23]

Lynnette sees the Heavenly Mother doctrine as presenting a limiting and constrained vision of what it means to be divine and female in the afterlife. Lynnette identifies the dangers of a doctrine that teaches that gender roles are eternal, while acknowledging that there could be some empowering aspects to the doctrine as well. She states, "Teachings about Heavenly Mother can as easily be used to reinforce traditional gender roles as to challenge them; the fact that we see no evidence of Heavenly Mother exercising any kind of power or authority, for example, might be one reason why we are reluctant to give priesthood authority to women on earth."[24] These troubling implications of the doctrine not only affect the way Mormons think of women's divine future, but also potentially diminish and constrain women's current realm of action and influence in the Church and family. Lynnette sums up her feelings,

> To put it bluntly, I sometimes think I might rather deal with the difficulties of having no Heavenly Mother at all, than with the challenges posed by the doctrine of a Heavenly Mother who is irrelevant to the Plan of Salvation, and who is either unable or unwilling to communicate with her children. With apologies to Eliza R. Snow, I find that it is this latter possibility, even more than the notion that in the heavens parents are single, that truly makes reason stare.[25]

Her final reference to Eliza R. Snow is a powerful statement of ambivalence, as she borrows well-loved language from Snow's famous Mormon hymn that mentions Heavenly Mother, thus showing her insider status, but then gives the phrasing her own logical twist.[26] This ending is emblematic of the way her post opens up space for creative theological analysis and discussions of logical implications of doctrines. When compared to the first post, this post falls further back along the ambivalence scale, as Lynnette is perfectly comfortable not attempting to justify the current Church policy of silence about Heavenly Mother, and she's also comfortable criticizing the doctrine in general. She is more willing to question the current status quo than the first poster's tentative and carefully spoken personal account.

Ambivalence and Creative Visualization

The last of the three most popular Mormon feminist blogs is the *Exponent II Blog*, now called *The Exponent*, which I co-founded in 2006 in an attempt to give the Mormon feminist *Exponent II* publication an online presence in this new technological age. One post on *The Exponent* simply asked women how they envisioned their Heavenly Mother. Out of the forty-six responses, about half the commenters said that they could not even begin to envision her, since she is so absent from Church discussions. Out of the rest of the commenters who could say something about her, one in particular stands out. Deborah described a Heavenly Mother very different from the way Mormons tend to envision the divine. Rather than an embodied personage, her Heavenly Mother is immanent and associated with nature. She states that for her, "the feminine divine takes hold less as a personage and more as an energy—a pure and powerful healing soul, surrounding us when we cry, playing with our hair in the wind, urging us to embrace compassion. More a presence than a person."[27]

This Heavenly Mother is disembodied in a strikingly non-Mormon way and has, sometimes through natural manifestations, direct contact with her children. On the one hand, this comment stands as an example of the way a distinctly Mormon idea in the Christian world (an embodied female divine) has been mutated and perhaps influenced by other religions' ideas about a disembodied and immanent divine force. On the other hand, it also hints at the idea, proposed by some Mormon feminists, that the Holy Spirit is actually Heavenly Mother. To some Mormon feminists, this reconception of the trinity—one that contains a mother, father, and child—is compelling given Mormonism's familial cosmology.[28]

Ambivalence and Practice in the Church Community

Finally, my own post on *The Exponent*, "God He, God She, God They: Reflections on Naming the Divine," stands as an example of adjusted and innovative practice within my congregation, arising from my discomfort with the androcentric God language that is prevalent during Mormon services and lessons. In this post I write that I feel uncomfortable praying to Heavenly Father, or even talking about Heavenly Father exclusively, because it does not feel right to ignore my other Parent. However, knowing the strong taboo against praying to Heavenly Mother, I realize that whatever changes I make to public prayers and public mentionings of Heavenly Mother have to be subtle and creative. I write, "I'm the one who is ultimately in charge of my spiritual progression, and if I'm hindered by androcentric language, I'm changing it to something more inclusive."[29] I go on to state that in church settings I will pray to God, not Heavenly Father. To me, "God is not a God He or a God She. It's a God They. A divine unit of male and female."[30] In church settings, I will also "replace Heavenly Father with Heavenly Parents as often as I possibly can, then switch to God when people start raising their eyebrows."

This post exhibits ambivalence about Heavenly Mother's invisibility, which has led to innovative language and adjusted prayer practices. Rather than just altering private behavior to include Heavenly Mother, I am altering public behavior. I am making compromises to my faith community by not mentioning her outright at church, but I am stretching and going beyond Church norms, which encourage the use of "Heavenly Father" over "God." This post highlights my process of moving beyond fear of social or divine repercussions for including Heavenly Mother in speech and prayers. Ambivalence has taught me the subtle art of creative negotiation with my faith community. Also distinct in this post is my somewhat public agenda to promote inclusive God language at church. My ambivalence has prompted me to take active, strategic steps to keep the doctrine of Heavenly Mother present in Mormons' minds and to promote more inclusive God language within my congregation.

Ambivalence and Creative Restructuring

While my own ambivalence leads me to model a more inclusive God and prayer language in church, other women, like Mraynes, are willing to push their Mormon communities further. Her personal experience of communing with God the Mother cemented in her a conviction of the importance of incorporating Heavenly Mother into Mormon women's spiritual lives. Mraynes ultimately proposes an entire reconception of the LDS Young Women program[31]—a reconception that incorporates explicit teachings of God the Mother as young women progress through various levels of priestesshood.

Mraynes's ambivalence about the current nearly invisible status of God the Mother blossomed when she experienced God the Mother personally during natural childbirth, "stroking my damp hair and holding me through the pain." Since that experience, Heavenly Mother "has been with [me] ever since, whispering in my ear, lovingly instructing me how to be a mother."[32] Mraynes's personal experience with her Mother cemented in her a conviction of the importance of knowing Heavenly Mother to the self-worth and identity of Mormon women. Thus, Mraynes in a blog post on *The Exponent* proposes an entire reconception of how we teach young Mormon women about their roles, their spiritual lives, and their divine potential.[33] In this post, she sketches out a whole new program for young women, one that mirrors the status and priesthood of young Mormon men. Mraynes's ambivalence in this post is giving birth to a vision of systemic inclusion of women, both in theology, by having young women learn and talk about Heavenly Mother, and in practice, by having young women recognized and ordained to priestesshood:[34]

> I strongly believe that the time for waiting is over—we can no longer continue hoping for further light and knowledge from men who are unable/ unwilling to acknowledge that women have an unique experience from men—we must begin seeking truth for ourselves. My intention here is to begin a dialog and a period of discernment in which we can join together as women, seeking to access the power of God in ways that allow us to live up to our full potential as goddesses in embryo.[35]

In this paragraph, Mraynes highlights her ambivalence. On the one hand, she embraces the uniquely Mormon idea that women are goddesses in embryo. On the other, she feels a deep sense of exclusion and constraint from her male Mormon leaders, whom she believes have chosen to not seek further light and knowledge about Heavenly Mother and women's roles in the Church. Her call for dialogue and joining together points once again to the unique nature of the blogging forum. On the blogs, with her identity somewhat obscured, she can initiate this conversation and solicit ideas from fellow Mormon feminists who live around the world, a conversation that would be either impossible or extremely limited without this technological medium. She continues,

> I believe we must start with an exploration of Heavenly Mother and what it means to be divinely female. We cannot know what God wants from women until we know who and what God Herself is. Once this is accomplished I believe that we can design a religious experience for women that is equivalent, though not the same as men's . . .
>   Girls would be given the power of God at age 12 just as boys are . . . [At this age] young women are ordained to a lower order of priestesshood. During this time young women will receive guidance in methods of prayer and will learn more about Heavenly Mother and the meaning of religious life to broaden and deepen the understanding of their relationship with God and God's children. They will participate in and provide meaningful service to the community.[36]

Mryanes goes on to outline other duties and training for young women as they age. Her sketch of a new program for young Mormon women is founded on a conviction that women must come to know Heavenly Mother and experience her. With that foundation, women can formulate a program that likewise teaches young women about their Mother. Her vision mirrors the training and status young Mormon men obtain within Mormonism. As a different

feminist, however, Mraynes does not seek to incorporate women into the existing male-dominated structure. Rather, she envisions a new female-centered,
female-controlled program that ultimately attempts to disentangle maleness
from spiritual authority and power within Mormonism.

Within the Mormon world, which is highly centralized by powerful male
leaders, this kind of re-envisioning of Mormon structures and programs is dar-
ing. It violates Mormon protocol and propriety, since Mormons believe that
revelation for Church practice and worship comes directly from God to the
president of the Church, his counselors, and the (all-male) Quorum of the
Twelve Apostles. In this way, Mormons embrace a strictly hierarchical and
top-down understanding of how God and the Church function. For a woman,
and a woman not even in any kind of leadership position within the Church, to
propose an entirely new reconception of the Young Women program in which
girls are ordained to priestesshood and God the Mother is acknowledged and
honored is an audacious act of Mormon feminist creativity.

Conclusion

From this selection of posts and comments from Mormon feminist blogs
regarding the topic of Heavenly Mother, we can see women's religious ambivalence manifesting itself in creative ways. Some women's ambivalence leads
them to theological innovation or speculation, as they muse over justifications for Heavenly Mother's absence, as they logically analyze the doctrine
itself for potential pitfalls, and as they reconfigure Heavenly Mother in their
minds in innovative ways. Other women's ambivalence leads them to innovative practice and adjusted ritual, as women pray to Heavenly Mother, compose
hymns about her, adjust definitions of the divine in order to create inclusive
God language, and propose a Mormon priestesshood grounded in teachings of
Heavenly Mother. By rethinking their relationships with Heavenly Mother and
creating these methods of remembering or communicating with her, several
of these women are spiritually nourishing themselves in a way that would be
frowned upon by their LDS leaders, while at the same time linking themselves
even more closely with their faith tradition. After all, Heavenly Mother is a
distinctly Mormon and unique idea within a Christian cosmology.

The blogging world is a particularly appropriate forum for Mormon wom-
en's ambivalence and religious creativity. Here, women from all over the world
can congregate in this virtual space to voice controversial ideas and express
their own stories and perspectives. And as they share their frustrations, their
triumphs, and the tragedies of their Mormon women's lives, these women have
the opportunity to step beyond their usual non-pastoral Church duties and minister to one another, advise one another, and offer sympathy and support to one
another. They also have the opportunity to offer up to one another new visions,
new roads, and new ways to navigate their Mormon lives. As one commenter
responding to Mraynes's priestesshood post poignantly writes, "How beautiful
are the paths I never allow myself to imagine!" This commenter encapsulates
what these blogs do. They give Mormon feminists permission to re-envision a

life, a church, and a tradition of inclusion and equality. What's more, they give them a safe and supportive community to do it within.

Notes

1. Mary Bednarowski, *The Religious Imagination of the American Woman* (Bloomington, IN: Indiana University Press, 1999).
2. Ibid., 20.
3. Mormons are discouraged from using materials in Church lessons that have not been correlated.
4. "LDS" stands for "Latter-Day Saints." The Church of Jesus Christ of Latter-Day Saints is the official name of the Utah-based Mormon Church. Throughout this paper, I use the terms Mormon and LDS synonymously.
5. The *Exponent II* newspaper, begun in the 1970s, was founded on the platform of Mormon faith and feminism. *Sunstone*, a liberal Mormon publication, has for decades been publishing Mormon feminist articles, as has *Dialogue: A Journal of Mormon Thought*. Several books also showcase Mormon feminist ambivalence, such as *Women and Authority: Re-Emerging Mormon Feminism*, edited by Maxine Hanks (Salt Lake City, UT: Signature, 1992); Margaret and Paul Toscano, *Strangers in Paradox: Explorations in Mormon Theology* (Salt Lake City, UT: Signature, 1990); and Janice Allred, *God the Mother: And Other Theological Essays* (Salt Lake City, UT: Signature, 1997).
6. In the 1990s and 2000, a handful of Mormon feminists and intellectuals were excommunicated for apostasy because of their refusal to conform to Church leaders' requests to stop writing and speaking about certain historical, feminist, or speculative topics. Hanks, Toscano, and Allred, mentioned in the note above, were all excommunicated.
7. Linda P. Wilcox, "The Mormon Concept of a Mother in Heaven," in *Women and Authority: Re-Emerging Mormon Feminism,* ed. Maxine Hanks (Salt Lake City, UT: Signature, 1992), 5.
8. Wilcox, 5.
9. Gordon B. Hinckley, "Daughters of God," *Ensign*, November 1991, http://lds.org/ensign/1991/11/daughters-of-god?lang=eng.
10. For more information on the Church-disciplining of several Mormon feminists, see Philip Lindholm, *Latter-day Dissent: At the Crossroads of Intellectual Inquiry and Ecclesiastical Authority* (Salt Lake City, UT: Greg Kofford Books, 2011). Margaret Toscano's PBS interview about her excommunication highlights the fact that her speaking and writing about Heavenly Mother, as well as other feminist issues, led to her excommunication, www.pbs.org/mormons/interviews/toscano.html.
11. Margaret Toscano discusses the serious consequences of this slow burial of Heavenly Mother, as the concept of deity becomes increasingly associated in rhetoric only with God the Father. Margaret Toscano, "Is There a Place for Heavenly Mother in Mormon Theology: An Investigation into Discourses of Power," *Sunstone*, July 2004, 16.
12. Joseph Smith, "The King Follett Discourse," http://mldb.byu.edu/follett.htm. While the King Follett discourse speaks only in masculine terms of humans progressing to become gods, LDS scripture in *Doctrine & Covenants* 132:20 makes it clear that both females and males have the opportunity to progress to godhood.
13. Margaret Toscano likewise mentions blogs as safe spaces for Mormon women to discuss their experiences with Heavenly Mother. She finds that women invariably describe their visionary experiences with God the Mother as empowering and spiritually transforming. Margaret Toscano, "Movement from the Margins: Contemporary Mormon Women's Visions of the Mother God," in *Spirit, Faith and Church: Women's Experiences in the English-Speaking World, 17th-21st Century*, ed.

Laurence Lux-Sterritt and Claire Sorin (Newcastle upon Tyne, UK: Cambridge Scholars Publishing, 2012), 207–226.

14. "On Praying to Heavenly Mother" (anonymous), *Feminist Mormon Housewives* (blog), May 30, 2007, www.feministmormonhousewives.org/2007/05/on-praying-to-mother-in-heaven/.
15. Ibid.
16. Ibid.
17. Ibid.
18. Wild Horses, May 31, 2007 (1:02 p.m.), comment on "On Praying to Heavenly Mother" (anonymous), *Feminist Mormon Housewives* (blog), May 30, 2007, www. feministmormonhousewives.org/2007/05/on-praying-to-mother-in-heaven/.
19. Lynnette, "Why I Don't Want to Believe in Heavenly Mother," *Zelophehad's Daughters* (blog), November 7, 2007, http://zelophehadsdaughters.com/2007/11/07/why-i-don%E2%80%99t-want-to-believe-in-heavenly-mother/.
20. Ibid.
21. Ibid.
22. Bednarowski, *The Religious Imagination*, 20.
23. Lynnette, "Why I Don't Want to Believe in Heavenly Mother."
24. In Mormonism's lay priesthood, every male age twelve and older is ordained to priesthood. Females are not ordained to priesthood; thus, women have limited opportunities for leadership within LDS congregations and in the general LDS Church structure.
25. Lynnette, "Why I Don't Want to Believe in Heavenly Mother."
26. Snow's lyrics state in the fourth verse, "In the heavens are parents single? No, the thought makes reason stare!/Truth is reason, truth eternal, tells me I've a mother there."
27. Deborah, September 2, 2006 (6:51 p.m.), comment on Jana, "Our Heavenly Mother," *The Exponent* (blog), September 2, 2006, www.the-exponent.com/our-heavenly-mother/.
28. See Janice Allred, "Toward a Mormon Theology of God the Mother," in *God the Mother: And Other Theological Essays,* ed. Janice Allred (Salt Lake City, UT: Signature Books, 1997).
29. Caroline, "God He, God She, and God They: Options for Naming the Divine," *The Exponent* (blog), September 24, 2008, www.the-exponent.com/god-he-god-she-and-god-they-options-for-naming-the-divine/.
30. While contemporary Mormon rhetoric equates the term "God" with Heavenly Father, some Mormons in the past have posited that God does consist of a male and a female divine unit working in concert with one another. Nineteenth-century apostle Erastus Snow (*Journal of Discourses*, March 1878) said, "There never was a God, and there never will be in all eternities, except they are made of these two component parts: a man and a woman; the male and the female."
31. In every LDS congregation, girls ages twelve to seventeen participate in the Young Women organization. This program follows a correlated curriculum overseen by Church leaders and hosts activities, services projects, and religious classes.
32. Mraynes, "Healing Through Motherhood," *Feminist Mormon Housewives* (blog), September 9, 2007, www.feministmormonhousewives.org/2007/09/healing-through-motherhood/.
33. Mraynes, "The Potential of Priestesshood," *The Exponent* (blog), July 21, 2012, www.the-exponent.com/the-potential-of-priesstesshood/.
34. Females are not ordained to priesthood or priestesshood in the contemporary LDS Church.
35. Mraynes, "The Potential of Priestesshood."
36. Ibid.

4   Being Undone by the Other
Feminisms, Blogs, and Critique

Xochitl Alvizo

Bringing together "feminism" and "religion" is often cause for consternation: what "feminism" are we talking about? Do we mean feminism as agency? power? resistance? The definitions can be so disparate that feminists may not recognize themselves in the feminism of another. It makes more sense to talk about feminism*s*, in the plural.[1] Adding the topic of religion to the discussion complexifies this even further for many feminists who understand feminisms in exclusively secular terms. For some, bringing religion into the mix is considered not only a matter of suspicion, but also "a dangerous affront" for seeking to impose on the many a normative morality determined by the religious few.[2] Religion is not often recognized as a friend of feminisms and is often identified as a primary cause of the injustices against which feminists direct their efforts. Thus, bringing these two topics together is a loaded endeavor. Nonetheless, in this essay, I will further complexify this crossroads by locating the discussion of feminisms and religion in the space of an online blog forum.[3]

Feminism and Religion[4] (*FAR*) is an online blog that daily publishes short articles written by feminist-identified scholars and activists in the areas of religion and spirituality.[5] In regard to its mission, the website states that the blog was established "in the hope that feminist scholars of religion—and all who are interested in the issues—will use this forum to share their ideas, insights, and experiences, so that this community of thinkers will be nurtured as we explore diverse and new directions." One of its main pages, titled "What Is Feminism?" is a short article by Rosemary Radford Ruether that expounds on a basic definition of feminism—the affirmation of the full humanity of women.[6] However, as one might imagine, participants diverge widely on how this definition is lived out and enacted as it concerns religion.

Using this blog as a mini case study, in this essay I explore the potential of blogs to serve as spaces in which feminists can engage one another across their feminist differences by practicing criticism in a way that leaves them open to transformation. My argument is that by expanding the definition of critique, feminists can actively participate in also expanding the borders of feminism and thereby uphold the full humanity of their feminist "other." To do this, I draw from the work of Saba Mahmood in her book, *Politics of Piety: The Islamic Revival and the Feminist Subject*, and from Angela Pears's book, *Feminist Christian Encounters: The Methods and Strategies of Feminist Informed Christian Theologies*, from which I learned to more accurately refer to feminism as *feminisms* in the plural.

Feminist Divides on the Blog

On *Feminism and Religion,* participants come from many different backgrounds, are of various sexualities and genders, are both religious and nonreligious, and have diverse and often conflicting definitions of feminisms. There are feminists who practice Goddess spirituality and are sometimes befuddled by feminists who choose to stay in patriarchal religions. There are some very committed Catholic, Protestant, Mormon, Muslim, and Jewish feminists working from within their respective traditions to reform them and bring about liberating change. Also among the regular contributors are a couple of atheist and agnostic persons who bring their contributions to the topic of feminism and religion from their non-religious perspectives, and Islamic scholars who do not claim the tradition as their own. Guest contributors and readers also add to the diversity of perspectives. Of special note are the readers who comment regularly in response to the blog posts; it is they who often more strongly set the tone for the discussion than do the authors of the post themselves. One such voice is that of secular feminists who continually call women out of religion altogether, especially patriarchal religions.

One reader who identifies as "Turtle Woman"[7] represents the feminist perspective that considers any religion of "the Book" to be fundamentally incompatible with feminisms. At times, she overwhelms with her incessant call for women to leave patriarchal religions.[8] She calls feminists who stay in these religions "liberal feminists," who in her estimation not only delude themselves that the tradition will change, but also actively contribute to the perpetuation and reinforcement of oppressive patriarchal institutions. She considers these feminists "odd and naïve," persons who want to be part of patriarchy but with a better job title and who "refuse to confront the global system of patriarchy SYSTEMATICALLY"[9] (emphasis hers). It appears that such feminists are the bane of her existence and yet she participates with them on the blog nonetheless.

Interestingly, though Turtle Woman comments quite frequently on the blog, others rarely address or respond to her comments directly. As a self-declared "radical feminist," she is not surprised by this. She explains: "Liberal feminists actually are afraid of what radical feminists have to say a lot of the time, I think it might be guilt for living with the enemy, or being able to tolerate the woman-hating churches to begin with."[10] Perhaps the chasm between these two kinds of feminisms and their respective practices in terms of their engagement or disengagement with religion is too great to cross. However, I would like to explore the possibility that one can not only engage across this difference, but can also do so in a way that undoes the certainty and rigidity with which one holds a particular definition of feminism.

Saba Mahmood Redefines Criticism

I was first inspired to pursue this project after reading Saba Mahmood's definition of critique in *Politics of Piety*. In this work, set out to be a study of the Islamic Revival movement in Egypt, Mahmood challenges the reader to reconsider feminist definitions of agency and resistance, concepts central to particular brands of feminisms that have largely been shaped by what she identifies as "secular-left politics." The particular context and culture of the Islamic Revival movement in Egypt and the complex workings of power at play there resulted in forms of agency and empowerment for the women involved that do not fit the definition of feminisms born of secular-left politics. Women there used the religious virtues of piety, feminine virtues from within their Islamic tradition such as shyness, modesty, and humility to achieve an increased public role and participation. Though at first Mahmood thought it implausible that women's subordination to these feminine virtues could actually serve as a form of agency that enabled the women to take a public role in the religious and political life of Egypt, she discovered it did precisely that.[11] Practice of these virtues paved the way for these women to be able to work outside their homes, teach classes, organize, and, in effect, lead a movement that increased their impact and influence in the public and political life of Egypt. Virtues that are often known only as means of submission and disempowerment were effectively employed by the women of this movement to enact a form of agency that a secular-left political bias could not achieve. This realization caused Mahmood to reconsider not only her understandings of these categories of feminisms—agency, resistance, and power—but also of the nature of critique itself.

Given that criticism is typically understood to be about "demolishing the opponent's position and exposing the implausibility of their argument,"[12] Mahmood thought it implausible that the practice of feminine virtues could be anything but oppressive. But as she turned her critical gaze back onto herself and questioned her own certainties about these virtues as being only instruments of women's oppression, she allowed for her feminist understanding of agency and the certainty of secular-left political feminisms to be undone in her encounter with the other. She came to see that the normative understanding of critique as the demolishment of the opponent's position is a limited and weak form of critique. She poses that what is most powerful is when criticism "leaves open the possibility that we might also be remade in the process of engaging another's worldview"—when we leave open the possibility that we "might come to learn things that we did not already know before we undertook the engagement with another."[13] Turning the critical gaze back upon ourselves is vital to this.

In promoting such an understanding of criticism, Mahmood emphasizes that there is no "singularity of vision that unites us [feminists]."[14] In effect, the feminist project must be left "productively open," for there will be various forms of human flourishing or empowering action that feminists will pursue.[15] No person or groups of persons can know the forms of agency, power, and resistance that will be appropriate in a particular time and place. In Mahmood's words, "the ability to effect change in the world and in oneself is historically and culturally specific"—and, therefore, feminist enactments cannot be fixed in advance but must emerge from within their various contexts.[16]

A similar perspective is offered by Angela Pears in her work *Feminist Christian Encounters: The Methods and Strategies of Feminist Informed Christian Theologies*. In this book, Pears sets out to identify strategies employed in feminist Christian encounters. Although many have found Christianity and feminisms to be incompatible with one another, Pears recognizes that many feminists do indeed bring the two together and analyzes how they do it. Similar to Mahmood, Pears begins her work by saying, "There is a need to avoid over-simplifying and homogenizing the diverse experiences of women in order to present feminisms and feminist theologies into some kind of unified and coherent system, which is a tendency that has so far often proved irresistible and highly destructive, and in many ways has stifled the promise of feminisms and feminist theologies to the extent that some would even contend that it has led to the end of feminisms as potentially liberative discourse or transformative social action."[17] Pears and Mahmood suggest that if feminisms are to continue to be potentially liberative discourses or lead to transforming social action, then feminisms cannot be restricted to any one single definition. Part of this conviction comes from the recognition that feminisms, even the "proudly claimed" secular-left political leaning feminisms, have at times produced "some spectacular human disasters."[18]

Expanding the Borders of Feminisms

With Mahmood's expanded definition of critique, is it possible for feminists to engage one another across their differences, to critique in a way that leaves them open to their own undoing and that expands the borders of what it means to be feminist, and to do so while still advancing feminist social action? Further, can this be practiced through one's participation on a blog? Turtle Woman, for example, is someone who practices the normative understanding of critique and seeks to expose the implausibility of another's argument. In many different ways on the *Feminism and Religion* blog, she insists that women should not expect to be respected, much less liberated, in male-prioritizing patriarchal religions—they are deluded to think so. Might she be willing to open herself up to being undone by her encounter with another and, as Mahmood proposes, have her feminism "remade in the process of engaging another's worldview"?[19] Might her participation on the blog open her up to the possibility of turning her critical gaze back on herself? Might such participation be possible for us?

Part of being undone by an encounter with a feminist other is to recognize one's limits in knowing and seeing, to be attentive to what might be outside of one's purview.[20] To turn one's critical gaze back on oneself is to be vigilant to the ways in which one's own definition of feminisms and its imposition on another may serve to reinscribe relational patterns of oppression that deny another's dignity, agency, and empowerment. Something is awry when feminists relate to one another as if they have a greater right to name the other's reality or feminist strategy. Not to allow another to name their own reality, to give word and expression to their experience, is to deny the other their right as a full human being. From the start of the movement, feminists have recognized that the right to name things for oneself from within one's own community is an act that asserts and affirms one's full dignity and full humanity. As such, feminists must be willing to keep the borders of their definitions flexible enough to make room for their feminist "other"—which in this case is their feminist sisters and brothers.

In promoting this openness to being undone by one's encounter with a feminist other, I am not wishing to promote a romantic or naively celebratory vision of sisterhood, but to promote a practice that does not simply speak of overturning embedded systems of hierarchy, exploitation, and domination, but enacts it in the very way that feminists engage with one another—even on a blog. I contend that the ways in which feminists participate on blog spaces contains within it the feminisms to which they ascribe. What people do, how they relate in cyberspace, itself embodies and makes real their particular feminist perspective. Participants are not discussing a concept or topic from which they disconnected; through their presence and engagement, they are practicing and enacting the very thing they are there to discuss. *How* blog participants engage with one another in this feminist-oriented blog space is revealing of their definition of feminisms. The topic at hand in that encounter is being lived out and lived into by each participant. Is there the possibility of expanding their feminist definitions?

Practicing Criticism on the Blog Space

Caroline Kline is a "perma"[21] (permanent contributor) and founding member of the *Feminism and Religion* website. She is a feminist woman who actively participates in The Church of Jesus Christ of Latter-Day Saints (Mormon Church). Almost exclusively, her posts are about her engagement and participation as a feminist in the Mormon Church. In one post discussing Mormon ideals, Caroline recalls how twelve years earlier, when she was not yet married, she had a difficult time making sense of the ideal that husbands should preside over their wives, as it seemed contradictory to another Mormon ideal that describes marriage as an equal partnership between a husband and a wife.[22] She was struggling with this ideal in conversation with her then-boyfriend (now husband). She remembers that, despite the ideal's implication to the contrary, she became convinced of her full humanity,

> I first articulated to myself a truth I would later often return to: that I am fully human, fully responsible before God, an agent in my own right, and an equal partner in the truest sense of the word. My future husband would need to see me as such for any marriage to survive. And God must see me as such as well.[23]

The point of her post was to stress the importance of asking questions of one's own religion and one's place within it, framing it as part of the responsibility of women who participate in traditions that they hope to see transform. She ended her post by expressing her hope for progress and change within the church and her own commitment with her other Mormon sisters to "work to uplift and empower all humans in our fold."[24]

Caroline is a feminist doing work within a patriarchal religious tradition to bring about change and transformation for a more-just and empowering situation for all people, women especially. As she does this, she strongly affirms her status as fully human and equal before others, before God. She received a variety of responses by people of different feminist definitions who engaged with her on this post. June Courage is a reader and regular commentator on the blog who according to her self-description is a former Catholic. She begins her comment by saying,

> OK, I'm gonna [*sic*] bring a storm down on my head, but I have to say what I have said before: ALL the religions of the Book, and their off-shoots, are structurally misogynist, and NO amount of tinkering with the system is going to change this. The only way for women is out . . .[25]

In her comment, June Courage effectively deems Caroline's chosen feminist enactment as invalid. June does not consider it a viable option to choose to stay and participate in reforming a tradition from within, as Caroline has done. Later within the same comment, June Courage states, "the religions of the Book offer women nothing more than the comfort blanket of obedience to a tradition which will give them refuge but no dignity." In contradiction to Caroline's own expression, June Courage's comment negates Caroline's conviction and affirmation of her own dignity.

In a similar manner, commenting on the same post, Turtle Woman also evaluates Caroline's reality for her and re-narrates her experience, stating,

> I don't do patriarchal religion or participate in groups that are run by patriarchs. They really can't be reformed. So we have to look at what the reasons for women's compromise and subservience to men is really all about. It is habit, it is the lock box of heteronormative family life, women's weakness for crumbs rather than liberation. Women's weakness and belief in things they grew up with and remain stuck in.

In this comment, Turtle Woman not only judges Caroline's right to name her own experience, but further denies any feminist empowerment that Caroline has claimed for herself with the Mormon tradition, calling her participation in the religion a matter of habit, compromise, subservience, and settling for crumbs. Some blog readers responded differently, their comments ranging from an expression of support to encouragement and an acknowledgement of commonality in experience. Barbara Ardinger, a perma on FAR who practices

Goddess Spirituality, left a short comment on Caroline's post simply stating, "Hooray for you and Sister Joan[26] and other women for asking questions!" Nancy Vedder-Shults, a reader and regular commentator on FAR, affirmed Caroline and also acknowledged the oppression caused to women by LDS church leaders,

> I think you are a very courageous woman, Caroline. As a feminist who came of age in the 1960s, I have seen what the LDS patriarchs did to the first women who questioned their authority. Sonia Johnson comes immediately to mind, a Mormon woman who supported the ERA and as a result, was excommunicated from the LDS. Her book *From Housewife to Heretic* was an eye-opener for many.

One last example of the diverse responses Caroline's post received is a comment from Bobbie Taylor, a feminist who identifies as a former Mormon. She has only commented twice on FAR, both times to Caroline's posts.[27] In this comment, Bobbie expresses commonality in experience and the difficulty that came with her own choice to leave a patriarchal religion,[28]

> Very eloquently stated. While I support every feminists [*sic*] right to either be a reform or revolutionary feminist (terms used by Carol Christ and Judith Plaskow) when it comes to their religious traditions, I myself had to leave a patriarchal religion as I saw no way that it could be reformed. It was very hard to do and even though I left it 5 years ago I am still struggling with finding another spiritual practice that satisfies my need for community, social justice, equality, and a comfortable relationship with the divine.

Some of these comments reflect the authors' willingness, if not their active practice, to turn the critical gaze back onto themselves. Their way of engaging with their feminist other contains within it an ethos of openness; of course, others' ways do not. Turtle Woman conveys certitude and even rigidity about the definition of feminisms to which she holds (which in this case might be properly referred to as the singular feminism). She seems to walk into the encounter with her mind already made up and is willing to discursively impose her opinion upon another. It is clear, however, that this is not the only manner in which one can engage with the feminist other. Also possible, as is reflected by Barbara, Nancy, and Bobbie's comments, is approaching the encounter without the assumption of the universal authority and rightness of one's position but engaging the other with "their right to have one's mind changed."[29] Indeed, all can bring forth wisdom and insight from their particular perspectives. And even if not universally appropriate for all, those insights may nonetheless enrich and inform the experience and situation of another. But it is not possible for feminisms to be experienced as potentially liberative if feminist-identified people, among whom I count myself, are not willing to recognize their own limits, make room for one another's feminist enactments, or turn the critical gaze back onto themselves—all of which I propose can and ought to be practiced in the micro space of a blog.

Conclusion

Toward the end of her book, Angela Pears says, "It seems that feminist informed theologies, and perhaps feminisms in general, are still quite a way from comfortable acceptance and recognition of the integrity and necessity of detailed critical analysis and deconstruction of themselves."[30] It may be that we are not prepared for the vulnerability that comes with our own deconstruction. It may be that Mahmood's expanded definition of critique with its built – in potential for our own undoing is more than we are willing to do. For that truly is the difficulty—to choose to be undone by another and to be willing to make room for our feminist other. Are we willing?

One difficulty with the medium of the blog space is the fact that people can simply choose not to engage. Even after a conversation has already begun across feminist differences, any of those involved can choose to disengage at any given moment. At the same time, many return to the conversation repeatedly, even when their rhetoric belies an unwillingness to be undone. Does that they show up indicate a possible willingness to listen and not just insist on their viewpoint?

The writers of the blog by the very act of writing a public piece are the first to open themselves to the vulnerability of being deconstructed. And then those who comment are not far behind, perhaps even when their rhetoric does not explicitly reflect that openness. Does the engagement itself count as an effort to make room for the feminist other, or is it necessary to reflect that openness in the rhetoric one uses? On FAR, even though Turtle Woman is one of the most frequent commentators, people do not generally respond to her. Is it because she does not reflect openness to being undone when she offers her critiques to others, or is it because of one's own fear of being undone by her? When she refers to "women's weakness for crumbs rather than liberation," in reference to those who stay in patriarchal religions, is the fear that her statement may be true simply too much to bear? Mahmood's experience with the women of the Islamic Revival movement in Egypt, women whose worldview was very different from her own, disrupted her understandings of agency and empowerment within her feminisms. I contend that it is worth grappling with baffling encounters with feminist others and worth opening oneself to the possibility of being undone, for one can use the "undoneness" that occurs to strengthen and deepen one's own feminist work and activism—religion included—and at the same time to expand the borders of that feminism. To do so is to give embodied witness to an ethic and vision for a world in which we do not discount, silence, or subsume the voice and experience of another. For what is at stake is the affirmation of all people's dignity as equal and full human beings.

Feminisms' liberative potential is increased when spaces are created in which participants may willingly be undone by their mutually "undoing" encounters, more than when the borders of feminisms are maintained. Practicing Mahmood's expanded understanding of criticism literally makes room for valuing another's different and often distant voice, not as an abstraction to which one has no relation, nor as a source of threat, but as a sister, a partner in the transformation of a world that begins with the very seeds of one's micro actions, even those that take place in the micro space of a blog. The aim sought in these feminist encounters across difference is well captured by a quote from Judith Butler's *Precarious Life* in her essay "Violence, Mourning, and Politics," when she reflects on the possibility of an international feminist coalition and the possibility of our encounter with one another.[31] She states,

> For if I am confounded by you, then you are already of me, and I am nowhere without you. I cannot muster the "we" except by finding the way in which I am tied to "you," by trying to translate but finding that my own language must break up and yield if I am to know you. You are what I gain through this disorientation and loss. This is how the human comes into being, again and again, as that which we have yet to know.[32]

To expand the borders of feminisms requires our undoing, our deconstruction, and the breaking open of our definitions. It is a difficult task indeed. But not to do so means that we give up the possibility of gaining one another as sisters, as subjects with whom we collaborate in the messiness of life—the living, the dying, the joyful, the painful, the healing, and the just—"that which we have yet to know."

Notes

1. I learned this from Angela Pears, *Feminist Christian Encounters: The Methods and Strategies of Feminist Informed Christian Theologies* (Hampshire, UK: Ashgate, 2004).
2. Saba Mahmood, *Politics of Piety: The Islamic Revival and the Feminist Subject* (Princeton, NJ: Princeton University Press, 2005), xi.
3. The word "blog" is short for weblog—a site on the World Wide Web onto which entries are published with as much frequency as desired. These are set up in a variety of formats by groups or individuals and range in topic and focus.
4. *Feminism and Religion* (blog), http://feminismandreligion.com.
5. I am one of the co-founders and project directors of the blog and currently a PhD candidate in Practical Theology at Boston University School of Theology.
6. Rosemary Radford Ruether, "What Is Feminism?" *Feminism and Religion* (blog), Accessed February 12, 2013, http://feminismandreligion.com/rosemary-radford-ruether-on-feminism/.
7. I will refer to Turtle Woman with female pronouns in order to be consistent with her online name, though there is no way of verifying if Turtle Woman is, in fact, a woman. Many people, if not most people, who comment use their full names and can easily be found through a Google search. Turtle Woman is one of the few who uses a pseudonym.
8. An internal search of the *Feminism and Religion* site shows 253 comments by Turtle Woman between August 13, 2011, and February 10, 2013. Turtle Woman's comments can also be found by searching for "site:feminismandreligion.com turtle

woman" on Google—this search turns up 299 results, some of which are comments by other readers in which Turtle Woman is referenced or addressed.

9. See comment in Amy Levine, "Liberalism as Feminist Religious Tradition: Friend or Foe?" *Feminism and Religion* (blog), May 2012, http://feminismandreligion. com/2012/05/10/liberalism-as-feminist-religious-tradition-friend-or-folly-by-amy-levin/.
10. Ibid., see comment section.
11. Mahmood, 5–6.
12. Mahmood, 36.
13. Mahmood, 36–37.
14. Mahmood, xi.
15. Mahmood, 39.
16. Mahmood, 14–15.
17. Pears, 9–10.
18. Mahmood, xi.
19. Mahmood, 37.
20. Mahmood, 199.
21. Caroline's posts, "Posts by Caroline Kline," *Feminism and Religion* (blog), http:// feminismandreligion.com/author/carolinekline/.
22. Caroline Kline, "We Are Responsible for Asking the Questions," *Feminism and Religion* (blog), July 2012, http://feminismandreligion.com/2012/07/03/we-are-responsible-for-asking-the-questions-by-caroline-kline/.
23. Ibid., see second paragraph.
24. Ibid., see last paragraph.
25. Ibid., see first comment.
26. Barbara Ardinger is referring to Sister Joan Chittister, whom Caroline referenced in her blog post.
27. A Google search of the *Feminism and Religion* blog site, "site:feminismandreligion. com Bobbie Taylor," shows the two results: http://tinyurl.com/cdjqmuy.
28. In a comment on another post, Bobbie Taylor writes about her choice to leave the Mormon faith. See Caroline Kline, "Mormonism's Heavenly Mother: Why I Stand By Her," *Feminism and Religion* (blog), June 2012, http://feminismandreligion. com/2012/06/05/mormonisms-heavenly-mother-why-i-stand-by-her-by-caroline-kline/.
29. I first heard this specific reference to having the "right" to have one's mind changed from Pamela Lightsey at a public lecture at Boston University School of Theology on January 24, 2013.
30. Pears, 176.
31. Judith Butler, *Precarious Life: The Powers of Mourning and Violence* (London: Verso, 2004).
32. Butler, 49.

5 The Catholic Church and Social Media

Embracing [Fighting] a Feminist Ideological Theo-Ethical Discourse and Discursive Activism

Michele Stopera Freyhauf

Social media embraces a feminist model of activism and builds community through experiential relationships and by reaching out to everyone, despite socio-political, economic, or religious categories. For the Vowed Religious,[1] this is not new—they embraced this type of activism during the civil rights movement in the 1970s, and capitalized on the use of social media in an effective manner today. Social media is a powerful forum for activism because it is inexpensive, immediate, and has a global reach, giving the Vowed Religious a means to promote the social gospel of Jesus.

The Vatican encouraged Catholics to use social media as a form of evangelization, outreach, and education. Unbeknown to the hierarchy, they are using a feminist tool that they know nothing about; a tool that has proven to educate, build community, and resulted in a pushback from the very people they seek to shepherd. They have garnered more criticism due to swift and punitive actions taken against the Vowed Religious and women, the result of which has been so heavy-handed that they have excommunicated anyone supporting the ordination of women without providing proper notice. In addition, they have gone so far as to publish comments that accuse their critics of being communists and embracing Nazi ideological views.[2]

In this essay, I will examine the ecclesiastical barriers of activism and use of social media by the Vowed Religious and the ordained, including the hierarchy. Through this exploration, measurable results emerge that show a group of Catholics who are no longer embracing the doctrine of blind obedience, but are flocking together, becoming educated, questioning, and, through their knowledge, beginning to promote change within the Church. What does the future Catholic Church look like in this new cyberworld? A banding together of a global Catholic community, or a schismatic movement that fractures the church in a way that has not been seen since the Protestant Reformation? The result depends on the Vatican's response, which under the papacy of Benedict XVI ruled with an iron fist, effectively alienating anyone who exercised their canonical right to follow their conscience and challenge Church doctrine.

Ecclesiastical Barriers on Activism

A study performed in 2000 examined traditional activism methods of the Vowed Religious and Ordained Men during the civil rights era. Until recently, the Vowed Religious enjoyed certain autonomy from diocesan Bishops and the Vatican. Ordained Men, on the other hand, vow obedience to their diocesan Bishop who, through the 1971 Synod of Bishops and later reiterated in 1993 by Pope John Paul II, are prohibited from engaging in activist activities, especially anything that is interpreted as political,

> Nevertheless, Jesus never wanted to be involved in a political movement, and fled from every attempt to draw him into earthly questions and affairs (cf. Jn 6:15). The kingdom he came to establish does not belong of this world (cf. Jn 18:36). For this reason he said to those who wanted him to take a stand regarding the civil power: "Give to Caesar what belongs to Caesar and to God what belongs to God."
>
> (Mt 22:21)[3]

Further reiterated in the *Catechism of the Catholic Church*, John Paul II differentiates the obligation and duty of the priests and laity, explaining,

> It is not the role of the pastors of the Church to intervene directly in the political structuring and organization of social life. This task is part of the vocation of the lay faithful, acting on their own initiative with their fellow citizens.
>
> (CCC 2442)[4]

Ordained Men who engage in any type of activism are at risk—risk of excommunication, alienating their parishioners, and financial ruin—as opposed to the Vowed Religious, who received warning by the Vatican for advocating "radical feminist views" but have no discernible financial risk,

> Bishops serve until promotion, retirement, or death. The Bishop is simultaneously responsible to higher Church authority and to the Church members. In the mission of the Church as a religious organization, diocesan priests are left out of the decision-making process determining leadership positions such as Bishop. Bishops' actions are not directly dependent on the priests' wishes. Rather, the Bishop is relatively more beholden to the Church hierarchy.[5]

Because of this, many Ordained Men must choose between their vocation and activism.

While they have, in theory, a canonical right to exercise their conscience, they are limited in expression by their priestly ministry.[6] Because of the innate conflicts and constraints that arose from the level of subjugation exercised by hierarchy, two-thirds of the priests who engaged in activism during the Civil Rights era left their vocation. This number is striking when you compare the Vowed Religious who left their vocation during the same time—which was roughly 1:9 or 11 percent.[7] Today, we see a continuation of this trend with a shrinking priesthood. Fewer men are choosing priesthood as a vocation, and for those who are ordained, many are leaving, either voluntarily or involuntarily, if they disobey to their superiors and follow their conscience.

Our world now sees punishment for exercising one's conscience; warnings are issued at a fast pace and excommunications are handed down for any Ordained Man who dissents from the teachings or interpretations of the hierarchy, causing most to endure financial ruin, and loss of status, vocation, salary, and diocesan pension, among other financial "perks" enjoyed by Ordained Men. This is clearly demonstrated with the recent excommunication of Father Roy Bourgeois, a member of the Maryknoll community for forty-five years and a priest for thirty years. Bourgeois exercised his right of conscience to support the ordination of women and was excommunicated in rapid fashion. Expelled from his Maryknoll community at age 75, Bourgeois also loses his source of income, including his pension.

The Vowed Religious, on the other hand, are considered to be laity—and thus under the definition provided by the Synod and John Paul II—have a duty to engage in activism in a way that reflects the Gospel teachings of Jesus. Unlike the priests, they are not forced to choose their vocation over their activism. However, imposed restrictions occur when their interpretation of the Gospels does not coincide with the understanding of the hierarchy. The recent warnings against feminist theologians and the Vowed Religious by the Congregation for the Doctrine of Faith (CDF) in 2012 are a clear demonstration of this stance.

In 2012, the CDF not only issued warnings against theologians such as Sister Margaret Farley, but also ruled against the Leadership of Catholic Women Religious (LCWR); 80 percent of the U.S. Vowed Religious Women belong to the LCWR.[8] The warning states that the LCWR undermines "Roman Catholic teaching with radical feminist themes and taken positions that undermined Catholic teaching on the all-male priesthood, marriage and homosexuality."[9] Sister Simone Campbell "believed the Vatican's harsh tone stemmed from anger about the nuns' support for President Barack Obama's healthcare reform"—a reform that the Bishops opposed.[10] Whatever the reason, this warning crossed a line in the sand and became a catalyst that started a fury of activity through the channels of social media—an avenue that not only supports the Vowed Religious in this recent action by the CDF, but which is also a tool used in their own activism.

Subordination and a Feminist Interpretive Framework

The Vowed Religious utilize a model of activism that is a participating democracy rooted in feminist ideals.[11] This was true in the Civil Rights era and is true today as they enjoy a measure of success using social media. To understand what this means, one must first understand the definition and understanding of feminist theory. Helene Tallon Russell states that feminist consciousness comes out of shared and personal experiences, not only through thinking, but also by participation.[12] Shared experiences of women become the interpretative framework, an epistemological source, and embodied knowledge in which to communicate and participate in social, political, and cultural contexts. Mary Daly elaborates that participation, as a primary epistemological source for feminist thoughts, necessitates a "profound alteration of consciousness and behavior—that is of the context in which words are spoken."[13]

Oppression influences this interpretative framework. Vowed Religious—or more accurately stated, women in general—are subordinate to men, especially within the hierarchy of the Catholic Church. The Catholic Church ascribes to a strict hierarchical structure whereby women, by their biological gender alone, are prohibited from most leadership positions and are always subordinate to Ordained Men. Amina Mama points out that "subordinated groups [are] empowered to articulate their realities and become subjects rather than objects of knowledge-production processes."[14] According to Mary E. Hunt, John Paul II "wrote that a woman cannot be thought of in 'criteria of understanding and judgment that do not pertain to her nature,'" in other words, "women are by nature subordinate so do not question it."[15]

The subordinate nature of women is clearly reflected in the Church hierarchy. Father Wojciech Giertych, a papal theologian for Pope Benedict XVI, states that maleness is essential to being a priest because, "a priest is supposed to serve as an image of Christ . . . priests love the church in a characteristically 'male way' when they show concern about structures"—structures which range from buildings to the relationship between church and state.[16] He diminished women who may feel called to priesthood. "Such a 'subjective' belief does not indicate the objective existence of a vocation."[17]

Unfortunately, the priesthood in the Catholic Church has subordinated and continues to oppress women because the hierarchy from priest to Pope symbolizes power. Power does not follow a feminist model, a model that focuses on recognizing the gifts of all participants, no matter their gender or status in life. When it comes to activism, one must do so cautiously so as not to fall victim to this same trap. Abuse of power was the very thing Jesus fought while on this earth. The Vowed Religious embody this adverse stance to power structures through their own community and mission. This mission, defined under *Gaudium et Spes* (*Hope and Joy*), is to be in solidarity with the whole human family, by serving the most downtrodden and disenfranchised members of society, focusing the social needs of the time.

Arguably, Jesus followed a feminist ideology and discourse in his earthly ministry; a ministry lived on a daily basis by the Vowed Religious who root their efforts within their own experiences and relationships within their respective communities. Hunt sees the totality of feminist ideology as a tree,

> the "roots" of feminism are in the oppression of women around the world, but the sprouts, leaves, branches, and the shade that the whole tree

provides are in the many forms of oppression that include racism, colonialism, ecocide, heterosexism, ableism, ageism, and in the myriad ways in which people are made poor by the greed and entitlement of others.[18]

This metaphor embodies Jesus in a way that differs from the "male way" that men love the Church, which Giertych defined as brick and mortar and working along governmental and hierarchical power structures.

Moving away from power, Kate Ott reflects on the understanding of an ethic that embodies a feminist ideology. She states, "Feminist theo-ethical discourse has from its beginning been concerned with how communities 'ought to be,' and perhaps more importantly, how we go about getting there."[19] Within the walls of oppression and subordination, Vowed Religious have always engaged in a feminist theo-ethical discourse through their very own communities. If we add "discursive activism" as defined by Frances Shaw, feminist embodiment through a theo-ethical discourse seeks to critique and change mainstream ideology; a perspective that intersects with multiple identities, "critical of multiple systems of oppression" while engaging with politics of many issues rooted in difference and exclusion.[20]

Social Media and the Vowed Religious

When the Second Vatican Council issued the conciliar document *Perfectae Caritatis*, (Perfect Charity, the decree on the adaptation and renewal for religious life), *aggiornamento* (bringing up to date) for the Vowed Religious was embraced.[21] Many orders removed their habits and moved out of convents to live among and with the faithful. However, this singular event became a catalyst for feminist changes within the Church. Motivated by faith and religious tradition, Catholic feminism adheres to the Gospel mandate for social justice, liberation, and radial equality.[22] The Vowed Religious care for the sick, live in poverty-stricken areas, serve the poor, and fight for the rights of the oppressed in a humble manner, never seeking credit individually or within their community for any successes. These women, who largely went unnoticed by the public for their works, emerged from a rigid hierarchical system "so rapidly and radically, that most of us did not catch up with them" until the CDF issued the warning against the LCWR.[23]

This warning has caused a stir in social media platforms—"The Vatican announcement has energized Catholic journalism and the left and right Catholic blogosphere."[24] Soon, social media sites were flooded with words of support and thanks for the Vowed Religious, who give of themselves faithfully and without expectation. When speaking of his female faith hero, Tony Blair stated that Catholic Sisters are "women of faith [who] make commitments, innovate, and take risks" at a grassroots level that can be both "demanding and sometimes dangerous."[25] They "champion human dignity when human dignity is the very last thing that people they are working with have experienced" and are "exemplar(s) of how religion can be a force for good in the world, champions of a networked Church coming to terms with problems of the contemporary world" as leaders.[26]

Because of the respect and impact that Vowed Religious had on so many people, the warning brought a flood of support. For example, James Martin took to Twitter and Facebook to show support for the Sisters who made such a difference in his life:

> Catholic Sisters are my heroes. They have been my teachers, spiritual directors, mentors, bosses and friends. I can barely begin to describe the admiration I have for these women . . . for what they have done for God, for the church, for what Catholics call the "people of God," and for me.[27]

His twitter initiative began with the hashtag #WhatSistersMeanToMe" starting with the "Ursuline nun who served as his spiritual director" and taught "him more about spirituality than any Jesuit."[28] He also mentioned:

- "The nuns murdered in El Salvador while serving the poor; Vowed Religious who live among the poor from the ghettos of New York;
- Maryknoll Sisters immersed in many years of ministry in remote villages of Nairobe, Kenya, and East Africa; and,
- Great nuns of history like St. Catherine of Siena—a Sister "who also ran afoul of the hierarchy of her day."[29]

Another one of his tweets sums up the Vowed Religious and their activism through social media in spite of the Vatican's warnings—"Catholic sisters teach me what it means to persevere without the benefit of institutional power."[30]

Thanks to social media, their importance and the oppression they face within the Church is in the forefront and the faithful are no longer willing to be quiet or accept with blind obedience words coming from a bunch of men who are largely seen as suffering from "Ivory Tower Syndrome." To say this another way, the ones making the rules are not the ones in the trenches doing the work, which makes them so far removed from the people that a disconnect exists between the interpretation of teachings and the real impact they have on the people. Instead of bearing witness to the women who live and work among the "least of these," as Jesus mandated, they bully a group of faithful women who bare witness to the complexities that people face on a daily basis.

From the warning issued against the vowed religious to the *latae sententiae* excommunication of any woman or Ordained Man who support the ordination of women, social media is a powerful tool that is changing the face of the Catholic Church. With the rise of the Internet, social media has "become a fact of life for civil society worldwide, involving many actors—regular citizens, activists, nongovernmental organizations, telecommunications firms, software providers, [and] governments."[31] People engage with the Internet, mainly through social media and networking sites, as a means of political and civil involvement.

Comparing this to activism in the mid-to-late 1960s, digital media has become a vital tool, because it is inexpensive, vast, and instantly accessible, which helps build momentum at a rapid pace.[32] As Mary E. Hunt states, "technology plus ideas and hard work can change the world as we know it."[33]

Social Media: An Embodiment of Feminist Ideology

According to Kate Ott, social media can be limited due to one's own "personal limits, societal structural limits, and . . . limits of the theological tradition."[34] Certainly, Ordained Men fall victim to the limits of structure and tradition; however, Vowed Religious have benefited and continue to capitalize on this new medium as a form of praxis. Gina Messina-Dysert states that "blogging is a meaningful mode of communication for women on many levels and should be understood as a feminist endeavor," empowers women through their expressions, and transcends geographical as well as cultural boundaries.[35] Adding to the idea of blogging, I would argue that social media itself is an embodiment of feminist ideology.

Returning to a term used in the previous section, the way the Vowed Religious use social media is rooted in feminist ideological theo-ethical discourse and discursive activism. Not only do the Vowed Religious embrace social media, but the Vatican has also embraced this technology as a tool of evangelization, reaching out to those who were considered to be unreachable. Has the Vatican unintentionally promoted the feminist model of activism or evangelism—developed community, used gifts and talents to transcend cultural and societal boundaries, pastoral care, collaboration, and promoted the Catholic Church and its teachings? Arguably yes, and, to much surprise, it has not worked to its favor.

The Use and Misuse of Social Media by the Catholic Church

From the Vatican to the laity, social media has become a tool of evangelization and a means of reaching out to the global community. Greg Kanda, a Deacon in the Catholic Church and blogger, stated,

> the Internet makes us acutely aware [that] the world is bigger than we realize and smaller than expect . . . we are bound together in ways we cannot imagine . . . we are catholic, which means we are universal, and that we are everything and everyone, for better and for worse.[36]

Dennis Poust also believes that social networking sites "helps us to keep our fingers on the pulse of the Catholics in the pews."[37] Initially, the Vatican embraced social media as a gift and tool of evangelization and catalyst for information.

In 2009, Pope Benedict XVI promoted the use of social media in his message delivered on the 43rd World Communication Day, stating, "these technologies are truly a gift to humanity and we must endeavor to ensure that the benefits they offer are put at the service of all human individuals and communities, especially those who are most disadvantaged and vulnerable."[38]

Through "Catholic Media Promotion Day" on March 15, 2011, Catholics who have a blog, podcast, or other social media account were asked to list three other social media sites for the purpose of increasing exposure to "solid, Catholic content on the internet." Pope Benedict once again stood behind social media, stating, "The contribution made by believers can be useful to the world of mass media, opening horizons of meaning and value which digital culture alone is incapable of seeing or representing."[39] The Vatican even launched several Twitter accounts in 2010 to share news and "inform about the life of the Church."[40]

Several members of the hierarchy also embraced social media. One example is Cardinal Timothy Dolan, who uses Twitter to speak to a wider and potentially younger group of people. Cardinal Dolan also uses Twitter under the name @CardinalDolan. His first tweet was sent May 8, 2012, and he tweets about twice a day, offering "religious meditations, plugs for his radio shows and occasional flares of gentle humor."[41] According to Archdiocese of New York spokesperson, Joseph Zwilling, "Dolan hopes the platform will help him reach new and perhaps younger audiences by extending 'an implicit invitation' to learn abut church teachings."[42]

Catholics have taken to social media to make friends, spread news, and learn as well as share their faith with others.[43] According to Alyson E. King and Avi Hyman, "one of the most exciting aspects of the Internet is its potential for the creation of communities that cut across the border and distance."[44] James Martin, SJ, is a prolific user of social media and states,

> Social media [is] the perfect place for people to weigh in when they feel voiceless . . . sometime Catholics don't feel that they have venues in which they can express their views"—something that is necessary because "everyone who is baptized is part of the church.[45]

Social media has allowed the laity, the "faithful" to engage in politics to promote Catholic teaching. New York State Catholic Conference communications director Dennis Poust states, "Facebook and Twitter have become integral to our advocacy," and, "email is quickly becoming an afterthought for online communications, particularly among the young."[46]

Embracing social media provided unexpected results for the Vatican. The biggest issue is that use of social media has shown how out of touch the hierarchy is through their unvetted interviews and statements that seem to mimic the bully in high school instead of representing Christ. Instead of using social media in a positive manner, there are many ordained or laity who used this mode of communication to promote hate and dissent, alienating Catholics who may disagree, instead of bridging gaps, dialoguing, and building a diverse community.

The result of this can be seen with the Congregation for the Doctrine of Faith, the United States Council of Catholic Bishops (USCCB), and other ordained in leadership operating with a heavy hand against anyone exercising activism that conflicts with their understanding of Church teaching, despite a person's canonical right to do so. Citing the online world as "the new wild west," the USCCB's Office of Digital Media created guidelines for how Catholics should engage in social media.[47] Because of this viewpoint of social media, Pope Benedict XVI called the Church to a more aggressive stance.

Conclusion: Social Media and a New and Emergent Catholic Church

While embracing social media, the hierarchy of the Catholic Church received a very unexpected result—a result that they are trying to remedy through guidelines, warnings, and threats. As previously established, social media is an embodiment of feminist ideology and a tool of activism. Because those who adhere to a hierarchical and autonomous existence have no understanding of what this means, embracing this tool backfired for those seeking to keep the faithful blindly obedient. Is the downfall due to their misunderstanding of what it means to be a feminist, what feminism is, and/or the meaning of discursive activism? Instead of embracing a feminist discursive activism and ideology as Jesus did, they are fighting to retain power and control over the Church, with no regard for the cost.

Focusing on the need for information and capabilities of social media, Catholics are banding together, becoming educated and informed, and learning to question many of the edicts handed down by the hierarchy or responses of those who are part of the hierarchical structure of the Church in an immediate nature. This has even impacted Ordained Men not only in North America, but also in Ireland, Australia, Germany, and Switzerland. These men are making a stance to support the Vowed Religious and the ordination of women in record numbers. Many are falling victim to the Vatican's iron fist with excommunications and warnings issued in rapid fashion.

The pushback from Catholics worldwide is intense, due to the Vatican's swift action and oppression against women and the Vowed Religious. Recently I learned through Facebook that Archbishop Gerhard Mueller, the new head of the Congregation for the Doctrine of Faith (CDF), issued a statement attacking the statements of any Catholic questioning this disproportionate treatment against women,

> North America and Europe are conducting a "concerted campaign" to discredit the Catholic Church that is resulting in open attacks against the priest . . . those attacking the Church borrow argument used by totalitarian ideologies such as Communism and Nazism against Christianity.[48]

Within hours, 176 comments were posted and it was shared through social media outlets almost 300 times, garnering a backlash that could further the divide.

The Vowed Religious, on the other hand, capitalized through this medium to raise awareness to human trafficking, oppression, and many other social justice issues. Sister Simone Campbell stated, "for me, to follow Jesus was to engage in my community that struggled for civil rights . . . to nourish my faith was to nourish my quest for justice, and my community does that."[49] They embody feminist ideology and theo-ethical discourse through discursive action. They become the embodiment of Jesus, more so then those that choose to oppress and silence them.

One thing is certain, change is in the air and social media is responsible for this change. Whether this means a smaller Roman Catholic Church or a future schismatic movement is dependent upon the openness of the hierarchy to engage with the faithful as Jesus mandated. If a schismatic movement occurs, this movement will be born out of the same abuse of power as the Great East-West Schism and Protestant Reformation and promises to see the same results; another division within the Catholic Church.

Notes

1. In the essay, I use the term "Vowed Religious" to mean U.S. Catholic Vowed Religious Sisters and Nuns, "Ordained Men" to mean Catholic priests, and "hierarchy" to mean anyone with ruling power or status of bishop and higher in the Roman Catholic Church. Catholics and Catholic Church is defined as Roman Catholic and not the Eastern Orthodox branches of Catholicism.
2. Associated Press, "Archbishop Gerhard Mueller: Critics Waging 'Pogrom' Against Church." *The Huffington Post,* February 2, 2013, www.huffingtonpost.com/2013/02/02/archbishop-gerhard-mueller-critics-waging-pogrom-against-church_n_2606241.html?1359822352&ncid=edlinkusaolp00000009.
3. John Paul II, "Priests Do Not Have a Political Mission" (sermon, General Audience, Vatican) July 28, 1993, www.vatican.va/holy_father/john_paul_ii/audiences/alpha/data/aud19930728en.html.
4. Ibid.
5. Marybeth C. Stalp and Bill Winders, "Power in the Margins: Gendered Organizational Effects on Religious Activism," *Review of Religious Research* 42, no. 1 (2000): 54.
6. Greg Kandra, "On Priests and Political Activism," *Patheos* (blog), August 31, 2012, www.patheos.com/blogs/deaconsbench/2012/08/on-priests-and-poltical-activism/.
7. Marybeth C. Stalp et al., 41.
8. June 3, 2012, the CDF issued a warning against Sister Margret Farley's book *Just Love: A Framework for Christian Sexual Ethics* because it contained teachings that do not conform with the Catholic Church.
9. David Pitt, "Nuns' Bus Tour Highlights Clash with Bishops over Their Activism," *Washington Post,* June 18, 2012, http://p.washingtines.com/news/2012/jun/18/nuns-bus-tour-highlights-class-with-bishops-over-t/.
10. Bruce Nolan, "Rev. James Martin, Jesuit Priest and Writer, Launches Twitter Campaign Supporting American Nuns' Work," *NOLA: Everything New Orleans,* April 24, 2012, http://blog.nola.com/religion_impact/print.html?entry=/2012/04/rev_james_martin_jesuit_priest.html.
11. Marybeth C. Stalp et al., 41.
12. Helene Tallon Russell, "Introduction to Feminist Theology," in *Creating Women's Theology: A Movement Engaging Process Thought,* ed. Monica A. Coleman, Nancy R. Howell, and Helene Tallon Russell (Eugene, OR: Pickwick Publications, 2011), 5.

13. Mary Daly, *Beyond God the Father: Toward a Philosophy of Women's Liberation,* 2nd ed. (Boston, MA: Beacon Press, 1985), xix.
14. Amina Mama, *Beyond the Masks: Race, Gender, and Subjectivity* (New York: Routledge, 1995), 14.
15. Mary E. Hunt, "Talking about Radical Feminism," *Feminist Studies in Religion* (blog), August 7, 2012, www.fsrinc.org/blog/talking-about-radical-feminism.
16. Francis X. Rocca "Why Not Women Priests? The Papal Theologian Explains," *Catholic News Agency,* February 2, 2013, www.catholicnews.com/data/stories/cns/1300417.htm.
17. Ibid.
18. Hunt, "Talking about Radical Feminism."
19. Kate Ott, "Special AAR Series Part I: Re-Envisioning the Academy as 'Open Source' Community," *Feminism and Religion* (blog), December 14, 2012, http://feminismandreligion.com/2012/12/14/special-aar-series-part-i-re-envisioning-the-academy-as-open-source-community-by-kate-ott-with-introduction-and-response-by-mary-hunt/.
20. Frances Shaw, "Discursive Politics Online: Political Creativity and Affective Networking in Australian Blogs" (PhD diss., University of South Wales, Australia, 2012), 8, in Academia.edu, www.academia.edu/2031938/Discursive_politics_online_political_creativity_and_affective_networking_in_Australian_feminist_blogs_PhD_Thesis.
21. Certainly women left their religious communities because they viewed the changes as difficult, but most embraced these changes. See Sandra Schneiders's explanation of this transition, which is understood as evolutionary in *Finding the Treasure: Locating Catholic Religious Life in a New Ecclesial and Cultural Context,* specifically Chapters 5 and 6.
22. Mary J. Henold, *Catholic and Feminist: The Surprising History of the American Catholic Feminists Movement* (Chapel Hill, NC: The University of North Carolina, 2008), Kindle Locations 133–134.
23. Jamie Manson, "What LCWR Teaches Us about Church Leadership: Grace on the Margins," *National Catholic Reporter,* August 16, 2012, http://ncronline.org/blogs/grace-margins/what-lcwr-teaches-us-about-church-leadership.
24. Nolan, "Rev. James Martin."
25. Tony Blair, "My Female Faith Hero: Catholic Sisters," *The Huffington Post: United Kingdom,* August 3, 2012, www.huffingtonpost.co.uk/tony-blair/tony-blair-international-womens-day-catholic-sisters_b_1330298.html.
26. Ibid.
27. James Martin, "What Sisters Mean to Me," *Washington Post,* April 26, 2012, www.washingtonpost.com/blogs/guest-voices/post/what-sisters-mean-to-me/2012/04/26/glQA9AMuiT_blog.html.
28. Ibid.
29. Nolan, "Rev. James Martin."
30. Martin, "What Sisters Mean to Me."
31. Clay Shirky, *The Political Power of Social Media: Technology, the Public Sphere, and Political Change* (New York: Council on Foreign Relations, January/February 2011), 1.
32. Kristin LaRiviere et al., "About Campus," *About Campus* (July–August 2012): 10–14.
33. Mary E. Hunt, "Special AAR Series Part I: Re-Envisioning the Academy as 'open Source' Community by Kate Ott with Introduction and Response by Mary Hunt," *Feminism and Religion* (blog), December 14, 2012, http://feminismandreligion.com/2012/12/14/special-aar-series-part-i-re-envisioning-the-academy-as-open-source-community-by-kate-ott-with-introduction-and-response-by-mary-hunt/.
34. Ott, "Special AAR Series Part I: Re-Envisioning the Academy as 'Open Source' Community."

35. Gina Messina-Dysert, "Special Series Part I: Women Blogging Theo/alogy," *Feminist Studies in Religion*, December 14, 2012, www.fsrinc.org/blog/special-series-part-i-women-blogging-theoalogy.
36. Kandra, "On Priests and Political Activism."
37. Dave Maluchnik, "State Catholic Conferences Support Bishop Herzog's Call to Engage Social Media," Catholic Online, www.catholic.org/printer_friendly.php?section=Cathcom&id=39335.
38. Pope Benedict XVI, "New Technologies, New Relationships: Promoting a Culture of Respect, Dialogue, and Friendship," The Vatican, www.vatican.va/holy_father/benedict_xvi/messages.
39. Billy Atwell, "New Online Catholic Campaigns Leverage Social Media," Catholic Online, www.catholic.org/printer_friendly.php?section=Cathcom&id=40636.
40. The Vatican launched six Twitter Channels in English, Spanish, Italian, French, German, and Portuguese. See "Vatican Launches New Twitter Channels to Inform about the Life of the Church," *Catholic News Agency*, March 23, 2010, www.catholicnewsagency.com/news/vatican_launches_new_twitter_channels_to_inform_about_the_life_of_the_church/.
41. Matt Flegenheimer, "Now, @cardinaldolan," *New York Times*, May 20, 2012, www.nytimes.com/2012/05/20/nyregion/cardinal-timothy-dolan-embraces-140-characters.html?_r=0.
42. Ibid.
43. "Vatican Launches New Twitter Channels."
44. Alyson E. King and Avi Hyman. "Women's Studies and the Internet: A Future with a History," *Resources for Feminist Research* 27, no. 1 (1995): 13.
45. Dalina Castellanos, "Catholics All A-Twitter about the Role of Nuns," *Los Angeles Times*, May 17, 2012, articles.latimes.com/print/2012/may/17/nation/la-na-nuns-20120518.
46. Maluchnik, "State Catholic Conferences Support Bishop Herzog's Call to Engage Social Media."
47. Randy Sly, "US Catholic Bishops Publish Social Media Guidelines for Catholics," Catholic Online, www.catholic.org/printer_friendly.php?section=Cathcom&id=37479.
48. Associated Press "Archbishop Gerhard Mueller: Critics Waging 'pogrom' Against Church," *The Huffington Post*, February 2, 2013, www.huffingtonpost.com/2013/02/02/archbishop-gerhard-mueller-critics-waging-pogrom-against-church_n_2606241.html?1359822352&ncid=edlinkusaolp00000009.
49. Dalina Castellanos, "Catholics All A-Twitter about the Role of Nuns."

6   From Typewriters to Social Networking

A Feminist Organization's Techno History

Mary E. Hunt

We never scratched in the sand with a stick. But when the Women's Alliance for Theology, Ethics and Ritual (WATER) began in Silver Spring, Maryland (suburban Washington, DC) in 1983, typewriters, albeit electric ones, were essential equipment. I write this chapter on a MacBook Air, same basic keyboard but a far cry from the old machines.

As feminists in religion reflect on our collective use of technology, I offer the history of one thirty-year-old organization's technological evolution as a case study in how rapid, relentless, and profound the changes are, and how important it is to keep our work accessible to those who need it most.

The founding document of WATER was a three-page proposal for the "Women's Theological Alliance" which I typed complete with White Out. For the uninitiated, White Out is a liquid correction fluid applied to paper when one makes a typo, allowed to dry, and then typed on again. We made copies of the original document at the neighborhood print shop for distribution. Voilà, we were in business.

Thirty years later, we handle routine communication on iPhones, Apple laptops and iPads, and printers that scan and fax. We utilize social media, including Facebook and Twitter. We maintain a website and strategize how to move our newsletter from print to digital mode. Google groups are tools of the trade; flash drives are indispensable.

The evolution has felt seamless, if obligatory at times—from floppy disks to compact ones, from fax to email, from printing photos to carrying them around on the phone. We plan to embed videos soon in our website. The implications at each step are not trivial, and the gestalt is telling. More people are aware of our work and involved in parts of it than ever before. This is how a 21st-century nonprofit functions.

In the midst of enthusiasm for techno wonders, it is wise to remember, however, that the pioneers in the field of feminist studies in religion—including Georgia Harkness, Nelle Morton, Pauli Murray, to name just a few—never sent an email. I am quite sure that Mary Daly never blogged a day in her life. Ideas still trump technology. Hard work is all. But technology plus ideas and hard work can change the world as we know it.

A review of this process tells the technology story of one small nonprofit organization. It also serves as an example of how feminist work in religion has changed, for better and for worse. For some readers, this history will be very familiar. For others, especially for younger colleagues, it will be eye opening to realize that what we take for granted today as ways of communicating are really quite new approaches. My staff colleague had to ask about several things mentioned in this chapter as she had simply never been acquainted with a phone with a cord or a messenger knocking on the door! The amazing part is how those of us who have lived these changes have managed to take them in stride and do the work that technology purports to facilitate.

From Typewriters to Computers

The WATER office opened at 8035 13th Street in Silver Spring, Maryland (suburban Washington, DC), in April 1983. This followed several months of working on the dining room table and in the study of Diann Neu's and my modest home in the same neighborhood. Our goal was to bring feminist religious values to the service of social change. We did not state it so succinctly in those days, but it was the work we set out to do that needed to be done. We gathered a dozen women together who helped to sketch out the need we had identified, and then we took responsibly for bringing it to life.

Both staff members, Diann and I, had typewriters that we brought from home. We had one telephone line with two phones that we never dreamed of carrying in our pockets. They were desk phones with cords so one sat and talked at her desk. We had pens and paper, a pencil sharpener, and, eventually, a paper cutter for equipment. I do not mean to make it sound like we were cave people writing on the walls, but compared with the standard 21st-century office resources, we were primitive at the outset.

Building alliances is person-by-person work, each of whom must be communicated with, informed, and invited to participate. We typed virtually all of our correspondence, placed them in envelopes, and stamped and mailed them. Whether we were responding to an inquiry, sending out a funding letter, or mailing off an article for publication, the process was labor intensive but quite routine. We licked a lot of stamps in those early years.

We met and got to know many people for whom what we were offering by way of feminist theo-ethical programs, projects, and publications, liturgies/rituals, counseling, and organizing was what they needed. WATER was on its way from an idea to a place where women could do our work in religiously based social change unfettered by the demands of university or denomination. As much as a place, WATER was and remains a symbol of women's autonomous, interdependent, and women-funded work in religion. That is the world-changing part, as many women (and some feminist men) take energy and inspiration from, not to mention make connection with, this work in order to do their own.

Short notes were handwritten and mailed in the 1980s and 1990s. Reports were typed and copied. In time, we wrote a newsletter that was typeset and mailed. As our contacts grew, we soon had enough (200) supporters so that we could send things by bulk mail at lower postal rates. There is one picture in our archives of the two co-directors braving a snowstorm with a wooden sled piled high with bags of newsletters en route to the post office. It helped to be young and strong to create this organization!

Phone calls were constant in the early years. We spent hours talking with colleagues around town and throughout the country. Long-distance charges were not cheap, but phoning was inexpensive enough to warrant calling when we needed discussion and/or an immediate answer. Conversations were crucial to planning programs, solidifying strategies, and figuring out how to fund what needed to be done. Friendships flourished among colleagues who inevitably spoke of personal matters when on the phone about work. We called colleagues abroad though only for very important reasons. Rates were prohibitive, and Skype was not yet a twinkle in anyone's eye.

In-person meetings were frequent in those years in Washington, DC. WATER would often host gatherings, or we would go to another group's office for collaborative work on conferences, publications, and the like. There were lots of programs as well, with speakers, discussion, and a wine-and-cheese reception following so that social time was built in. Those events are rare these days.

Personal relationships were foundational and important in much of our work. Granted, we were not a huge crowd of theologically interested feminists, but we spent a lot of time getting to know one another that stood us in good stead for collaboration and networking. If it was the work that brought us together, it was the connections with one another that sustained the work.

From its founding, WATER's vision and praxis were global, given my formative experiences of teaching and engaging in activism in Latin America. We travelled extensively in Western Europe, and eventually to Australia and New Zealand. International travel was an important way to meet colleagues and expand our work. WATER staff took many trips to teach and learn in Argentina, Chile, Uruguay, and later Brazil and Cuba. Of course, colleagues from around the world came to WATER as well.

Travel technology progressed apace, so that going abroad became increasingly common and affordable as the Alliance grew. International colleagues formed an important part of the Alliance, a loosely structured network of feminists in religion. There was no substitute for the personal relationships that connected WATER with centers like Con-spirando in Chile[1] and the Frauenstudien und Bildungszentrum in der EKD (Women's Studies and Education Center of the German Protestant Church) in Germany.[2] Those connections continue at this writing, but the advent of computers brought about big changes in the dynamics and fabric of our work.

From Computers to Social Networks

WATER got its first computer in the late 1980s. It was a memorable day when the machine and printer took up the better part of the car in which we drove it home. Diann Neu and I were in awe of the thing, rather like having a baby and not knowing quite what to do with it. We were en route to the theater that night, so we toasted it with wine and worried a bit as we left about how it would fare in our absence.

One computer led to another, each one successively smaller and more powerful over the years. But it is hard to overestimate the changes that computers occasioned in our field and in the world. Everyone now did tasks previously done by secretaries and administrative assistants. This meant that many women were out of jobs and that many other women had more work than ever to do. Luckily, we had never become dependent on others to do our clerical work, so we made the change seamlessly.

Keeping one's calendar involved a pen and not keystrokes. Making more than one copy of a document used to require carbon paper, and eventually photocopying. Now it could be done with the push of a button and the whirl of a printer. In those days before laser, we made do with dot matrix printers, though the print quality was sketchy. Donor records and address lists were transferred from ledger books and sticky labels to databases and mail merges.

A small staff could do a lot more of the office work that goes into making a nonprofit run efficiently. Our success at expanding our networks, increasing our programs and publications, and upping our public profile was possible because of technology. We used to joke that the Vatican thought WATER was about the size of a medium university when in fact we were a staff of three or four along with interns and visiting scholars.

Facsimile machines were relatively short-lived in the 1990s as the communication mode of choice. Their original thermal paper was not very reliable, so plain-paper faxes replaced them. There was a certain novelty in being able to write a letter and fax it to the recipient instantly in any part of the world. I recall talking several friends and colleagues into buying fax machines so that we could correspond more efficiently. The ability to move documents from one office to another rapidly and with signatures that were legal even if copied was a welcome fax innovation. Messengers—those bike-riding, bag-toting errand people—were mostly put out of business. We have not seen one in years, though in the early days even nonprofit organizations used them quite frequently to expedite business around town.

Electronic mail and the Internet changed everything. What began as military and government technologies rapidly became widely available commercially. Email eclipsed faxes for ease and speed, and was cheaper to boot. WATER and many other nonprofits started to use email in the mid-1990s. It took several years for a critical mass of people to get online, as simply sending an email did no good if there were no recipients! But gradually, email addresses replaced postal ones for regular correspondence.

This dynamic had important implications for our international work. Many of our colleagues in other countries, particularly in developing countries, were without access to computers and email until well into the new century. So we had to be explicit about our outreach, tailoring it to the media available and erring on the side of inclusion by snail mailing as well as emailing our constituents.

Email has added exponentially to the communication volume in our work and subtracted dramatically from our post office bill. Emails have all but replaced the many paper mailings of program announcements we used to send and receive. It is the way in which we "talk" with our colleagues, such that telephone conversations are fewer and far between. Committees that are part of our coalition work do most of their business by email.

WATER's listserv, one of the early and still popular ones in the field, is a useful interactive way to share information and ideas. Vertical Response is our one-way mailing mode, the way we advertise programs and projects without expecting replies. Google and other groups send and receive massive amounts of information, far more than any of us processed in the days of snail mail and overnight express services.

Texting, the communication of choice of most young people, plays a relatively limited role in our work, since most of our messages are longer than a few lines. Nonetheless, we text when necessary, since it is one more way to reach out and share information.

Internet websites are the other major innovation of the computer age that have made WATER[3] and sister organizations accessible broadly. Websites began as online brochures of sorts—brief overviews of organizations with information on how to contact them in person. They are now what people come to equate with an organization itself. We are our websites. Most people will never visit the WATER office on the third floor of the World Building at 8121 Georgia Avenue in Silver Spring, MD 20910 USA. But the number of "hits" on our site grows daily, as people use our resources and connect with our Alliance.

Many of our programs are offered both in person and on the telephone. Monthly teleconferences with leading feminists in the field gather dozens of people around the lunch hour for substantive input and discussion. We have hosted Margaret Miles, Nancy Pineda-Madrid, Judith Plaskow, and Traci West, to mention only a few of the dozens who have graced our airwaves. Recordings and notes of the sessions are available on our website[4] for use in classrooms and study groups.

We even make liturgies, rituals, and meditation available in both person and phone forms. At first it seemed counter-intuitive to be sitting in silence with people hundreds of miles away. But it works well, linking people who would otherwise be alone with a group gathered in the WATER office. Likewise, we doubted that liturgies and rituals would convey well over the phone, but they do.

We have resisted filming such events so as not to create religion as a spectator sport, but that is under discussion and likely to be next. We find Skype, WebEx, and other video platforms more distracting than the simpler audio set ups. But as the technology improves, we will undoubtedly give them a try. There are certain events, for example lectures and funerals, for which we have been grateful to have access to that technology rather than miss the moment.

When we started our site, we had a web designer who handled content and format. Now our staff persons make the changes and add new content on a regular basis with the far more streamlined and easier to use technology that is available. Control over the platform as well as the material means that we can communicate via our site much as we once did with a newsletter or report, updating daily if we wish. While this is common today, it is important to underscore how quickly this capacity has come about. The proliferation of websites is nothing less than the elimination of most organizations' print materials and the invitation to share information widely. Of course, it is predicated on the notion that everyone has web access, which puts some limit on accessibility for those in countries where Internet access is less common.

One challenge in all of this is the venerable newsletter. Our quarterly WATERwheel[5] was printed for more than twenty years. Its eight-page format included a substantive article, an innovative liturgy, news of the organization, an annotated list of resources, and the like. Much of that information is now on our website, creating a two-pronged dilemma. First, how do we get the information to people who do not go to our website or who prefer to hold such material in their hands? Second, how do we charge a fee for receiving our materials when people are accustomed to reading everything for free on the Internet? These are important questions. We seek to balance access for all and just compensation in order to keep our work going. Answers are complex and still in formation.

WATER's resource center, named for Carol Blythe Murdock, our longtime editor, includes six thousand-plus print books, journals, and CDs, all for the borrowing. Most of these volumes have come as review copies from publishers who hope that we will promote their works in our newsletter, bibliographies, and programs. They are catalogued at Librarything.com[6] for easy reference. Some visiting scholars come to the office to use the library for their research, as it is one of the few places where feminist resources in religion are readily available in such quantity.

Many of our publications are also still in print, for example, *New Feminist Christianity: Many Voices, Many Views.*[7] But the big shift now in publishing is toward digital platforms like Kindle, Nook, and iBooks, so we have to rethink our approach both to collecting other volumes and distributing our own resources. For a while longer it appears as if both print and digital versions will continue to be feasible and necessary. Just as many of our colleagues did not have computers or Internet access until years after we did, so today many people still want print versions of books and journals because they do not have easy access to portable readers. But that is changing at lightening speed around the world.

A related change is the arrival of blogs as a normative way of engaging in conversation. WATER has a blog called *WATER Voices* that we encourage our colleagues to use.[8] We contribute to some blogs as well, including the *Feminist Studies in Religion Forum*[9] and *Feminism and Religion.*[10] They both feature up-to-the-minute work in the field. Blogs have the advantage of being interactive so that responses to short pieces can be instantaneous. Both blogs have comment policies that keep some editorial control over what gets put up.

Social networks are the latest, and at this writing, most popular new ways to connect. WATER uses both Facebook and Twitter to communicate with our Alliance and other colleagues. We are not as frequent in our postings as some groups, nor are we as vigilant in our reading of this media, but they are critical to expanding our audience, especially for including young people. There is an egalitarian dimension to social networking that appeals to our feminist sensibilities and an excitement about the posts that catches our attention. The fact that, at least theoretically, everyone has access to the blog rings a feminist bell. Likewise, the encouragements to try out ideas, see what others think, and have the possibility to change what has been written are all positives from a feminist perspective.

There is something boring at times about the endless scrolling of brief tidbits that leaves at least this writer longing for more sustained conversation. Nonetheless, access to such a wide range of materials can be a plus because simply gathering it is a big job. I find that efforts to make academic publishing more accessible and the ability to document easily the common blog post mean that the genres of academic and popular writing are converging more than they diverge. This has interesting implications when it comes to "weighing" publications for hiring, tenure, promotion, and the like. While in former times only academic articles were taken seriously, now I think we have to rethink criteria, since so many pieces are academic but are published online.

After thirty years, we at WATER are still eager to try new ways to bring about feminist religiously grounded social change. This history of our efforts serves as an example of how it can be done and as proof that organizations can and must stay current with the available technology. Some further reflection on the implications of such a commitment and what is ahead is in order.

From Social Networks to the Stars

Technology is not neutral. It costs a lot of money to have the latest equipment to be able to use social media easily, to be able to work on the road, to be able to communicate easily with virtually anyone. It takes a good deal of training to use technology well. Older people are always on the steep side of the learning curve. Poor people do without. Young people of a certain social stratum are the leaders in this work, and organizations like WATER need them. Those dynamics separate out the haves from the have-nots in ways we seek to change.

There is an irony in feminist studies in religion being as dependent as we are on technology. For example, if the phone lines are down, we cannot have WATER's monthly teleconferences.[11] We need the electric power and telephone lines that have their roots deep in capitalist patriarchy to which we are indebted and indentured. So it is, though we work toward getting off the grid as much as we can.

I feel certain nostalgia for in-person meetings and telephone calls, even while I realize that more people can be involved using the new technologies.

But are they involved as deeply and as fully, I wonder, when we are at such remove from one another? What do we give up in terms of quality of the Alliance community for quantity of people connected? Is an office even necessary any longer if so much of our interaction is virtual? Is our resource center redundant now that we can fit hundreds of books on a device we can carry in a purse?

Time will tell on these and related questions. WATER and other feminist organizations have to make the hard choices that face every group that wants to continue its mission in a rapidly changing world. On the one hand, the goal remains the same: to bring feminist religious resources to the service of social change. On the other hand, the means of doing so have changed dramatically in the first thirty years of this organization's history.

It is not so much for me as a co-founder and co-director to analyze our impact. Rather, I can say that we have followed two guiding principles in how we have handled the changes: we use resources responsibility and we share resources widely. I think those criteria will continue to stand us, and our successors if we have any, in good stead.

Notes

1. See http://conspirando.cl.
2. See www.fsbz.de.
3. See WATER's website at http://waterwomensalliance.org.
4. See www.waterwomensalliance.org/teleconferences-audio-and-notes/.
5. WATERwheel can be accessed at www.waterwomensalliance.org/waterwheel/.
6. WATER's resources can be access on Librarything.com at www.librarything.com/home/waterlibrary.
7. Mary E. Hunt and Diann L. Neu (eds.), *New Feminist Christianity: Many Voices, Many Views* (Woodstock, VT: SkyLight Paths Publishing, 2010).
8. *WATER Voices* can be accessed at www.watervoicesblog.blogspot.com.
9. *Feminist Studies in Religion Forum* can be accessed at www.fsrinc.org/. Access "Talking About Radical Feminism" by Mary E. Hunt at www.fsrinc.org/blog/talking-about-radical-feminism.
10. *Feminism and Religion* can be accessed at http://feminismandreligion.com. Access "Narrative Textiles and Women's Stories" by Mary E. Hunt at http://feminismandreligion.com/2012/06/01/narrative-textiles-and-womens-stories-by-mary-e-hunt/.
11. WATER Teleconferences can be accessed at www.waterwomensalliance.org/teleconferences/.

7 Television, Social Networking, and Cultural Criticism

Alternative Methodologies for Feminist Scholarship

Elise M. Edwards

Interactive possibilities provided by the Internet have altered the way that television shows are presented to the viewing public. At one end of the spectrum of interactivity, viewers are asked to provide content or guide the direction of a series. Sports, entertainment news, and talk shows frequently incorporate material obtained online into the show as an indicator of viewer response or commentary. In these cases, viewers are asked to send messages, video clips, and poll results through Twitter, Facebook, email, or the show's website. At the other end of the spectrum, viewers submit reactions to the show, but these are not directly tied to the content of the programming itself. They are designed to promote community through common dialogue of reactions and commentary, such as when episodes are re-aired as social network editions that display online comments about the action unfolding on the screen as the television viewer watches. Similarly, some networks and media publications have live blogging and commenting features on their websites to stimulate real-time discussion of programs.[1] Both ends of the interactive spectrum prioritize viewer response. Facebook, Twitter, and blogs that recap and review television shows and specials allow viewers to share reactions to the shows. For scholars who engage in cultural criticism, these reactions can become sources in themselves, to be placed alongside the cultural object (the television program) for interpretation. In the field of religion, this type of cultural criticism can be incorporated into scholarship about lived religion, ethical theory and practice, comparative analysis between religious texts and cultural objects, and other work that examines women's lives and their religiously informed conceptions of the world.

Emerging forms of online discourse also encourage interactions that can be incorporated into scholarly work through a cyclical process of review and discussion. If scholars of religion can learn to critically incorporate the sources that reflect engaged viewership into their scholarship, then they gain access not only to new sources, but also an alternative, collaborative method of writing. By publishing their reflections in blogs and online communities, they subject their writing to review and comment from a public that may include not only scholarly peer reviewers, but also their own social networks of friends and followers from different fields, educational backgrounds, and religious orientations. This essay discusses the ways that social networking sites and blogs can function in practices of attentive television watching, collective reflection, and collaborative writing and will demonstrate that these practices express feminist values and are alternative methodologies to religious scholarship.

Attentive Watching

The practice of attentive watching is viewers' close inspection of media so that they can offer commentary and reactions to the images, narrative, and messages promulgated by the show. Attentive watching is a new application of a skill that has been proposed by feminists for decades. In the 1980s, feminist activists and scholars became increasingly concerned with public imagery and representations of women in popular media, art, and pornography. Margaret Miles made an important contribution to this work for religious studies in 1985's *Image as Insight: Visual Understanding in Western Christianity and Secular Culture* by investigating historical religious images to discover the messages from which "ordinary" persons constructed a sense of self. Although most of the book presents a new interpretation of historical images, its final chapter discusses the critical use of images by contemporary people. The title, *Image as Insight*, is a variation of the phrase "eyesight as insight" from Rudolf Arnheim's *Art and Visual Perception*. This phrase captures Miles's assertion that training people to see is important to developing and understanding religious sensibilities: "Because religion involves both concepts and altered perceptions [of the meaning and value of the sensible world], training of the eye and the mind is fundamental to the quickening of religious sensibility."[2]

Miles's method of training in image use has three stages. The first step is becoming aware of the messages received from the images with which one lives.[3] The second step is asking questions about how media use contributes to the cultural tasks of providing exemplary models for women's lives and whether these tasks coordinate individual desires to support the larger community. Feminists must ask whether the models for women's lives and the formation of individuals into community pursue affirming, inclusive ends or idolatrous, oppressive ones. Miles phrases the questions as,

> Is my sense of social and political responsibility informed or developed by the images I contemplate daily? . . . Can I locate, in my daily fare of image, a supply of images that affirm me and help me explore what it means to be a woman of my age in my culture?[4]

She notes that steps one and two may result in a feminist's sacrifice of images that titillate without informing or that attract one to dangerous or destructive values and goals. The third step is selecting and developing a repertoire of images that supports personal and social transformation. They may need to develop their own images as part of a constructive feminist practice. The third step is beyond the scope of attentive watching that I discuss here, but it, too, can be aided by the use of online tools. Imagery from blogs, interactive media projects, and feminist content on YouTube can supply alternative images to replace anti-feminist television programming.

Attentive watching as a source of religious scholarship relies on two presuppositions: (1) Images serve more than an illustrative, decorative, or entertainment-oriented function. Public media influences the way its audience conceptualizes and engages in daily practices as it offers "ideas and images for the understanding of our relationships with other human beings, the community and the world."[5] (2) Religion is merely a set of dogmas or institutions. It is a way of making sense of the world that is captured by Clifford Geertz's definition of the term.[6] In *When Religion Meets New Media*, Heidi Campbell explains that this definition of religion is so appealing to scholars of media, religion, and culture because, "This means religion possesses the ability to transform people's conceptions of the everyday world and provides a basis for justifying those actions and understanding of reality."[7] Understanding religion as a meaning-making practice and framework is a useful starting point for analysis of how people use images to understand, reinterpret, and re-present their religious sensibilities through other media forms.

Social networking sites and blogs can become forums for viewers to share insights developed from attentive television viewing during or shortly after a program's telecast. In addition to Twitter updates (140-character statements) and status updates on Facebook, LinkedIn, and other networking platforms, viewers can use commenting features on blogs, columns, and recap sites to express their reactions. On Twitter, users send out "tweets" with hashtags (#) as a way of identifying keywords, concepts, or commentary about their statements that can then be used as a way to search for related items and group them. For example, a tweet about CBS's television show *The Good Wife* could contain a hashtag for the show's name, #TheGoodWife and also a reaction to its content. (For example, when I searched for Twitter posts with the hashtag #TheGoodWife, I found a tweet that read "Watching #TheGoodWife. 60 years ago it would have been about a woman standing quietly in a kitchen smiling, all Stepford . . . #GoodChange." The hashtag #GoodChange is the viewer's commentary about depictions of women on television.) Tweets relevant to a topic can be searched by using hashtags or a keyword in Twitter's search bar. Twitter also displays trending topics, the most popular hashtags, and words across the platform. Users can contribute their own perspectives on popular discussions as well as identify what other people on the site are discussing. When tweets about timely topics are posted, users often initiate an online dialogue about the popular discussion item by responding to others' tweets with their own, or "retweeting" them, which shares them with other followers. On blogs and sites like Facebook, dialogue primarily assumes the form of comments about a specific post. The "owner" or moderator of the page has the ability to delete or reply to objectionable content, and privacy settings may prevent comments from being visible to the larger public.

Some of these types of social media outlets promote a sustained attention to a television program's visual presentation. For example, the online community that follows recaps of ABC's *Dancing with the Stars* on *Entertainment*

Weekly's website, EW.com, searches for "hidden gems" in the show's live broadcast. Hidden gems can be to actual crystals, sequins, and sparkles placed in atypical locations on a performer's body (in the hair, behind the ears, etc.) or the show's set. But commonly, viewers identify hidden gems that are notable, ten unintentional occurrences onscreen, such as reactions from audience or cast members' shenanigans in the background of a camera shot. Gem hunters then submit their hidden gems by commenting on the site's recap page or endorsing others' submissions. A list of "Hidden Gems of the Week" is then posted with screenshots on the following day for all site participants—even those who did not watch the telecast—to review and discuss. The hidden gem phenomenon reveals an existing practice of attentive viewing. However, for this type of watching and sharing to become an exercise in attentive watching, participants would have to apply a critical lens to their viewing.

Discernment transforms the practice of attention into a critical practice. Cultural critic bell hooks notes that discernment is necessary for critical thinking: "[Discernment] is a way of approaching ideas that aims to understand core, underlying truths, not simply that superficial truth that may be most obviously visible."[8] For attentive watching to be critical, viewers must move first from passive observation to attentive observation and then to critical engagement. These two steps have the potential to redirect the consumption-oriented messages of many television programs into the evaluation of its representations in light of religious—and feminist—sensibilities.

Viewers with religious sensibilities become discerning viewers who can offer feminist critique by attending to the affective power of a program and the messages it conveys in its text and subtext. Noting the affective power of a television show encourages viewers to reflect on a television show's message at a personal level. A reaction to the affective power of a program indicates that something being conveyed is either disturbing or edifying. In the case of a negative reaction to a show, a sense of shame, unease, self-doubt, or anxiety may be useful for identifying the religious sensibilities of the viewer that are in conflict with the show. Critics can ask: What is presented in the show that conflicts with specific religious beliefs and practices? For feminist scholars, assessing the affect becomes important because it acknowledges the significance of non-textual communication, which can be overlooked in religious discourse, particularly for religions "of the Book."

Analysis of the text and subtext of a show requires particular attention to what is verbally stated and written on the screen (text) and what is assumed, suggested, or promoted by the action or narrative content that unfolds (subtext).[9] Problematic messages from a feminist and media justice perspective include: depictions of female bodies that emphasizes their sexuality—particularly in comparison with male bodies on display—or depictions that idealize a narrowly defined idealized norm (tall, very thin, European features, and light skin, for example) and exoticize women who fall outside this norm; romanticized portrayals of heterosexual marriage that characterize singleness and LGBTQ relationships as aberrations to be remedied onscreen by dating coaches, matchmakers, and competitions for a "prized" bachelor or bachelorette; media representations that stereotype, degrade, or in some other way marginalize women, people of color, the poor, LGBTQ persons, the disabled, and immigrants; and product placement of items that dramatically improve quality of life. Cultural critic Jennifer L. Pozner notes that the fairytale/princess trope so ubiquitous in reality television is also problematic from a feminist perspective because it undermines the agency of women.[10]

There are several works in the areas of feminist literary criticism, media studies, television studies, and cultural criticism that articulate ways of using and critiquing popular media and discuss particular works and their issues regarding the representation of women. It is beyond the scope of this essay to delve deeply into that body of work, but I have included some of those works in my references. To succinctly express the kind of questions critics should be using to assess television, I use six categories articulated by Pozner that are particularly relevant to reality television:

1. Framing: Critical assessment of the narrative message central to the series and the construction of each episode to support the master narrative.
2. Casting: Consideration of how the characters chosen reinforce stereotypes.
3. Exclusion: Evaluation of the diversity of ages, genders, races, ethnicities, appearance, sexual orientations, professional backgrounds, physical abilities or health status, nationalities, and expressed ideologies of the cast members to identify who is excluded from participation and how master narratives are supported by the selected cast.
4. Methodology: Assessment of the storytelling devices employed to support the master narrative.
5. Advertising: Attention to who profits from the show, which products are integrated into the show's content and commercials, and how these products relate to the show's master narrative.
6. Impact: Analysis of the show's potential or actual impact on the self, other viewers, public policy, and culture. It also entails consideration of who the intended audience is and how impact could vary depending on the demographic of the audience.[11]

These categories are useful for provoking discussion about correspondence between a show's affect, text, or subtext and the religious sensibilities of the critic. Whether the feminist criticism comes from a person who has their own religious commitments or a scholar who has an academic interest in religion, the engaged critic will likely explore issues around women's agency, purpose, and representation.

Although it is sometimes assumed that members of religious communities respond to media images in passive ways, Campbell challenges this view and uses the position she defines to ground her work. She argues that criticism from religious communities reveals an active engagement with technology and the media communicated through it,

While I do not discount that technologies can encourage certain values or behaviors, coming from the intentions of their designers who may seek to promote certain uses or being built into the logic of the technology itself [. . .] these occurrences do not necessarily dictate the outcomes of technology use amongst their users . . . [Th]is perspective seems to assume that media users are passive and do not make thoughtful choices about how, why, and to what end they will use the media technology that they are presented with.[12]

Campbell's research demonstrates that religious individuals and communities "make distinctive choices about their relationship with technology in light of their faith, community history, and contemporary way of life."[13]

Collective Reflection

Technologies that allow viewers to engage in critical use of television images and critique them through social media allow collaborative approaches to generating academic work to emerge. Because these insights are shared, traditional models about the use of sources and need to be redefined to move transcend the model of the lone scholar. A dialogical model is preferable to a hierarchical one because it corresponds with feminist commitments to shared power. And so exchanges in online communities, such as the *Feminism and Religion* blog (FeminismAndReligion.com), should support mutual instruction between the writer and the commenters to a post.

When a writer shares her thoughts with a community of readers, Facebook friends, and Twitter followers, the responding community often initiates a dialogical interaction that makes analysis more collaborative. They offer support, confirmation, correction, and censure. Writers should not uncritically accept their assessments and incorporate them into projects that develop from the writing (after all, many reviews and comments are issued by networks, groups, and individuals with anti-feminist agendas), but they can use comments to gauge what resonates, or as a source upon which to do critical reflection. Collective reflection not only embodies feminist praxis, but it also may incorporate methodologies articulated by scholars in womanist ethics. Womanist ethics privileges personal experience and interpretation by black women as a source against dominant, "normative" readings of culture. Incorporating viewer reaction and commentary honors the radical subjectivity and expressive agency of a show's audience.

Womanist pedagogy, in particular, illuminates why diverse voices who participate in attentive watching should be incorporated into scholarship. Ethicist Melanie Harris identifies a connection between the development of critical thinking skills and the importance of welcoming a diversity of voices to interrogate ethical themes in her essay "Womanist Wholeness and Community." Speaking of the womanist pedagogy she adopts when teaching religion courses,

Harris explains that her process for enhancing students' critical thinking skills begins with "setting a communal and respectful atmosphere" to encourage active participation.[14] The diversity of participants' experiences is honored, which creates space for their individual reflections on how their cultural, racial, economic, and social background influence their religious orientations and beliefs. Applying this womanist pedagogy beyond the classroom to an online environment for learning and growth (which presumably is what blogs like *Feminism and Religion* aim to be), individual reflections on social location posted online invite readers to "locate themselves in conversation with the essay and the writer"[15] and also in conversation with the images and messages from television that are discussed in their work. The religious-oriented dialogue that can emerge from these interactions can provoke moral stances and feminist critiques, and also acknowledge the influence of the unique contributions of particular, socially located voices. Brought together, these voices offer a broader understanding of the impact and reception of anti-feminist imagery and its possible remedy.

When engaging in collaborative reflection online, feminists must be vigilant to practices of exclusion. They should ask, "Who is invisible in this particular project?"[16] It would be a mistake to assume that the reactions of the audience who is posting online are proportionately representative of the larger viewing audience. Online responses only reflect a segment of the viewing population, namely those who have access to the Internet and an interest in engaging in these types of online communities. There is also a presumption of the audience's literacy and access to a computer or smartphone in a timeframe appropriate for a response. Participation in live blogging requires that the viewer watch the live show in the time zone that corresponds to the live blogging and have access to the Internet during that time period. The demographic composition of an audience in categories of age, gender, and race will vary depending on the time a show is aired, as will the ease of access to the Internet the various demographics have while the show is airing.

One final caution should be stated regarding the collaborative nature of work that is based on viewer's attentive watching and engaged commentary. Scholars should be aware of the potential for backlash, not just because the dialogue they seek to promote is based on a feminist agenda, but because they intellectualize media that many viewers use for entertainment. The intended dialogue could easily degenerate into a condescending lecture, followed by reactions of anger and frustration. There is an inherent tension between the desire for "mindless entertainment" and the desire to identify patriarchal structures behind television imagery. Feminist scholars need not limit their work to receptive online communities, although that is one strategy. Another strategy would be to contextualize their work, adopting the ethos of the community in which one is siting their discourse.[17] Wit, humor, and creativity in approach can make feminist commentary interesting and compelling on sites where an entertainment mindset predominates.

Collaborative Writing

In this final section, I focus more specifically on the collaborative nature of blogging, and draw from my personal experiences on *Feminism and Religion*[18] to discuss the difficulties and opportunities blogging presents. Blogging allows quick response to current events. It puts pressure on the scholar who blogs to bravely voice opinions without relying on as many sources as a traditional research project. As part of a community, a blogger also comments on others' work and the dialogical process of reflection can enable the process of writing traditional academic pieces (essays, journal articles, book reviews, and books) to become more collaborative. When blog readers give and receive comments, their insights can function in a manner similar to more established routes of feedback (e.g., presenting conference papers or circulating drafts to peers and mentors). Blogging opens a writer's work to new audiences, which can enhance her own critical thinking skills. As bell hooks notes, "Collaborating with diverse thinkers to work toward a greater understanding of the dynamics of race, gender, and class is essential for those of us who want to move beyond one-dimensional ways of thinking, being, and living."[19] Collaboration in writing, as in analysis and reflection, is the practical application of feminist commitments to shared power.

In the 2011–2012 academic year, I experimented with conversations about a particular topic across social media sites, in the *Feminism and Religion* blog, and at an academic conference. I submitted a proposal for a paper for a *Feminism and Religion* panel at a student research conference, to develop a theological understanding of transformative aesthetics and discuss how it might be used in Christian communities. In the paper, I would examine a television special, *Black Girls Rock!*, and explain its relevance to the topic. When the proposal was accepted, I used searches on Twitter and Facebook to ascertain audience responses. I then composed and posted a blog entry about the special. This yielded some interaction with the blogging community, many of whom did not watch the special when it aired. The next step was presenting the paper at the conference. It was well received and I reported back to the blog to gain more commentary before revising the essay into a finished article that would be published online in the conference proceedings. Although I had high hopes for the effectiveness of this interactive writing process, I struggled to find commentary that would contribute substantively to the content of my work. This taught me about the challenges of collaborative writing.

Throughout the process, I should have paid more attention to audience, timeframe, and rhetorical technique to solicit constructive criticism online. With the issue with audience was that I found myself writing about *Black Girls Rock!* to an online community that had not watched the program. *Black Girls Rock!* was a special presentation on Black Entertainment Television (BET) that aired in November 2011, highlighting achievements made by women of color. The commenters on *Feminism and Religion* were unfamiliar with the program, but they did support its message based on discussion of it in my blog entry. An audience familiar with the program, perhaps one developed on BET.com or on the website of the Black Girls Rock! foundation, would have garnered more critical engagement. Critical engagement cannot be expected from an audience who has not had the opportunity to be attentive viewers. Although this seems obvious in hindsight, I had hoped to generate questions about the program that would provoke me to revisit the analysis from my attentive watching. But because the audience I communicated was never engaged in the program I discussed, they could not provide the dialogue to support a collaborative process at any stage in the essay's composition.

Another problem was that I wrote the piece months after the presentation aired. Timeliness is a key issue in blogging, and I found it is also critical for gathering reaction from social media sites. I found myself looking for sources that were written months prior to my analysis. While this is acceptable in academic writing, it distorts the lifespan of the social currency of some cultural works. This is especially true for television specials, premieres, finales, and significant episodes that generate immediate reaction. Reactions may be very heated near the show's air date, but may demonstrate a precipitous decline and little long-term impact. It can be particularly difficult to determine the short-term and long-term impact of a show and the messages it conveys. For social media commentary, I encourage bloggers to use timely sources and topics.

I also encourage scholars entering the world of blogging to devote sufficient energy to learning writing skills that are relevant to this particular genre. Like other forms of writing, blogging is a craft that is improved as one gains experience doing it. Mary Hocks refers to the specialized composition process for online writings as "digital rhetoric." Digital rhetorical skills should include how to communicate effectively online with diverse audiences and how to build Internet communities for activism. Online writers should know how to frame their work to generate reader response. My posts about *Black Girls Rock!* may have generated more discussion if they were composed differently. In addition, feminists who engage in collaborative writing online need to know how to skillfully incorporate sources that are not their own and link to similar writings across the Internet, building digital conversations. Thus, the concern about digital rhetoric is interconnected with the issues of timeliness and appropriate audiences.

Conclusion

Engaged viewers who choose to use social media technology to share responses about television programs can illuminate connections between religious sensibilities and media imagery. As active users of technology, social media responders can become dialogue partners with scholars, identifying and shaping the direction of religious discourse about media content through their exchanges. While an attentive viewer identifies what is compelling, interesting, and thought-provoking in a show's content, the critical viewer connects those statements to questions of faith and modes of living that can be redirected back to the original group who offered the comments. To keep this from being a paternalistic, one-sided instruction, groups of viewers and critics will ideally exist within a common community that promotes mutual respect, like a network of friends, a community of blog readers, or a social media network of another form.

Notes

1. Examples of this include the "We Sync" feature on WEtv.com, the website for Women's Entertainment Television, and live blogging on EW.com, the website for *Entertainment Weekly* magazine led by the writers who write the publication's show recaps.
2. Margaret R. Miles, *Image as Insight: Visual Understanding in Western Christianity and Secular Culture* (Boston, MA: Beacon Press, 1985), 4.
3. Ibid., 147.
4. Ibid., 148.
5. Ibid., 128.
6. He defines religion as: "(1) a system of symbols which acts to (2) establish powerful, pervasive, and long-lasting moods and motivations in men by (3) formulating conceptions of a general order of existence and (4) clothing these conceptions with such an aura of factuality that (5) the moods and motivations seem uniquely realistic." Clifford Geertz, *Religion as a Cultural System: Anthropological Approaches to the Study of Religion* (London: Tavistock, 1985), 176.
7. Heidi A. Campbell, *When Religion Meets New Media*, Kindle ed., Media, Religion, and Culture (New York: Routledge, 2010), 7.
8. bell hooks, *Teaching Critical Thinking: Practical Wisdom*, Kindle ed. (New York: Routledge, 2010). Kindle Locations 205–06. In this chapter on critical thinking, hooks builds from the work of Richard Paul and Linda Elder in *The Miniature Guide to Critical Thinking: Concepts and Tools* and Dennis Rader in *Teaching Redefined*.
9. Jennifer L. Pozner, *Reality Bites Back: The Troubling Truth about Guilty Pleasure TV*, Kindle ed. (Berkeley, CA: Seal Press, 2010). Kindle Location 4847. Pozner references www.medialiteracyproject.org.
10. Ibid., Kindle Locations 582–584.
11. Ibid., Kindle Locations 4869–4889. Pozner's work differs in tone from other books about feminism and television criticism. It presents strategies for making change while addressing an audience that *enjoys* watching the shows she criticizes. Also, her insights are easily applicable to online forums, which is not surprising considering that Pozner is a managing editor of *WIMN's Voices*, a blog on women and the media and that this book grew out of WIMN's (Women in Media and News) media analysis program.
12. Campbell, *When Religion Meets New Media*, 6.
13. Ibid.
14. Melanie L. Harris, "Womanist Wholeness and Community," in *Faith, Feminism, and Scholarship: The Next Generation*, ed. Melanie L. Harris and Kate M. Ott (New York: Palgrave Macmillan, 2011), 133–134.
15. Ibid., 134.
16. Mary Hocks, summarizing some of the issues "cyberfeminists" face, writes, "Cyberfeminism can simply reproduce the White, middle-class feminism that has dominated academia since the second wave. It's definitely class-based in terms of unequal access and digital divide issues." Mary Hocks, "Cyberfeminism Intersects Writing Research: Studies in Digital Rhetoric," in *Webbing Cyberfeminist*

Practice: Communities, Pedagogies, and Social Action, ed. Kristine Blair, Radhika Gajjala, and Christine Tulley, *New Dimensions in Computers and Composition* (Cresskill, NJ: Hampton Press, 2009), 236.

17. Ibid., 241. Hocks discusses the rhetorical appeal to *ethos*.

18. *Feminism and Religion* can be accessed at http://feminismandreligion.com and my blog posts can be accessed at http://feminismandreligion.com/author/elisemichonne/.

19. hooks, *Teaching Critical Thinking*, Kindle Locations 524–526.

8 Finding Ancestor Connection via the Internet

Carol P. Christ

While technology has enabled people across the world to find connections among the living, it has also created new opportunities for the living to make connections with the dead. Ancestor connection is an important part of traditional religions, but in our increasingly mobile world, people are losing connections with the stories of their ancestors. This is particularly true in the immigrant nations of the New World, but migration due to war, poverty, and persecution is now a worldwide phenomenon. In traditional societies, stories are passed down from generation to generation, and memories are rooted in places that connect the generations to each other. Such places might be the family home, the family farm, the family olive grove, the local church or synagogue, the village cemetery, the swimming hole, the kissing rock, the old oak tree, or the mountain that rises above the village. In our world, the Internet is providing opportunities for those of us who have lost our family ties due to immigration and emigration, both chosen and forced, to reconnect with ancestors and the places where they lived.

While tracing ancestors has become a widespread pastime and hobby, the reasons ancestor connection is important in human life remain largely unarticulated by those who spend untold hours creating family trees. On the popular television series *Who Do You Think You Are?* participants regularly state that the journey of discovery of their family history has "changed" their understanding of "who they are." But beyond stating that they feel "stronger," they are usually at a loss for words. In this essay, I will share information about how the Internet can aid the ancestral search and lead to connections with living relatives, share my own ancestral journey, and reflect on the deeper spiritual meanings of ancestor connection from the perspective of feminist and ecofeminist theologies.

In the early days of second-wave feminism, women created a ritual of naming our mother lines. "I am Carol, daughter of Janet, daughter of Lena, daughter of Dora." This ritual is a powerful affirmation that the women—whose names were lost in the patriarchal tradition of tracing fatherlines and of naming women only by their relationships with fathers and husbands—deserve to be remembered. Even when I knew only three names in my mother line, I found this ritual incredibly powerful. I am also connected to my mother line through things I have inherited. When my grandmother died, I asked my mother for her silverware. Though my grandmother used the "good" silverware only on Sundays and special occasions, I have used it nearly every day for over forty years. For me, this ritual of daily use sparks fond memories of my grandmother's table laden with food and of her generous presence at family gatherings. After my mother died, I filled my home with her things, knowing that this would help to keep her memory alive in me. Thoughts of my mother have been ever-present in my conscious mind nearly every day since her death for more than twenty years now.

Following one of my lectures on the earth as the body of Goddess, womanist theologian Karen Baker-Fletcher asked a question that provoked me to expand the scope of my thinking about ancestor connection. Baker-Fletcher stated that as an African American woman, she knew that ancestor reverence was part of traditional African religions. She said that she thought the ancestors were a missing link in ecofeminist theologies.[1] As I was already aware of the power of my connection to my mother and grandmother, I intuitively felt that she was right. However, I had not the slightest idea of how to articulate the relationship between reverence for the earth and reverence for the ancestors.

As I pondered the ancestors, I made the ritual of naming our mother lines central in the Goddess pilgrimages I lead in Crete. A few women in my groups began adding their memberships in one of the clans of the "seven daughters of Eve" to their mother lines. Conversations about this sparked me to read Bryan Sykes's book of the same name,[2] and to begin thinking about human migration out of Africa. To our ritual of naming our mother lines, I added a refrain: "I come from a long line of women, known and unknown, stretching back to Africa." Speaking this refrain again and again prompted me to wonder about the women "known and unknown" in my family lines.

The *National Geographic* test of my mitochondrial DNA that is passed from mothers to their children—but passed on only by daughters—showed that I am in the group known as "T2." Bryan Sykes explains that this means that I am descended from a woman he calls "Tara," who may have lived in Northern Italy about 18,000 years ago. Tara's DNA has been passed in an unbroken female line from mother to daughter to daughter again all the way down to me and about 9 percent of all Europeans. Tara was a descendant of Africans who migrated out of Africa about 50,000 years ago. Her lineage goes back to the "African Eve" who lived about 200,000 years ago, who is the single ancestress of all living human beings. The *National Geographic* documentary[3] connected African ancestors who migrated to Australia, Asia, and Europe to the San people, commonly known as the "African Bushmen [and Bushwomen]." Film footage of the San people helped me to begin to visualize ancestors in the African bush, ancestors walking out of Africa, and ancestors coming to live in the caves of Europe during the last ice age. I then tried to imagine the "long line of women" that connected them to me.

Over the past few years, I have spent countless hours on the Internet searching for more recent ancestors. Before accessing web technology, I looked for family records and asked for family stories. In my family, stories of ancestors were not frequently told. My maternal grandmother's family left the farm in Michigan in the early part of the 20th century. Grammy and Uncle Emery told stories about the farm, but we never returned to see it. My maternal grandfather left his family in Kansas City when he went to work for the Wells Fargo as a young boy; his later career with the Railway Express meant that my mother's family moved frequently. My father's parents left their families in New York when they moved to San Francisco during the Depression. My Nannie, my paternal grandmother, was "as Irish as the day is long," but I never met the Irish family she left behind in New York. My maternal grandfather acknowledged his Swedish heritage, but that was all. After Alex Hayley's *Roots* played on television in the late 1970s, I asked my father about his family. His response was, "We are all American now." Through my genealogical research, I understand that my father chose to shield me from painful memories.

Despite my California family's separation from ancestral roots, my Uncle Emery, my grandmother's brother, researched his paternal line, the Searing family, in the 1950s. For reasons I did not fully understand, I treasured and periodically reread the history of the family he gave to my mother. However, since Uncle Emery listed places, names, and dates with little history attached, I failed to connect the genealogy he uncovered to places where I lived or visited or to the parts of American history I knew. I did not realize that my family's ancestor Simon Searing was a Puritan like those who founded Yale Divinity School where I studied, or that he came to the United States only a decade after the first pilgrims landed in New England. Simon was one of the original members of the Hempstead Colony, but I did not realize that this was the same Hempstead where I visited family (not related to him) while I was a graduate student. Similarly, though I "felt" strong family connections when I lived in New York City, I did not know that my father's family had lived in the Lower East Side and in Williamsburg, Brooklyn, in the tenements. Nor did I know that I could have looked for Searing roots in nearby Saratoga Springs when I visited friends in Albany, or that I was very close to the family farm in Lyons when I visited a friend who taught at Central Michigan State.

I began my search for ancestors with Uncle Emery's document. I also asked my father what he remembered. This time he told me the names of his grandparents and the names of his father's and mother's siblings, as well as stories about the Iloff family farm in Cherry Ridge, Honesdale, Pennsylvania; about Lord Kelly's gambling and suicide in Ireland that left his family destitute; and about his grandfather Christ having left Germany because he was a socialist. Even the smallest clue can prove useful. Places of birth and names of family members help you to verify that you have found the right family on the census. Places of origin can lead to records in "the old country."

Someone told me about FamilySearch.org, which is a free Internet resource provided by the Mormon Church. I began my research there. Typing in the names my father gave me, I found his father's and mother's families on census records in New York and Brooklyn. At first I just jotted down dates and places, but gradually I discovered that if you look closely at the original documents which are often available by a click on a link, you can find details which, depending on the year of the census, may include date of immigration, occupation, date and month of birth, country of birth, date of marriage, and number of others living in the household—sometimes a street address is written on the top or side of the sheet. You can search for a street address on street maps and you can even see what the area looks like today on Google Earth.

About a year after I began my search, I became aware of the television program *Who Do You Think You Are?* with US, UK, Australian, and other versions, which can be viewed or found online. I also found the series by Henry Louis Gates *African American Lives, Faces of America,* and *Finding Your Roots.* These programs helped me to understand the importance of setting a family search in the context of history. I soon discovered that there is a wealth of history to be found online using web technology. One of the first questions I asked myself was whether my ancestors took land from Native Americans. Typing Hempstead Colony into a search, I was amazed to find transcriptions of the early records of the settlement, including the "deed of purchase" of the land from the Indians.[4] Reading through these records, I found Simon Searing's name on a list of the original residents of the colony and discovered that he was once fined for selling wine to Indians. Further searches revealed that wars with the Indians were ongoing in the early days of the colony and that the deed of sale was probably a "peace" or victory treaty. My ancestors did take land from Native Americans.

Uncle Emery had said that the Searing family's origins were Quaker. I discovered that the Hempstead Colony was founded by independent Puritans who left the Stamford Colony after a dispute. Many in the colony, including my ancestors, became Quakers a few decades later. One search leads to another. I found links to family trees and summaries of research by other people who like me were related to Simon Searing of Hempstead. Among documents copied by a distant relative, I found the will of a John Searing, a Quaker slaveholder who left his "oldest negro boy" to his wife Elizabeth and directed that his other slaves be sold. In her will, his wife Elizabeth left a "negro man" to her son, a "negro girl" to her daughter, and a second "negro girl" to her granddaughter, who may have been only a girl herself. I was stunned. I had always assumed that slavery pertained to the American south. I did not expect to find that any of my ancestors held slaves.[5] I knew that Quakers were among the leaders of the abolitionist movement. I certainly did not expect to find Quakers holding slaves in New York!

Another few searches led me to an article on slaveholding in New York[6] that indicated that slaveholding was widespread in New York before the Revolutionary War. Other research led to the documentary film *Traces of the Trade.*[7] It explained that even after the slavery was abolished in most of the northern states, the economy of the north was still very much tied in with the slave trade: slave ships were built in the north; the chains that tied the slaves into the holds of the ships were made in the north; the cotton mills where new immigrants worked were supplied with cotton by slave plantations; and so on. Further research showed that I am related to Henry Pearsall who was also among the early settlers in the Hempstead Colony. Henry Pearsall is likely (though this is not certain) to be the son of Thomas Pearsall of Virginia, who at one time held a monopoly on the tobacco trade to England. The Pearsall family, a powerful aristocratic family in England, was one of the architects of the slave trade.[8]

I did not begin my family search with hopes of finding royal, wealthy, or heroic ancestors. But neither did I expect to find slaveholders and architects of the slave trade. It is an understatement to say that this discovery gave me pause. As I examined my feelings, I found that the predominant one was not, as I might have expected, "guilt" for what my ancestors had done. Instead I felt "a clear space opening in my mind." In this clear space, I began to understand how deeply I am linked to the history of America, the country where I was born, the country where my ancestors lived. I understood more clearly than I had before that "I" come from people who were involved in great evil. No longer can I imagine that "I" come from people who were only or primarily good. I have ancestors who were slaveholders, and I have ancestors who were abolitionists. If I want to feel proud of the Quaker abolitionists, I must also, as they did, take responsibility for the evil done by the Quaker slaveholders: I must pledge myself to repair the web.

I was researching various family lines at the same time. I began to find out more about my father's family in New York. My father's mother Mary Rita Inglis was the daughter of James Inglis. Her father was the son of James Inglis, a Scottish seaman, and Annie Corliss from Ireland. A search for the origin of the Inglis family surname led me to an online Inglis family message board. There, I discovered a message posted ten years earlier by someone named Hattie who was looking for the family of Mary Rita Inglis who married John Irving Christ—my father's parents. Hattie is a third-cousin about my age who still lives in New York's Lower East Side: we are both descended from James Inglis the seaman and Annie Corliss.[9] We corresponded by email, and she helped me fill in one branch of the family tree. Hattie sent me family photographs and stories and birth and death certificates she had collected in New York City. I was surprised to discover that almost all of the family's death certificates contained the notation "tenement," along with words like diphtheria, malnutrition, and tuberculosis. Hattie explained that the Lower East Side where our ancestors lived was the poorest area of New York City at the time. From further searches I discovered that tenements in the 1850s had no central heating and no bathrooms, and that often the only windows opened to internal light wells, which were also used for dumping garbage. My cousin also told me about other useful Internet genealogy locations, including Italian and German genealogy groups that provide access to vital records, including marriages and deaths, for New York; she also told me about Castlegarden.org, which has records from the place of entry for immigrants before Ellis Island opened in 1892. I look forward to meeting my cousin Hattie the next time I visit New York.

Our great-great-grandmother Annie Corliss bore nine children in the tenements on the Lower East Side. She must have struggled to feed, clothe, and keep track of them without any help or support when her husband was away at sea. This too gave me pause. I was surprised to see Annie smiling coquettishly in the photograph sent by my cousin, in which our great-great-grandfather, the seaman, looks tired and worn out. A search revealed that the surname "Corliss" means "careless" or without care. This led me to think that Annie had the Irish spirit immortalized in the song "When Irish Eyes Are Smiling." I listened to a rendition of the song on YouTube. It seemed to describe Annie's eyes and her ability to triumph over her suffering. I memorized the song, and for about a month, I sang it to myself several times a day. Through this ritual, Annie's spirit took root in my body, and I internalized a part of my Irish heritage. I swore that suffering would never get me down again.

I had always known that my father's grandfather died when my grandfather was a baby. Hattie found his death certificate. George Christ, age 32, died at home of tuberculosis, four months after my grandfather's birth. He left five small children. A notation on the death certificate said that he had been ill for a year. The home was a tenement. I remembered that a Greek older lady friend had once described how her father had died of tuberculosis while lying on a couch coughing up blood in the living room of the house where I was living at the time. I pictured my grandfather's mother Catherine Iloff Christ caring for four small children and a husband who was dying and coughing up blood, all during her pregnancy, and while my grandfather was a tiny nursing infant. I was stunned. Where did she find the money to feed her family and the courage to carry on? George Christ was buried in Most Holy Trinity Cemetery. A search revealed that Betty Smith, who wrote *A Tree Grows in Brooklyn,* was brought up in the Most Holy Trinity Church. I watched the film of the novel and learned that tenements in Williamsburg, Brooklyn, had a living room, a bedroom, and a kitchen. If my grandfather's father was dying on a couch in the living room, then his mother and all the children must have slept together in the bedroom.

My great-grandmother Catherine Iloff was born on a dairy farm in Cherry Ridge, Pennsylvania. My father and his cousins have fond memories of their visits to the farm, where they stayed with relatives known as "the Switzer girls," who had their own small farms. Catherine's father, Henry Iloff had nine children with Catherine's mother, Catherina, and nine with his second wife, Johanna—of whom fifteen survived to adulthood. As my searches revealed, Iloff is not a common name in the United States; I suspect that anyone with connections to the Iloff surname is a descendant of old Henry. Two Iloff family Facebook groups have between them over 100 members—and both are new. Through a message board, I met Debra, who founded the Iloff-Ball-Lintner group. She is a third-cousin, descended from Catherine's sister Mary Iloff. Our ancestor Henry told census-takers that he was born in France and in Prussia in 1820 and in 1822. Searches finally led me to a Heinrich Eiloff, born in St. Nikolaus, Saarland, now in Germany, but in Prussia in 1820. Heinrich's father's family came from the other side of the Saar River in Rosbruck,

Moselle, France. As I could find no other possible connections, I assumed that my great-great-grandfather was Heinrich Eiloff. A search of the German telephone book (which is also available online) revealed that there are only about fifty telephones registered to Eiloffs in all of Germany, five of them in St. Nikolaus. I guessed that they were relatives of Heinrich, but I hesitated to call, as I do not speak German. Continuing to search, I discovered a Pedigree Submission on FamilySearch that traced the family of Heinrich's mother, Catharina Lux, back to the 1600s in several small towns the Saar River valley. Photographs on the Internet showed all of the towns in the area to be picturesque. I found this incredibly exciting, but these connections would only be valid if our Henry Iloff was the Heinrich Eiloff I had found.

At some point, I had gathered all the data readily available through FamilySearch. I knew I could find more information if I joined Ancestry.com, because FamilySearch often told me that some documents could only be viewed through Ancestry. I hesitated, because the fees are substantial. I had reached dead ends on several of my family lines. I could not trace the Inglis family in Scotland or the Corliss family in Ireland. I had several clues tracing my great-great-grandfather "Lord Kelly" to the Essex Lawn estate in Roscommon, but no proof.[10] I also had not been able to trace specific Christ family ancestors in Germany, though the name is not uncommon. I decided to contact cousins on my father's side of the family to see if any of them had done genealogical research. I had interesting conversations with two Christ second-cousins I might have met once or twice when I was younger: I remembered their father and mother. They were pleased to receive the information I had, but had nothing to offer me.

A half-cousin of my father, who is a grandson of Catherine Iloff by her second marriage, is the only family member I contacted who had done any research. Though "Uncle Don" had focused on his paternal line, he had asked his mother Emily to write down everything she knew about her side of the family. She knew a lot about the children of Henry Iloff by both of his wives and also had information about the "Switzer girls." I sent this information on to Debra, the third-cousin from the Iloff family, who was able to verify that her ancestor Mary was a daughter of Henry's first wife. It has been very nice to be back in touch with Uncle Don, who was part of family gatherings in Hempstead when I was in graduate school. He was pleased to receive my information about the Eiloff and Lux families in Saarland. He attended a family reunion in Pennsylvania organized by third-cousin Debra.

Through Facebook I have met another third-cousin, Marcia, who organized the Iloff Family Facebook group. She and her mother recently visited the area where the Iloff farm was located and discovered that all the buildings had been torn down. Emailing back and forth with Marcia inspired me to call the Eiloffs in St. Nikolaus to see if any of them knew anything about a Henry in America. A German friend agreed to call for me. The man who answered our first call was perplexed to be receiving a call from a German woman calling from Greece claiming to represent an American woman who might be distant ancestor. But when my friend explained to him that I only wanted to find my family and perhaps visit them, he relaxed. He said that he indeed had heard the story of Heinrich who went off to America more than 150 years ago. He was certain that there were people in St. Nikolaus who would know more about the lines of relationship. He said he would ask around and that we should call back in two months to see what he had found. When my friend told him that Heinrich had eighteen children, he laughed and said the whole family was like that. He stated that as far as he knew the family name was German, and said that he had never heard anything to confirm speculations by American Iloffs that the family name might be Russian. I shared all of this information with third-cousins Debra and Marcia. Debra hopes we can visit to St. Nikolaus together with another cousin in the near future.

Excited to have the Iloff/Eiloff connection confirmed, I decided to join Ancestry.com to see what else I might find about my ancestors. On my first day, I started filling in the information I had collected over several years of searching on the Ancestry.com family tree form. The Ancestry tree form and several others are available for free on the Internet. I had not used any of them previously. These forms are infinitely expandable and make it easy to keep track of names, dates, and relationships. The Ancestry tree also has places to add documents, photographs, family stories. I am in the process of writing up all of the information I have found so far so that I can attach to my tree. Once I do this, other Ancestry members and my immediate family members will be able to read them.

I didn't realize until after I joined Ancestry that it offers far more than a document archive with search engine. When you enter names and dates onto your Ancestry family tree, Ancestry automatically searches all of their files for you. Ancestry is also a family social network site. It connects you to others whose family trees have the same ancestors in them. These people are all cousins of one degree or another. You can email them via the site, and they decide if they wish to answer. On my first day on Ancestry, I was connected to a family tree that had been posted by someone with the same surname as one of my mother's cousins. I immediately emailed this person and was reconnected with a second-cousin I had not seen since I was a child playing croquet with him on my grandmother's lawn. I suspect the possibility of connecting with cousins, second-cousins, and cousins to the nth degree is one of the reasons so many people stay on Ancestry.com long after they have found the information they originally thought they were seeking. A friend who has been a member for a long time told me that he has 10,000 people on his family tree now, as he follows up all the branches of the living and the dead, just for the fun of it. He also said that you never know when Ancestry will get access to new documents or whether a new person might join who has access to information you don't have. When that happens, what had seemed to be a deadend on your tree can open up.

In my ancestral journey I have learned that my ancestors came to America from Germany, Sweden, Ireland, England, Scotland, and France. In some cases, I know their places of origin from online birth records. In other cases, I do not. I have Huguenot, Puritan, Quaker, and Christian Science ancestors for whom religious belief was extremely important. Other ancestors married back and forth across Protestant and Catholic lines without apparent concern for religious differences. I have ancestors who took land from Native Americans. I have ancestors who were slaveholders. I have ancestors who were abolitionists. I have ancestors who fled religious or political persecution and ancestors who fled poverty and starvation. I have a few ancestors who were rich and many who were very poor. I have learned that I am deeply connected to the history of the United States in ways that I am proud of and in ways that I am not.

Like others who have found ancestors whose stories had been lost, I feel that my sense of "who I am" has "changed," and I feel "stronger" for knowing who some of my ancestors are. I feel pride in stories of strength and triumph in difficult circumstances. Knowing my family's relationships to the troubled history of the United States, I feel renewed commitment to ending the ongoing suffering of the descendants of slaves and Native Americans. Remembering ancestors is one way of recognizing our interdependence in the web of life. None of us "made ourselves." We all came from somewhere. Our ancestors live on in us both in the genetic inheritance written in our DNA and in conscious and unconscious memories and stories told and untold that shape our lives. The more we know about those who came before us, the more we know who we are, and who we can become.

For some time, I puzzled about how to understand connection to ancestors. African spiritual practices such as possession by ancestors seem to imply that the ancestors live on in a place "other than this world" after they die, from which they communicate with the living. A vivid dream in which my mother spoke to me after her death suggested this, too. The idea that ancestors live on after death conflicts with my sense that death is the end of individual life.[11] In recent years, I have come to believe that it is sufficient to say that the "place" where ancestors live is "in us." In us, "they" can even grow and change as our memories and our relationships to our memories change. Thus, I understand that when my mother said things in a dream that she had never said in life, I was transforming my relationship to her.

Pondering Karen Baker-Fletcher's question about the relation of ancestors to nature in the body of Goddess, I have come to see that while it is true to say that "we all come from the Goddess," it is also true that we each come from the bodies of specific mothers, with genetic inheritance from both of our parents. A long line of ancestors, female and male, made decisions, or had decisions made for them, that determined our places of birth. Our ancestors were connected, as we are connected, to specific places. Our lives are shaped, as theirs were shaped, by the conditions for life in a particular place. Our parents and grandparents consciously and unconsciously bequeathed to us complex patterns of feeling, forged in care and neglect, in love and the abuse of love, in hope and despair, in justice and injustice that have travelled down the generations to us.

We can remember and thank the ancestors whose lives made ours possible. We are stronger when we recognize the long line of ancestors who transmitted to us the gift of life, along with particular histories in specific places in the body of our mother earth, and genetic inheritances, which are both widely shared and totally unique. "I am Carol Patrice Christ, born in Pasadena, California, daughter of Janet Claire Bergman, born in El Paso, Texas; daughter of Lena Marie Searing, born in Lyons, Michigan; daughter of Dora Sofia Bahlke, born in Alma, Michigan; daughter of Mary Hundt, who came to Michigan from Parum, Mecklenburg, Germany; daughter of grandmother Schumann, born in Mecklenburg, in the clan of Tara, in a long line of women, known and unknown, stretching back to Africa. I am grateful for the gift of life they passed on to me."[12]

Notes

1. See her *Sisters of Dust, Sisters of Spirit: Womanist Wordings on God and Creation* (Minneapolis, MN: Fortress Press, 1998). Although Baker-Fletcher grew up with stories of her ancestors, Louis Henry Gates's programs indicate that this is not the case for all African Americans.
2. Bryan Sykes, *The Seven Daughters of Eve* (New York: Norton, 2001).
3. "The Human Journey," DVD with Spencer Wells, produced by the National Geographic Society and distributed as part of the Genographic Project.
4. Peter Ross, *Hempstead: A History of Long Island* (New York: Lewis Pub. Co., 1902), transcribed for the Internet by Coralynn Brown, http://dunhamwilcox.net/ny/hempstead_hist.htm. Also see www.rootsweb.ancestry.com/~nynassa2/annals3.htm.
5. As it turns out, John was a brother of my direct ancestor Jonathan, who may or may not have held slaves himself. Members of the Pearsall family whose children married Searings more than once, also held slaves. John's will was dated April 22, 1746, Elizabeth's, November 27, 1760. Records transcribed in "McCurdy Family Lineage," http://mccurdyfamilylineage.com/ancestry/p5434.htm http://mccurdyfamilylineage.com/ancestry/p182.htm. Also see my article, "A Daughter of the American Revolution and a Daughter of Quaker Slave Holders," http://feminismandreligion.com/2012/06/04/a-daughter-of-the-american-revolution-and-a-daughter-of-quaker-slave-owners-in-long-island-new-york-by-carol-p-christ/.
6. Ann Hartell, "Slavery on Long Island," *Nassau County Historical Journal* (Fall, 1943), transcribed http://longislandgenealogy.com/Slav.htm.
7. *Traces of the Trade: A Story from the Deep North*, www.tracesofthetrade.org/synopsis/.
8. "Thomas Pearsall: England and Virginia," http://home.teleport.com/~grafe/Pearsalls/Pearsalls/England.Virginia.html.
9. First-cousins have the same grandparents; second-cousins the same great-grandparents; third-cousins the same great-great-grandparents, and so on. Once-removed (or twice and so on) means you are in different generations: my father's first-cousin is my first-cousin once-removed. My father's first-cousin's children are my second-cousins.
10. There are quite a few Kellys on the Irish Landed Estates Database www.landedestates.ie/LandedEstates/jsp/estate-list.jsp. My great-grandmother always referred to her father as Lord Kelly, no first name. Joannis/John and Brigittae Kelly of Roscommon were Roman Catholic, as was my great-grandmother, and had a daughter Elizabeth Ann born in February, 1867, the date my great-grandmother gave to the census. John Kelly of Essex Lawn had a will in probate in 1874, which would fit with the story that he died when my great-grandmother was a child. He left

a married daughter and five other daughters, which fits with the story my father remembered. However, I have not yet found information confirming or disconfirming the story of gambling debts and suicide.

11. See "The Last Dualism: Life and Death in Goddess Feminist Theology," in *Journal of Feminist Studies in Religion* 27, no. 1 (Spring 2011): 129–145.

12. I end the essay with an affirmation of my augmented knowledge of my mother line as I can now speak it in a women's circle in Crete. In other contexts, the mother and father lines could both be included, or specific ancestors could be singled out.

Part II

Feminism and Alternative Communities

9   Private Space, Public Forum

A Netnographic Exploration of Muslim American Women, Access, and Agency in "Islamic" Cyberspace

Kristina Benson

This article engages in a netnographic case study using *fatawa* from two of the most popular Islam-related sites for American Muslims: Islamicity.com and SuhaibWebb.com. The first of these sites, Islamicity, was launched in 1995 and is operated by the Human Assistance and Development International, a nonprofit organization incorporated in California in 1991 with the goal of "[providing] a non-sectarian, comprehensive and holistic view of Islam and Muslims to a global audience."[1] In addition to posting prayer times, articles about Islam, and translated editions of the Quran, it hosts a prolific "Ask Imam" section where various scholars answer questions posed by the Muslim community. The site is also home to a vibrant discussion board where tens of thousands of users have created over 150,000 posts spread across fifty-eight different subfora.

The second website, SuhaibWebb.com, is named after its founder, an American convert to Islam who serves as Imam at the Islamic Society of Boston Cultural Center. Named "Best Blog" by the Brass Crescent in 2009, the site posts lectures, articles, *fatawa*, and essays, and "is dedicated to enhancing the spiritual and religious development of Muslims through sound, balanced & moderate Islamic teachings. It seeks to bridge orthodox and contemporary Islamic knowledge, bringing to light issues of cultural, social and political relevance to Muslims in the West."[2] Unlike Islamicity.com, SuhaibWebb.com has no forum or message board, but readers are invited to respond to and discuss site content in the Comments section below each posted *fatawa*, article, or essay.

These two sites provide an ideal case study into the dialectic between Islam, women, and computer-mediated environments in the post-9/11 milieu. While the scope of this study is, of course, narrow, we can still draw some tentative conclusions about the unique opportunities that cyberspace has presented to American Muslim women and to American Islam due to the enduring nature of these sites, their popularity, and the prolific amount of content they offer and produce, allowing us to draw some tentative conclusions.

First, the ongoing translation and online dissemination of Arabic sources into English has given American Muslim women the ability to consume religious literature that was previously unavailable to anyone lacking a mastery of classical Arabic or access to Islamic texts. For the time being, English is the *lingua franca* of the Internet,³ and traditional authorities in Islam, even in the Middle East, often choose to present their ideas in English to enable a global reach.

Second, the Internet enables American Muslim women to read and respond to these Islamic sources, knowledge, and ideas in a milieu detached from physical space, allowing them to access discussions and participate in conversations that historically have taken place primarily in homosocial, male-only settings. In Islamicate cultures, the intermingling of the sexes in *physical* space remains heavily regulated compared to "Western" cultures; intermingling of the sexes in *cyberspace*, however, falls outside the scope of this regulation. The digital dissemination of lectures, texts, and conversations, therefore, presents significant opportunities for women to not only *consume* but also *produce* religious knowledge in a heterosocial setting and to a heterosocial audience.

Third, the asynchronous, de-spatialized nature of online interaction contributes to the obfuscation of knowledge production and knowledge consumption, giving women new forms of active and passive agency. For example, when women comment on a posted article or *fatawa,* and when they "Like" or "Share" content, they are both *consuming* and *producing* knowledge. Muslim women's interaction with Islam-focused articles, their contributions to message boards, and their participation on comment threads occur in a heterosocial milieu, further empowering them to influence the trajectory of conversations, respond to sources of authority, and destabilize top-down hierarchies of religious production. Women's presence as countable members of an online audience can also influence the nature of content produced by Islam-oriented websites. Even women who choose not to directly interact with site content, therefore, still have an opportunity to influence the crafting of religious knowledge simply by their mere online presence—a presence that may not be possible in a de-spatialized context.

In sum, a confluence of factors have allowed American Muslim women unprecedented *access* to religious knowledge, and with it, new forms of *agency* within the context of its production. Such access and agency, it should be noted, comes at a key moment, given that Internet has only recently emerged as a destination for actors wishing to participate in the consumption and production of knowledge. This emergence coincides with the events of 9/11, which not only made Islam salient in the public imagination, but also launched conversations about the nature of Islam, its role in American Muslim life, and its development in a diasporic context.

After pausing to discuss the methodological framework employed in this article and a brief review of netnographic literature, the following sections will consider the nature of American Muslim women's access and agency, its deviation from historical precedent, and its ramifications for American Muslims and American Islam.

Access: English, Space, and Place

Within the context of Islamic culture and thought, it is not an exaggeration to say Arabic has traditionally been regarded as nothing short of a God-given language,[4] and the centrality of Arabic to the historical development of Islamic jurisprudence, culture, and philosophical thought cannot be overstated. This attitude, as well as the idea that Islam is permanently yoked to Arabic, has been prevalent for centuries, even in non-Arab countries and among non-Arab scholars and thinkers. For example, Turkish Islamic thinker Sakib Arslan "held that the community was defined by its religion, and since Arabs formed the core of the Islamic *umma* [community], Arabic was the true language of Islam, so that every Muslim had to learn Arabic."[5]

To be sure, a serious scholar of Islam must still be comfortable reading and understanding Arabic, however, there is evidence that fluency in Arabic has become optional for Muslim laypeople interested in learning about the faith. Thanks to the combined efforts of South Asian Islamic governments,[6] Muslim educational foundations, and various Islamic publishers, a scarcity of English-language Islamic resources are a "thing of the past."[7] Therefore, although prayer in Arabic is still considered mandatory—even for Muslims who do not understand or speak Arabic—Muslims wishing to consume or produce authoritative religious knowledge are now able to do so in English and reach a global audience capable of understanding and responding to their views.

Muslim intellectuals, *muftis*,[8] and Imams[9] have also realized that English, as the lingua franca of the Internet, has emerged as a "preferred medium to call attention to new ideas. One leading Arab religious intellectual recently observed that knowing English and being taken seriously by English-speakers, Muslim and non-Muslim alike, enables the proliferation of new ideas even within the "Islamic world."[10] While religious authorities may still address local audiences using Arabic, they will often favor English over Arabic or even French when trying to obtain a more cosmopolitan reach.[11]

The availability of these English-language Islamic materials is particularly significant for American Muslims, as the creation of an English-speaking Islamic milieu "de-emphasizes an Arab/Middle Eastern Arabic speaking monopoly on Arabic discourse, opening up debate and discussion between Muslims worldwide."[12] Furthermore, the fact that this English-speaking Islamic milieu occurs online in a deterritorialized format allows Muslim American *women* to question *fatawa* and engage in critical discussions without transgressing social norms that attach women to "private" spaces, a practice that has, until recently, limited women's access to physical spaces historically associated with the production of religious knowledge.[13] Put differently, the translation of materials into English allows American Muslims to read them, while the online dissemination thereof allows American Muslim *women* to *discuss, react to, question,* and *interpret* these materials in a heterosocial field, in front of or in a dialectic with a large audience, without violating religious or cultural norms surrounding the gendered division of space.

This too is a significant deviation from hundreds of years of tradition: while there is no formal clergy in Islam, there has historically been a jurist class who relied on a combination of factors, including low rates of literacy, "to maintain a virtual monopoly on the production of authoritative religious knowledge."[14]

In the classical period of Islamic jurisprudence, a majority of religious knowledge was transmitted orally between men, with a scholar granting his student an *ijaza* (licence) to pass on the texts of his teacher.[15] Later, when charitable schools for Quranic recitation and interpretation were established, they were boys' schools; girls of the same social class, on the other hand, were generally sent to sewing and embroidery schools.[16] Occasionally, upper-class women were taught informally by male relatives, or were permitted to hire a tutor to teach them the art of Quranic exegesis, however these were exceptions to the rule, and throughout the classical period it was fairly rare even for a wealthy woman to claim mastery of the Islamic sciences or be in a position to teach other women with any authority.[17]

Eventually, increased urban literacy, acting in concert with introduction of the printing press in the modern era, allowed for the scholars' *interpretive* stranglehold to be broken;[18] however, the *producers* of original knowledge were still limited to those who had access to printing presses and the ability to express oneself publicly without risking social opprobrium. With few exceptions, therefore, men retained their monopoly on authoritative religious production.[19]

The male monopoly over religious knowledge has continued to exist insofar as physical space is concerned, given that production and consumption of Islamic knowledge are generally "male" spaces: while daily prayer is mandatory for all Muslims; for example, Friday congregational prayer is technically only mandatory for Muslim men. Women are not generally permitted to lead prayers before a mixed audience, and while women are permitted to attend prayers, American women will most often do so in a separate space allocated to women and children where they either listen to the male prayer leader from behind a screen, through a public address system, or watch him on a television placed at the front of the room. [20]

For example, Islamicity.com has a section called "Q&A (Ask the Imam)" wherein members of the online community ask the Imam or *mufti*- in-residence for his opinion on religious matters. Today, as in the pre-colonial era, the responses will be most likely written by private individuals who have chosen to dedicate themselves to studying Islam and are not appointed for a state government in pursuit of achieving specific religious goals. Although the markers of authority have changed somewhat, their authority is derived solely from the trust of the public and their reputations as a knowledgeable, pious people who had engaged in rigorous study of the sources and had a strong command of Arabic.[21] Their answers to the community's questions ideally include a sophisticated analysis of the sources and result in a publicly disseminated, non-binding recommendation called *fatwa* (pl. *fatawa*). Ideally, when composing his (or occasionally, her) *fatawa*, the *mufti* will draw from key authoritative texts in Islamic law, which are the Qur'an and the *Hadith*,[22] in addition to applying various epistemologies and methodological tools depending on his sectarian affiliation. These might include *'urf* (local custom), *ijma* (the consensus of scholars), *maslaha* (perceptions of the public good), *qiyas* (analogy), or *ijtihad* (independent reasoning).

The "Ask Imam" and *fatawa* sections of Islam-oriented websites, therefore, are continuing a centuries-old tradition within the framework of a digital milieu. The "Ask Imam" section of Islamicity has an impressive archive of questions and answers dating back to 1995, when the site was launched, and at present there are approximately 8,000 questions categorized by topic, date, or keyword. No less than 342 of these questions can be found under the topic "women," and most of these ask about women's ability to "go out," work in public, pray in public, pray in a heterosocial setting, or work in a setting with non-*mahram*[23] men. In other words, most of the 342 questions about women are concerned with women's occupation of *physical, non-domestic space.*

The *mufti's* answer, after revisiting the question several times and in relation to a variety of contexts, is that women are discouraged from entering public space, or alternatively that women may do so but with (occasionally profound) limitations. For example, while the *mufti* acknowledges in one *fatwa* that women may enter a mosque so long as they pray in a space that is separate from the men, he suggests in two other *fatawa* that women will ideally choose to pray at home:

Question date: *5/31/2008*
Topic: *Entering Masjid [mosque]*

Question: *why the muslim women not allowed to enter mashjid [mosque] ?*

Answer *. . . There is no harm in reserving a section of the mosque for men and another section for women. Women used to pray behind the Prophet's mosque in Madeenah at the back rows . . . There is no doubt that separating men from women is considered as a better way of preventing men and women from seeing each other and a way of increasing attention to prayer and a better way of performing this great act of worship by both parties, especially at this time when corruption and temptations are widespread . . . If a barrier or curtain is put between them and men, that is better on the condition that it should not prevent the sight and sound.*

Women, therefore, are theoretically permitted to enter the mosque under certain conditions, however, a year later the Imam advised that in practice, women should choose not to:

Question date: *6/22/2009*
Topic: *Prayer: women in congregation*

Question: *can a women be an imam to other women during prayers?*

Answer: *. . . It is permissible for women to go out and pray in the mosque with men, although their Prayer at home is better, because the Prophet, peace and* *blessings be upon him, said: "Do not prevent the women from going out to the mosques, even though their homes are better for them."*[24]

The Imam returned to the issue approximately a year later, again affirming that while women are permitted to pray in congregation, it is better that they stay at home:

Question date: 9/19/2010
Topic: Prayer women prayer in public places [sic]

Question: Are women allowed to pray in public places?

Answer: . . . Moslem women are allowed to pray in public places. But it is preferred and recommended to pray at home.[25]

While these and other *fatawa* stress the importance of physically separating men from women, none of the 8,000+ *fatawa* address the problem posed by computer-mediated interaction and its implication for the division of physical space, given that cyberspaces impossibly obfuscates the difference between "private" and "public." Islamicity's own message board, for example, has more than 21,000 members—many of them women—engaging in heterosocial interaction in more than fifty subfora. At times, they discuss fairly intimate problems, share their feelings about challenges in their lives, and ask each other for help in resolving various matters, many of them profoundly personal. All of these interactions and all of these shared problems, moreover, are visible to anyone with an Internet connection, rendering them "public" in most senses of the word.

Even so, consuming, producing, and sharing knowledge with non-*mahram* men in non-private *physical* spaces may be problematic, but doing so in non-private *cyberspaces*, for the time being, is not. The untethering of social interaction and knowledge dissemination from the physical world, therefore, has profound ramifications for women, who are now able to consume any form of religious knowledge, regardless of its original site of production, if it is rendered in digital form and disseminated online.

This brings us to the point that the consumption of knowledge is impossibly co-present with the *production* of knowledge in an online setting, allowing Muslim women to quickly translate *access* into *agency*. This *agency* is enabled and articulated in a variety of ways and can take a variety of forms; these will be discussed in the following section.

Agency: Audience, Response, and Knowledge Generation in Cyberspace

Inclusion in online, Islam-focused communities is particularly significant for Muslim women given that users are interacting with each other and about material under discussion in a manner that blurs *consuming* and *producing*. As

Nancy Baym observed in her netnographic study of an online group of soap opera fans, online communities devoted to appreciating a certain text, craft, skill, or ideology are "communities of practice" in every sense of the term, given that they are organized and defined according to common interests and are generally devoted to the sharing and trading of information.[26]

The Internet's obfuscation between "private" and "public" domains, furthermore, not only gives women *access* to settings that were previously conceptualized as homosocial spaces for knowledge consumption (as aforementioned), but also gives women new opportunities to exert *agency* over the kind of knowledge being produced. These opportunities can be broadly categorized as *reactive agency*, wherein women respond (or choose not to respond) to content that has been posted by the site administrator, and *active agency*, wherein women generate and post content as a site administrator, or at the invitation thereof.

The importance of reactive agency should not be minimized. A vast majority of websites earn money by the amount of "impressions" or "clicks" they receive from unique visitors.[27] The more visitors they receive, the higher they rank in Google search results for terms relevant to their content—in this case, terms like "Islam" or "Imam." Higher Google search results lead to a higher number of "impressions," which in turn leads to a higher Google search ranking, and so on. Alternatively, a website can choose not to include ads but in this case, the website is acting less as a source of revenue than as a brand amplification platform, and will almost always encourage visitors to repost content on their own social media accounts and "follow" site administrators on their respective Twitter feeds, Facebook pages, and YouTube channels.

While decision to visit or not visit a website seems like a small one, the proportion of American women visiting a given site may be linked to the inclusion of more "progressive" attitudes toward gender, as well as the presence of more women writers, given that site administrators are directly and indirectly incentivized to accommodate their visitors. According to Alexa, a metric for judging Internet reach, male users, for example, are disproportionately represented in Islamicity's audience.

In the first four months of 2013, sixty-eight articles were posted on Islamicity. com. The only one written by a woman was an article reposted from the *Guardian* website. The rest were either authored by men, or by "staff."

SuhaibWebb, on the other hand, is popular among young American Muslims and, according to Alexa, is disproportionately visited by women.

At present, there are ten women listed as contributors out of a total of twenty-two, including two women who commenters—male and female alike—consistently address and refer to as *sheikhas*, the female version of *sheikh*. The presence of a female audience, therefore, may be framed as *passive,* given that it may involve as little as the passive consumption of knowledge, or even the mere choice to click on a given headline or article and become a counted member of a website's audience. However, the choice to click on a given headline or article is co-present with *active* agency, given that doing so may give women more opportunities to produce religious knowledge within the context of a credible, authoritative website, absent the various pressures to refrain from entering heterosocial spaces. In other words, the presence of a female audience may invite content that caters to women, including but not limited to content written *by* women.

The presence of a disproportionately female audience may also influence not *who* is producing the knowledge, but *what kind* of knowledge they are producing. Returning to the issue of whether or not women are encouraged to pray at home rather than at the mosque, a question similar to those answered on Islamicity was posed to the Imam-in-residence at Suhaibbwebb. It was answered in Arabic by an Egyptian *mufti,* Shaykh Muhammad al-Hassan al-Dido, and translated and abridged by Suhaib Webb himself, stating:

Date: *March 26, 2010*

Question: *Some jurists say that the increased reward for praying in the masjid [mosque] does not apply to women because of the known hadith, "A woman's prayer in her house is better than in her courtyard, and her prayer in her own room is better than her prayer in the rest of the house" (reported by Abu Dawud). Does this hadith apply to all women?*

Answer: *The more favorable opinion is that it does not apply to every woman . . . Women also gain more reward for praying in the masjid, just like men. This is especially true when the masajid in our times have designated areas for women. During the Prophet's time the men and women were not separated in the masjid; the women simply prayed in rows behind the men.*

Women, in other words, are not transgressing male space when they pray in congregation at the mosque. To be sure, Islamicity's *fatawa* on the matter—that it is "better" for women to pray at home—is not necessarily a fringe stance if taken within the historical context of Islamic jurisprudence: the classical and colonial periods of Islam, jurists have had varying opinions as to the circumstances under which women could pray in the mosque, with some scholars against all women praying anywhere but their homes, and others solely opposed to the congregational prayers of attractive women.[28] Very few, however, discouraged all women from attending mosque under any circumstance.[29] Twentieth- and twenty-first-century muftis, however, have issued *fatawa* encouraging women's mosque attendance, pointing out that the physical seclusion of women in their homes leads to their political and social alienation, disempowerment, and disenfranchisement.[30] Additionally, the global trend—for American Muslims as well as for Muslims in South Asia and the Middle East—is toward greater accommodation of women's congregational prayer.[31] Suhaibb Webb's opinion that women can and should attend mosque as they wish, therefore, should not be seen as an outlier or radically outside the tradition of Islamic spiritual practice.

While it is difficult to conclude at this point that such a *fatawa* is *caused* by the presence of a female audience, a disproportionately female audience may be *correlated* with more progressive views on gender, and with opportunities for women scholars to present their views to a heterosocial audience within the framework of an authoritative medium.

Concluding Notes and Observations

As scholar Gary Bunt noted, new issues have emerged from the creation of online communities devoted to Muslims and discussions of Islam. The "digital *umma*" and "Cyber Islamic Environments" have emerged as Muslims—like members of other religions—have created online communities and sites of computer-mediated interaction. These communities often, but not always, feature a "horizontal knowledge model" reliant on collaboration and peer-to-peer networking. They have destabilized top-down frameworks of authority, reconfigured pre-existing hierarchies, exposed the faithful to new sources of religious authority, and introduced new venues for creating religious knowledge.[32] New spaces enable laypeople to develop religious literacy, discuss issues of concern, offer support in times of crisis, form social coalitions, and interrogate religious norms and practices. iPhone apps, IRCs,[33] Facebook groups, IslamTube, and other sites offer Muslims the ability to remain perpetually connected to each other, their mosque, or their religious communities, potentially decompartmentalizing religious practice from the rest of daily life.[34]

Public conversations have long had a special role in the Muslim world, allowing the religious and political elite to take public ideas of community, identity, and leadership into account when crafting policy or interpreting Shar'ia law.[35] Message boards and space for commenter activity can be seen as a 21st-century articulation of this tradition, allowing Muslim women unprecedented opportunities to exploit and influence the very visible tension between Islamic law as interpreted "from above" and living law as it experienced "from below." All of this occurs in an extra-spatial, English-speaking, asynchronous framework, enabling participation that was not possible for women when the production of religious knowledge took place almost solely in Arabic and in homosocial, male-only settings. Cyberspace, with its obfuscation of "public" and "private" space, empower women to deviate from their culturally sanctioned, domestic roles and participate in the "public" dissemination and production of religions knowledge online.

Notes

1. Islamicity, "Islamicity Facebook Page," www.facebook.com/islamicity/info.
2. See SuhaibWebb.com: "Your Virtual Mosque," www.suhaibwebb.com.
3. At present, English remains the most-used language on the Web. For a brief discussion about English on the Web, see: Jane O'Brien, "Learn English Online: How The Internet Is Changing Language," in *BBC News Magazine*, December 13, 2012, www.bbc.co.uk/news/magazine-20332763.

4. Anwar G. Chejne, *The Arabic Language: Its Role in History* (Minneapolis, MN: University of Minnesota, 1969), 253.

5. Kees Versteegh and C.H.M. Versteegh, *The Arabic Language* (New York: Columbia University Press, 1997), 177.

6. Peter Mandaville, "Reimagining Islam in Diaspora: The Politics of Mediated Community," *International Communication Gazette* 63 (2001): 63, 169.

7. Abdul Hamid Lofti, "Spreading the Word," in *Muslim Minorities in the West: Visible and Invisible*, ed. Yvonne Yazbeck Haddad and Jane Idleman Smith (Walnut Creek, CA: Altamira Press, 2002), 3.

8. A *mufti* is literally "one who issues *fatwa.*" *Fatwa* (pl. *fatawa)* will be discussed in a later section in detail, however, for now suffice it to say that *fatawa* are nonbinding religious recommendations disseminated to the community by scholars and jurists. These recommendations are issued in response to questions posed by laypeople about issues of concern.

9. For the purposes of this paper, an Imam is someone who leads prayer. While he or she may also be a scholar or jurist, she or he can also simply be an esteemed member of the community considered sufficiently learned and morally fit to do so.

10. Dale F. Eickelman and Jon W. Anderson, "Redefining Muslim Publics," in *New Media in the Muslim World: The Emerging Public Sphere.* 2nd Edition, ed. Dale F. Eickelman and Jon W. Anderson (Indianapolis, IN: Indiana University Press, 2003), 8.

11. Yves Gonzalez-Quizano, "The Birth of a Media Ecosystem: Lebanon in the Internet Age," in *New Media in the Muslim World: The Emerging Public Sphere.* 2nd Edition, ed. Dale F. Eickelman and Jon W. Anderson (Indianapolis, IN: Indiana University Press, 2003), 61–79, 68.

12. Alexis Kort, "Dar Al-Cyber Islam: Women, Domestic Violence, and the Islamic Reformation on the World Wide Web," *Journal of Muslim Minority Affairs* 25, no. 3 (December 2005): 364.

13. There are, of course, exceptions and I do not mean to suggest that there has never been a single heterosocial space devoted to imbibing Islamic knowledge. Throughout time and space, however, it is safe to say that a vast majority of such spaces were "male" spaces, and in many communities, still are.

14. Mandaville, "Reimagining Islam," 176.

15. Ibid.

16. Leila Ahmed, *Woman and Gender in Islam: Historical Roots of a Modern Debate* (New Haven, CT: Yale University, 1992), 113.

17. Leila Ahmed, *Woman and Gender in Islam,* 113.

18. Mandaville, "Reimagining Islam," 176.

19. See Margot Badran, *Feminism in Islam: Secular and Religious Convergences* (New York: One World Publications, 2009).

20. To be sure, it is problematic to unequivocally link public space to power and assume that women are inherently disempowered or oppressed by virtue of their existence in homosocial settings. It should also be mentioned that women's voices are represented in canonical Islamic texts, and that the prophet's wife Aisha was a prolific transmitter of *ahadith.*[19] Nevertheless, public *physical* space is still overwhelmingly considered male space, and American Muslim women's entrance into public spaces or "male" spaces—even in the present-day United States, and even in spaces devoted to worshipping, producing religious knowledge, or consuming religious knowledge—is frequently regarded as a potentially transgressive act that may necessitate careful negotiation.

21. Wael B. Hallaq, *Origins and Evolutions of Islamic Law* (Cambridge, UK: Cambridge University Press, 2004), 87–88.

22. The *Hadith* are the collected observations of what the Prophet did and said while he was alive.

23. *Mahram* men are men to which women are closely related, either by marriage or kinship ties.
24. Islamicity, "Q&A (Ask Imam)." Last modified June 22, 2009, www.islamicity.com/qa/action.lasso.asp?-db=services&-lay=Ask&-op=eq&number=32585&-format=detailpop.shtml&-find.
25. Ibid.
26. Nancy Baym, *Tune in, Log On: Soaps, Fandom, and Online Community* (Thousand Oaks, London, and New Delhi: SAGE, 2000), 3.
27. See Albrecht Enders et al., "The Long Tail of Social Networking; Revenue Models of Social Networking Sites," in *European Management Journal* 26, no. 3 (2008): 199–211, http://dx.doi.org/10.1016/j.emj.2008.02.002.
28. Marion Holmes, *Katz Prayer in Islamic Thought and Practice* (New York: Cambridge University Press, 2013), 201.
29. Ibid.
30. Ibid., 207.
31. Ibid., 209.
32. Gary Bunt, *iMuslims: Rewiring the House of Islam* (Chapel Hill: University of North Carolina Press, 2009), 2.
33. IRC stands for Internet Relay Chat, which facilities computers to communicate with each other. It is often used by groups of people to communicate in a discussion forum, generally referred to as a "channel," but can also be used for file sharing, chatting, data transfer, and instant messaging between two or more computers.
34. Ibid., 10
35. Eickelman and Anderson, "New Muslim Publics," 2.

10 Faith from Nowhere

Feminist Ecclesiological Reflections on the "Liquid Catholicism" of New Media

Brett C. Hoover

Christianity arrives electronically these days. It comes via browser, online video, blog, text, email, and podcast. Many believers—especially in the United States—use this *new media*, though not all to the same extent or in the same way. Some envision themselves as accessing online toolkits of information, addenda to spiritual lives and faith communities centered elsewhere. Others identify themselves as personally participating in virtual communities, some even eschewing the live versions and using the term "virtual church." However the users of Christian new media describe their experience today, it has become a widespread *practice* of faith, that is, a repeated and patterned meaningful activity.

Theological examination of practice is frequently associated with the work of practical theologians in the academy—such as the Americans Don Browning, Claire Wolfteich, and Tom Beaudoin, or the British feminist theologian Elaine Graham.[1] Practical theologians presume that practices like new media use have theological significance shaped by both their social context and their engagement with Christian tradition. Many feminist theologians—inside and outside of practical theology—share a concern with examining Christian practice. Many want to determine, in Rosemary Radford Ruether's memorable phrase, whether Christian practice promotes or "denies, diminishes, or distorts the full humanity of women."[2] In this essay, I ask about the ecclesiological significance of the *practice* of using Christian new media, particularly as informed by strands of feminist theological reflection on both practice itself and on the Church.

While widespread today, the use of Christian new media proves a difficult practice to explore and evaluate.[3] The immediacy and ubiquity of the Internet obscure the (often gendered) communities, contexts, and relationships from which these media arise. New platforms arrive all the time, and old platforms either disappear or linger unaltered in virtual limbo. Thus, new media can seem like they deliver a faith without context—a "faith from nowhere." While there is no such thing as a "faith from nowhere," we do have to find some way to critically address something that appears so diffuse and unmoored. I recommend turning to a concrete case study, and this essay examines the use of a single new media platform—the Roman Catholic new media platform *BustedHalo*®—especially in its early days. I was involved in its development from 2000–2004, first as one of the designers and then later as editor-in-chief of the website. The platform, launched in late 2001, survives still, and remains addressed to young Catholics in their twenties and thirties. This case study will explore how use of the platform functions as an *ecclesial* experience—a gathering of believers. Though the use of BustedHalo—like many Christian practices—has contributed to both the promotion and diminishment of the full humanity of women, its trajectory in Christian new media suggests considerable hope for more of the former and less of the latter.

Theological "Takes" on New Media

Theological consideration of new media often focuses on the individualistic nature of its use, even suggesting that new media use promotes a solipsistic, "churchless Christianity."[4] Feminist theologians might well agree. Any insufficiently relational accounting of human life contradicts cherished feminist theological anthropology.[5] On the other hand, constructing new media as a form of "churchless" or solipsistic Christianity overlooks the actual human processes by which new media come to be and are maintained. Human beings do not create or use new media apart from the networks and communities to which they belong. Christian new media necessarily involve concrete communities and networks of faith. They come from somewhere, and that somewhere matters. Thus, in the end, we have to take Christian new media platforms seriously as an *ecclesial* experience rooted in particular communities. We might wish to know what *kind* of ecclesial experience new media platforms present. How can we evaluate them vis-à-vis Ruether's criterion of promoting or diminishing the full humanity of women?

In all honesty, we the founders of BustedHalo did not reflect much on the ecclesial experience we initially hoped to generate. We did not intend to design a "virtual church," that is, a distinct community of faith in cyberspace. We wanted instead to develop an online community in only the most minimal way, enough to sustain a conversation that critically engaged young people's experience of Catholicism. The earliest mission statement of the sponsoring ministry concluded, "Through our pastoral and 'virtual' ministry with young adults and with the pastoral ministers that accompany them, we aim to encourage their exploration of spirituality, their listening to and support of one another, their discovery of the rich depths of Catholic and other traditions, and their participation in communities of faith." Of course, as hermeneuticists have long reminded us, the intentions of an author or designer remain only one factor in the development of any interpreted message. The world of the "text" itself and the world that it addresses remain just as crucial.[6] Here, I hope to engage the text and world of BustedHalo by exploring its *use* by believers. In other words, how did use of the BustedHalo platform construct and communicate a Roman Catholic ecclesial experience, and how can we understand that experience from feminist perspectives?

To reflect on the social practice of the *use* of BustedHalo, I turn to practical theology. Reflection on the theological significance of social practice has been a mainstay of practical theological method from the beginning. Practical theology emerged within Protestant pastoral theology in Europe and the United States in the late 1970s and early 1980s as a critical response to more text-driven theology. It was not the only approach to do so. Practice-oriented theological approaches, for example, also emerged in U.S. Hispanic/Latino/a theology, often rooted in the practice of popular religion.[7] The *mujerista* theology of the late Ada María Isasi-Díaz, in particular, engaged social theory and/ or the social sciences to interpret practice, just as practical theology does.[8] Here, however, I will make particular use of the British feminist practical theologian Elaine Graham's theology of Christian practice. I also engage Pete Ward's ecclesiology of a "liquid church" as a tool for understanding the *ecclesial* nature of the practice of using new media. This ecclesiological perspective comes from Ward's experience in the new-media-saturated Emergent Church Movement (ECM). The innovation and institutional fluidity of this perspective does not, however, place it outside the long history of patriarchal-kyriarchal theologies of church. The "liquid church" of new media must still take seriously critical feminist perspectives on the historic church as we have known it.

The Social Context of New Media

Any responsible theological exploration of the practice of using new media requires placing that practice in its proper social and ecclesial context. Elaine Graham writes, "Christians act in ways they believe to be good, just and true because they inhabit a community which aspires to realize a particular vision of ultimate value—in their case, the reality of God."[9] That vision is always "situated"; it arises from a concrete communal experience of faith.[10] Indeed, BustedHalo's vision arose from those who created it—a group of lay employees and clerical members of a Roman Catholic religious order, the Paulist Fathers, a congregation long associated with preaching and use of the media.[11] The creators—all middle-class whites—lived and worked in urban centers—New York City and Washington, DC. They belonged to social networks of accountability within Roman Catholicism—principally, networks for Catholic young adult ministry and Catholic media. Members of these networks shared a belief in the transformational potential of people having conversations—public and private—about Catholic Christian faith.

But the networks themselves only partially explain how this emphasis on encouraging faith conversation unfolded in the creation of BustedHalo as a new media platform. We operated in a transitional online environment in those days, one that encouraged modest ambitions but still boasted relatively uncluttered fields of play. On the one hand, the "startup" bubble had burst; overheated claims about the reach and transformational character of Internet resources no longer impressed. Thus, we did not imagine ourselves starting a faith revolution or founding a church online but simply creating effective resources to spur faith conversation among young people. Religious resources on the web remained limited at the time. With determination and imaginative design, we expected to have a broad impact. Finally, the new media boom—with its focus on branded platforms, interlocking media, social networking, podcasting, and Internet video—had not yet begun in earnest. Like most religious groups, we initially focused our energy on website development and traffic—Web 1.0. Only later did BustedHalo come to encompass satellite radio, podcasting, and Internet video and to relate extensively to social networking platforms.

The Beginning of BustedHalo[12]

BustedHalo itself came about when, in late 1999, the leadership of the Paulists held a focus group to brainstorm about augmenting their ministerial outreach to young Catholics. They gathered young professionals, college students, campus ministers, and priests and lay people working with young people—women and men—in New York City. The group made several recommendations, chief among them that the Paulists create a spirituality website from the perspective of young people. The group saw that Internet communication was increasingly the preferred medium of the young, yet the Catholic landscape of cyberspace at the time was dominated by a small number of websites with question-and-answer formats, "Baltimore Catechisms of the Web" that often employed language and resources from before the Second Vatican Council.

Hoping to create something different, the Paulists assembled two teams to work on the project together—the already existing Paulist Media Works (PMW) in Washington, DC, and a new national young adult outreach based in New York City called Paulist Young Adult Ministries (PYAM). Both teams were themselves a mix of lay media professionals (all but one women) and Paulist priests (all men). PMW was embedded in decades-old networks of Catholic broadcasters, journalists, and public relations experts. PYAM's staff participated in Catholic young adult ministry networks of that era, which largely addressed the concerns of middle-class young professionals, most white or Asian. PMW and PYAM did extensive research in preparation for the launch of BustedHalo. PMW looked at existing religious websites and design approaches while PYAM conducted geographically dispersed focus groups with young Catholic women and men. Several hundred young people—a disproportionately female, racially and ethnically diverse but socioeconomically homogeneous group recruited through church and media networks—participated in an online survey.

The results of the research surprised the creators. Young Catholics wanted *information* from a Catholic website rather than media personalities or interactivity. A new design and a domain name emerged from this months-long process. The domain name, BustedHalo, was suggested in a young-adult focus group at a predominantly Puerto Rican parish in the Bronx; it tested well among young people, who associated it with recognition of the humanity of spiritual seekers.[13] The eventual design included (1) an electronic magazine with ever-changing articles on spirituality, relationships, culture, current events, and the arts; and (2) a mildly irreverent catechetical section written by young people involved in graduate theological education, with appropriate expertise in areas such as liturgy, Scripture, and personal prayer. The website also included an interfaith trivia game called "Dante's Trivia Inferno," where answers propelled the visitor on a spiritual elevator back and forth between heaven, purgatory, and hell.

The site was launched in December of 2001. PYAM drew traffic to Busted-Halo through existing Catholic ministry networks (such as the Catholic Campus Ministry Association), and in the summer of 2002 hosted a demonstration booth at World Youth Day in Toronto. At the same time, PYAM did "guerilla promotions" at events focused on young people (such as distributing material at the Head of the Charles Regatta in the Boston area) and conducted an online advertising campaign on the site of the satirical newspaper *The Onion* (and later at The Hunger Site, a charity donation website). By early 2004, it had hosted more than 200,000 unique visitors. Today, the website has more than 22,000 unique "likes" on Facebook.[14]

We soon found that *use* of the site centered on reading the catechetical sections and the short essays on spirituality in everyday life, the arts, and current events produced by our staff of young writers from diverse backgrounds. Most people visited as individuals, but Catholic institutions also promoted the website in their internal networks as a resource for ministry. One rural and resource-poor diocese in the southern United States used BustedHalo to resource catechists and religious education students. According to the website's current editor, Barbara Wheeler, confirmation teachers, Catholic schools, and Protestant pastors still use the catechetical materials on BustedHalo.com— now including a great deal of video—as pastoral tools. Not all use centered on passive reading. The PYAM staff also answered and sometimes posted the answers to religious questions sent to us by email, the so-called "Question Box." In some cases, this rose to virtual pastoral counseling, as people shared serious problems and asked advice back and forth via email. Young Catholics also communicated how BustedHalo offered them a connection to other young Catholics, rare in some areas. One young couple wrote:

> [We] really enjoy BustedHalo and it often provides the basis for our nightly theological discussions. Also, as the youngest (by far) student in my scripture program (as well as most of the other Church-related activities I participate in) it is so nice to hear from other people my own age and reflect on their perspectives.[15]

The most interactive part of the site, the message boards, initially drew many people not associated with formal religion, but an early surge of opinionated participation by traditionalist Catholics reversed that trend.[16]

BustedHalo as Liquid Catholicism

Little in contemporary Roman Catholic ecclesiology helps to orient one to the place of new media like BustedHalo in the contemporary church. Instead, I turn to ecclesiological reflection on the experience of the media-savvy Emerging Church Movement (ECM). According to sociologist Gerardo Martí, the ECM is a tiny but influential ecclesial movement that emerged in the 1990s as a critique of stable church structures, principally those associated with mainstream evangelicalism in the United States and the Anglican and Methodist churches in the United Kingdom.[17] Were it not a Catholic endeavor, BustedHalo might appear to have come from the playbook of the ECM.

Anglican theologian Pete Ward, heavily influenced by the ECM, writes of a need for a "liquid church" in late modernity. His terms are reminiscent of BustedHalo's fluid style and lack of clear mooring in concrete faith communities,

> We need to shift from seeing church as a gathering of people meeting in one place at one time—that is, a congregation—to a notion of church as a series of relationships and communications. This image implies something like a network or a web rather than an assembly of people.[18]

Ward sees church as network as an appropriate response to Zygmunt Bauman's understanding of late modernity as a "liquifying" of the solid, settled modernity of industrial capitalism—the Weberian world of factory, capital, and the bureaucratization of government and business.[19] He believes that a liquid church better serves the liquid modernity of global capital, flexible labor, and ever-changing patterns of material consumption.[20] Whether or not the situation he describes is unique to the contemporary era remains open to question. Sociologist Grace Davie reads a remarkably similar set of dilemmas in the failure of the churches to respond to the alleged "solid modernity" of the industrial revolution,

> The forms and structures of religion that worked so well in the long-term stabilities of pre-modern Europe, came under severe strain at the time of the industrial revolution. Rapid industrialization, and the equally fast urbanization that went with it, were devastating for institutional structures that were anchored in place . . . disastrous for churches in which the rural parish was central. Quite simply they were unable to move fast enough into the rapidly growing cities where their "people" now resided.[21]

Ward's articulation of a less geographically rooted and institutionally structured Christianity might seem congenial to feminist ambivalence about the institutional structures of Christianity. But feminist ambivalence rests more on the marginalization of women within institutional structures (a marginalization often summarized as *clericalism*) rather than any perceived irrelevance of institutions per se. "From the earliest days of the Christian church," writes Natalie Watson, "the development of hierarchical and clerical structures has run in parallel with the increasing marginalization and oppression of women and their discourses of faith."[22] "However," notes Rosemary Radford Ruether, "this does not mean that institutionalization as such is illegitimate. The spirit-filled community deludes itself by imagining that it can live without any historical structure at all."[23] Thus, while Ward's contention that the established churches need to adapt to a more fluid social environment needs to be taken seriously, such adaptations will themselves create institutional structures. Those structures still require critical evaluation rooted in judgment about how well they serve the full humanity of women (and men).

Nevertheless, Ward's notion of a liquid church may prove helpful in understanding BustedHalo and other new media platforms. BustedHalo grew out of concerns parallel to those of the ECM, concerns that young Catholics in the United States had significant trouble identifying with the heavily institutionalized Catholicism of the modern era. At the time of BustedHalo's creation, a number of book-length studies and commentaries emphasized the disaffiliation, individualism, and suspicion of institutions of young Catholics.[24] BustedHalo.com's current mission statement acknowledges, "We live in an age filled with seekers who are desperately trying to find deeper meaning in their lives but whose journey has little to do with traditional religious institutions." This concern inspired BustedHalo's lively catechetical resources (such as the trivia game), but also its electronic magazine, focused on creating open-ended conversation about spirituality. According to the mission statement, "We are committed to creating a forum that is: open, informed, unexpected, unpredictable, balanced, and thought-provoking."

The fluid and conversational tone of our earliest articles seemed to match this ambition. Much of the content was characterized (and still is) by rhetorical reversals and personal "takes" on everything from films to politics to church events. A young writer wrote about the spiritual appeal of the ever-innocent SpongeBob Squarepants. Another reflected on how her local faith community's practicing of praising married people at Sunday worship evoked multiple emotions in her as she awaited her decree of divorce. These articles provided message board opportunities for users to respond, and website articles still provide such opportunities, though now they occur through comment sections, emails, and Facebook pages. Then and now, conversational networks arose and subsided on the website. Then and now, emails referred to conversations with other young people within a social group. All these practices on BustedHalo might indeed be termed "liquid Catholicism," an ecclesial experience rooted in a provisional and de-centered dialogue along informal Catholic social networks constantly assembling and disassembling. Dispersed social networks created space at BustedHalo for greater participation by young people unrelated or only marginally related to more visible and centralized forms of Catholicism. BustedHalo only occasionally drew the attention of a hierarchical leadership more comfortable at traditional ecclesial sites.

Nevertheless, this form of "liquid Catholicism" remains unlike the Emerging Church Movement in that it includes little overt deconstruction of institutional Catholicism or any explicit criticism of church as a gathering in place. At BustedHalo, the practice of building networks of conversation has always been and continues to be accompanied by clarity about institutional Catholic identity, active leadership by Paulist priests, and a desire to see young seekers affiliated with institutional Catholicism through parishes and other communities in place. The "About Us" section today reads as follows:

> Under the direction of Fr. Dave Dwyer, CSP, Busted Halo® Ministries helps young adults explore their spirituality, listen to and encourage one another, discover (or re-discover) the rich depths of Catholic tradition, and connect to communities of faith where their unique gifts will be respected and used, and where they will find support on their journey towards God.

In the beginning, the centerpiece of the site was the "FaithGuides" section (now "Googling God"), which presented catechetical material about Scripture and liturgy with an edgy tone but consonant with official Catholic teaching. The section on liturgy ("Mass Class") still includes the following introduction:

> The Mass is a big deal for Catholics. According to the General Instruction on the Roman Missal, which is sort of the official user's guide to the Mass, it is central both to the communal life of the Catholic Church and also to the individual experience of each Catholic. It's the "high point" of our ability to worship God and God's ability to "sanctify," or make holy the world in which we live . . . Of course, we think it's a good time too.

The director of BustedHalo's sponsoring ministry, with decision-making authority, was and still is a Paulist priest. The site continues to offer suggestions for parishes to attend.

Thus, BustedHalo from the beginning offered the "liquidity" of conversational networks but within a framework deferential to the stability of institutional Catholicism. This tension might be further probed using Elaine Graham's feminist dialectic between *disclosure* and foreclosure. Thus, then and now, visitors to BustedHalo have found a strong emphasis on what Graham characterizes as disclosive conversation, "forms of practical reasoning which illuminate inclusive strategies and policies, enable the articulation of formerly hidden needs and experiences, but retain a responsible sense of their own provisionality."[25] BustedHalo, after all, was created in part to give a provisional voice to the often-invisible concerns of young Catholics. "We want people to actually have conversations [about faith]," argues Barbara Wheeler, and she notes that the site requires only the most minimal registration information before people can comment. During my editorial tenure, we had writers' conferences characterized by free-flowing conversation and brainstorming. At one, a young writer initiated talk of the representation of sexuality in Catholic writing. This resulted in an article about the unhelpful tension between restriction and romanticism in Catholic writing about sex, a tension she attributed to authorship by clerical celibates who either do not have sex or have it furtively. Reflecting on her own experience as a married young adult and that of friends, she wrote about the quotidian nature of sex and sexuality for many Catholics.

This kind of open conversation impressed visitors more accustomed to sites with a more univocal Catholic perspective. One visitor emailed, "Frankly when it comes to Catholicism on the Web, there is a lot of malarkey out there, so keep fighting the good fight."[26]

But disclosive practice at BustedHalo always existed in tension with a tendency toward foreclosure, what Graham describes as "practices [that] deny the association of knowledge with power and the violation of undifferentiated meaning wrought by the imposition of unitary identity."[27] Susan Abraham argues that these are manifestations of an "imperial church," "presenting one singular aspect of the tradition in place of the whole of the tradition."[28] They do not exhibit awareness of the relationship between asserted knowledge and power. At BustedHalo, we did not escape such foreclosive tendencies. Editors sometimes simply avoided topics we imagined might land us in trouble with the church hierarchy. We answered questions submitted by email with "official teaching" from church documents without acknowledging the complex history of that teaching or without offering alternative perspectives. Some foreclosive practices emerged more specific to the liquid environment of the Internet. In our first months of existence at BustedHalo, a de-centralized network of traditionalist Catholics consistently intimidated visitors with their strict, unitary assertions of what was Catholic and with their personal assertions of who was not Catholic. Wheeler cites a more recent example of traditionalist critics blasting a blogger who argued against imposing strict standards of modesty of dress for women ministering at church. In both cases, however, it bears mentioning that clarity among BustedHalo's leadership about its mission of facilitating open conversation led to interventions that reversed the movement toward foreclosure. In the first case, I (as editor) went as far as to shut down the message boards for an entire month and reopen them with trusted moderators watching over them. Overall, the use of BustedHalo has meant sustained, liberating conversation about Christian faith but with occasional lapses into narrowing or foreclosing that conversation.

BustedHalo as Virtual Church

But does that kind of conversation make a new media platform like Busted-Halo a *church*? In a 2006 account, co-founder Michael Hayes and I wrote of the early days of BustedHalo, "Our hope was . . . to entice people into returning to the site and forming a kind of 'virtual community.'"[29] And so it did. Then and now, visitors returned, commented, emailed, and posted in response to others' posts. They formed alliances and rivalries. In a fluid way, BustedHalo had become a community. By 2006, despite our early reluctance to see BustedHalo as anything besides a set of resources, we found ourselves using the term "virtual church" to describe it. We had to acknowledge that it did, in fact, gather believers in a kind of community or congregation, even if that gathering did not constitute a *church/ekklesia* in a fuller, more traditional sense. BustedHalo had an ecclesial reality to it. But what kind of ecclesial reality was it?

Church remains a highly contested term in many circles. The Vatican document *Dominus Iesus* allows the term only for ecclesial bodies it deems to possess "a valid episcopate and the genuine and integral substance of the Eucharistic mystery."[30] As already noted, feminist theologians have contested the term for other reasons,

> What does it mean for women to rethink what it means to be church? Where do we start and what are we aiming for? The starting point is one of fundamental ambivalence. It is possible to read the history of the church as one of women's suffering, of an institution that has gone out of its way to exclude, to marginalize, to oppress women often purely on the grounds of their being women.[31]

Susan Abraham sees the same problem in traditional articulations of the four marks of the church: "As a feminist and Catholic theologian from India, I am convinced that we have to challenge the narrow and gendered interpretation of the marks of the church by infusing the church's catholicity with justice through a more capacious theological imagination, in order to rethink the problem of gendered and colonial ecclesiology."[32] For decades, Elisabeth Schüssler Fiorenza has argued that this imperial or patriarchal structure of church must be contrasted to and opposed by a discipleship of equals manifested in an *ekklesia* of women.[33] Letty Russell spoke of the need for a "church in the round" that eschews inequalities and emphasizes the hospitality of equals.[34] Somewhat critical of North Atlantic feminist theologies, Ada Maria Isasi-Díaz and María Pilar Aquino have long argued for the experience of church as solidarity with all who struggle for liberation.[35]

Whether viewed through the lens of official church documents or feminist theologies, we must first understand that BustedHalo functioned (and continues to function) as a *virtual* gathering of believers, one gathered through communications technology rather than specific worship sites. As such, BustedHalo closely resembles the "liquid church" of Pete Ward, an interconnected network of nodes,

> Networks, according to Manuel Castells, are made up of lines of communication that connect a series of nodes. The nodes represent individuals, organizations, communication systems, or even political structures. Networks produce and are produced by the explosion in communication technologies."[36]

For Ward, liquid church is still church. He opts for the organic metaphor of *circulation* to describe the distribution of power and influence over the interlocking networks and nodes of liquid church. He also explicitly ties that "circulation" to Patristic notions about being drawn into Trinitarian life. For Ward, the fluid liquid dynamics of circulation imitate *perichoresis,* the interpenetrating dance of the three persons of the Trinity.[37] Of course, perichoresis also appears with some frequency in feminist theological reflection. Its implications for a relational theological anthropology and an egalitarian ethics have been explored and critiqued.[38] But does a circulation of content and influence over a wide and unpredictable path via new media really constitute being drawn into Trinitarian life?

Some theologians critical of new media would strongly argue that it could not be so. Kam Ming Wong, like many, worries that the *superficiality* of virtual faith communities—their lack of intimacy, interdependence, and structures of accountability—renders them incapable of drawing human beings into a true Trinitarian life of communion. "The focus of virtual community is nevertheless on information, contacts and encounters rather than meaningful human relationships."[39] Kam rightly notes that identities can be managed or occulted. "The sense of person-to-person encounter that constitutes the powerful dimension of our moral experience is neglected."[40] Of course, people routinely manage their identities in face-to-face encounters as well. And many parishes and congregations provide little in the way of accountability, equality, interdependence, or meaningful human relationships. Decades ago, Johannes Metz noted how churches in Western nations easily domesticate their Christian life with one another—he called this "bourgeois religion"—and lose all sense of the radical demands of Christian discipleship.[41] In other words, the superficiality of ecclesial community remains a larger modern cultural problem, not one restricted to Internet-based communities.

Christian theologians with feminist commitments might ask if the de-emphasis on embodiment in virtual communities proves an obstacle to their drawing people into Trinitarian life. Theological constructions of embodiment have long concerned feminist theologians of diverse backgrounds.[42] Decades ago, Christine Gudorf argued that ascetical mind–body dualism in Christian history has distanced human bodies from God in a way contrary to both the doctrine of the Incarnation and biblical traditions of God's uncomfortably *physical* presence with human beings (Genesis 3:8–19; Genesis 32:22–31; Exodus 33:12–23; Job 38:1).[43] Others have objected to gender complementarity arrangements that assigned theology to a male world of activity and cognitive rationality contrasted with a seemingly passive realm of female embodiment.[44] In this manner, Western theology has often promoted a "disembodied knowing" that totalizes its perspective.[45]

But virtual churches often subvert this kind of dualism. Crowdsourcing and the episodic presentation of perspectives do not lend themselves to totalized, gendered perspectives. A "faith from nowhere" does not easily get diverted into distinct and unequal realms for men and women. Indeed, women's contributions to blogging and social media overall have overtaken those of men.[46] True, new media sometimes create space for a disparagement of women's bodies (e.g., competitive ratings of women's physical appearance) that reinforces dualistic perspectives, especially in the world of online gaming.[47] But this approach hardly appears the norm in virtual religious groups (and was never tolerated at BustedHalo). At BustedHalo as in much of today's Internet, women blog as much as men do. They were evenly balanced with men among the original writers. Women are now among the chief decision makers at BustedHalo—including the current website editor and radio producer.

Even if virtual communities like BustedHalo subvert unjust gender complementarities, they may nevertheless subtly contribute to a social imaginary of human life conducted at a distance from embodied experience. Gary A. Mann worries about a trend toward what he calls "tech-gnosticism,"

> Our age of technological culture has had a profound impact on culture by its disembodying of knowledge and its disregard for of the sensual knowledge presented through human affectivity and sensory experience . . . Tech-gnosticism is the exponential expansion of such a disembodying technical reason that can create a virtual world without body.[48]

Mann even wonders if virtual technologies are offering us a "redemptive myth" of salvation as deliverance from the limits and problems of the body and the physical world.[49] Such a redemptive myth could prove profoundly destructive to Christian soteriology. As Elisabeth Moltmann-Wedel argues, "Salvation concerns the whole person, since according to the New Testament the salvation of the soul is not yet salvation. The message of Jesus relates to human beings in their totality, in their bodies, in which the soul dwells and gives them life."[50]

Sacramentality provides a theological lens for examining and evaluating embodiment in ecclesial experience, including in virtual ecclesial experience. Sacramentality sees the physical creation as ever invested with potentially revelatory significance.[51] Sacramental moments offer an ecclesial echo of Christian salvation.[52] Some Catholic feminist theologians have described sacramentality as part of the very "theological grammar" of Catholicism (and of Christian Orthodoxy, as well), that is, the embedded ways in which Catholics should and do construct our faith tradition.[53] But their attention to sacramentality also includes the recognition that sacramental practices themselves may reveal and reinforce liberation, or they may reveal and reinforce oppression (or both). For feminist theologians, sacramental practice must meet criteria of justice, that is, that relationships respect the dignity and full personhood of women and men.[54]

In the 1990s, "cyberfeminists" were sanguine about the power of the Internet in and of itself to subvert gendered institutions and establish more just social relations. "While they admit that technology as a male domain had often been used in a way that reinforced women's status as locked in the domestic life, they view the Net [sic] as a site where subversion of existing gender relations can be incubated."[55] Yet even as this optimism waned a bit, cyberfeminists have not given up on online communities but rather insisted on the need for a robust analysis of power relations there—especially those between men and women. "Cyberfeminism necessitates an awareness of how power plays not only in different locations online but also in institutions that shape the layout and experience of cyberspace."[56] Perhaps more than other early scholars of the Internet, they recognized that the experience of people in concrete communities and institutions shapes the power relations of the Internet.

Like the early cyberfeminists, Pete Ward has faith in the way the Internet and other networks of liquid modernity broadly distribute knowledge and power. Yet he, too, admits the importance of power analysis: "Who holds the power in the network depends on who controls the switches; in this new, fluid environment there are multiple switches, and so power is diffused rather than concentrated."[57] Seen through the lens of Ward's terminology, BustedHalo had different persons—the editor, the Paulist president, persuasive visitors, traditionalist networks of visitors—who controlled the "switches," that is, the places where the flow of information was shaped and channeled. True, the "collar at the helm" policy—assumed in much of Catholic new media and in place at BustedHalo from my own time there on—associates apostolic leadership with an exclusive clerical class that makes it appear that the most serious discipleship takes place through ordained men's bodies. On the other hand, at BustedHalo as at other virtual churches, other "switches"—a Protestant laywoman editor, female bloggers, the pastoral leaders who visit and promote the site along their networks, even those lay people who pan the site in their traditionalist networks—are so broadly distributed that the flow of power and influence does not prove as predictable in its effects and movements as in a relatively fixed geographical network of congregations or parishes. That almost inevitably makes it easier for a more just set of relationships to flourish—more open conversations and a multiplicity of perspectives.

As crucial as this criterion of just relationships may be, it remains insufficient. Because sacramentality addresses the revelatory potential in created things, critical assessment requires not only judgments of justice but also judgments more properly described as aesthetic. Nancy Dallavalle describes this as a question of catholicity, of discerning a rich and inspiring fullness—an inner wholeness—in embodied ecclesial practice. "Catholic theology and Catholic tradition are not only unjust, they are, in many cases paltry, flat, stultified, boring—a far cry from the ideal of a richly textured tradition of symbol and gesture and speech that draws people into a community of praise."[58] Dallavalle invokes this "catholic" criterion of richness or fullness against an imposed uniformity that drives away the richness of diverse Christian experiences forming a tradition in fractious but beautiful co-existence. But her point also invites us to consider how the use of new media constitutes an ecclesial practice rich and full enough to evoke the broadness, ambiguity, and mystery of human experience of God.[59]

New media use presents aesthetic limitations. Especially in the early days of the Internet, virtual church—like much of virtual life—privileged the use of the free-floating written word. Websites unleashed a virtual torrent of emphatic and often decontextualized words—posted texts followed by text-based responses. In many cases, no author or editor was identified. Many of the trappings of a rich, sensual experience were absent—nonverbal cues, specific contextual information, color, and texture. At BustedHalo, we did identify our writers and editors, but use focused on written articles and occasional commentary on message boards. But users of new media today—including virtual ecclesial platforms like BustedHalo—have a qualitatively different experience. They watch embedded video, see stylized photos and images, and hear a tonal range via podcasting and Internet or satellite radio. They see vibrant colors, hear offbeat perspectives, and listen to divergent voices. One pastor, for example, saw the humorous banter on the absurdities and delights of everyday life as a key feature of the BustedHalo radio program. The BustedHalo website became famous for its embedded videos of spiritual questions posed to passersby on the streets of New York City. New media is able to facilitate gatherings of the faithful that evoke a Christian life that is fluid, surprising, and colorful. New media often deliver video and audio of the sights and sounds of large-scale events (BustedHalo went to World Youth Day in Rio de Janeiro in 2013). Other virtual churches include live streaming of worship and facilitate video conferencing. In short, higher bandwidth and increasing transmission of video and sound make the churches of Web 2.0 a more sensually rich and immediate sacramental experience.

Back to Practice

This essay began with a question about how the *practice* of using Christian new media constructs and communicates an ecclesial experience. We looked at the use of the BustedHalo new media platform as a concrete case study. Case studies in their particularity always run the risk of proving more idiosyncratic than generalizable. Nevertheless, BustedHalo, as a loose platform of diverse media and interconnected users, possesses a structural similarity to most other Christian new media. One of the most frequent theological criticisms of such media is that they foster a privatized, individualistic notion of Christian faith, a "churchless Christianity."[60] But I have argued here that, even on the Internet, these practices are communal—created and used by people consciously operating in social networks, some of which are face-to-face communities. BustedHalo and other virtual communities do not exist in free-floating cyberspace, even if they give off that impression.

Thus, on the one hand, virtual communities like BustedHalo will manifest the same ambivalences that appear in the social networks and face-to-face communities that initiate and maintain them. BustedHalo demonstrated the same tension between disclosive practices—that is, provisionally interpreted communal practices that evoke inclusion and reveal hidden concerns—and foreclosive practices—those that shut down movement toward liberation by imposing univocal interpretations—that occurred in the ministry organizations and social networks that lay behind it.[61] While new media may seem like an experience of "faith from nowhere" that occludes the power dynamics of the real communities and institutions behind it, they also, by virtue of the broad distribution of power in their virtual networks, have more dialogue and a multiplicity of perspectives built into their very structure. While always at risk of separating ecclesial experience from embodiment, new media especially in more recent incarnations come closer to what Nancy Dallavalle calls "the metaphorically dense, highly sexualized, graced and scandalous sacramental flood of belief and believers that caused James Joyce appropriately to characterize Roman Catholicism as 'here comes everybody.'"[62]

Whatever their limitations or advantages, virtual communities like BustedHalo show no likelihood of disappearing. Christians committed to feminist ideals would be foolish to disregard new media completely or condemn it moralistically. Instead, we do well to continue to refine our Christian practice of the use of new media. One necessary refinement would be to surface recognition of the social networks already involved in the production and use of Christian new media. This helps to avoid the impression of faith coming from nowhere, particularly when that "nowhere" comes with an assertion of univocal orthodoxy. Writers and other gatekeepers ("switches" in Ward's liquid terminology) must learn to explicitly identify their communities of accountability as part of the stories they tell. If content providers refuse to engage in this kind of public reflection, they should be forced to do so as moderators and fellow users "out" the social networks that shape them. In the different social environment of the public immigration debate, for example, the Southern Poverty Law Center successfully issued public reports on the unsavory communities to which frequently quoted anti-immigration "experts" belong.[63]

Such refinement of practice matters in a world ever more characterized by digitally based relationships. Christians involved in virtual communities are just as tasked with re-imagining and re-embodying those communities in the light of Jesus's proclamation of God's Reign as Christians involved in geographically rooted communities. We need not only an alternative vision of a more just and richly beautiful ecclesial life but also to embody that vision in some (albeit imperfect) way. "Redemption must be enacted."[64] The above reflections constitute only the barest beginning of efforts toward inviting our communities—virtual or real-life—to more closely resemble the Body of Christ manifesting the delicate dance of egalitarian Trinitarian love.

Notes

1. See, for example, Don S. Browning, *A Fundamental Practical Theology: Descriptive and Strategic Proposals* (Minneapolis, MN: Fortress, 1991); Claire Wolfteich, *Navigating New Terrain: Work and Women's Spiritual Lives* (New York: Paulist, 2002); Tom Beaudoin, *Consuming Faith: Integrating Who We Are with What We Buy* (Lanham, MD: Sheed and Ward, 2003); and Elaine Graham, *Transforming Practice: Pastoral Theology in an Age of Uncertainty* (Eugene, OR: Wipf and Stock, 2002).
2. Rosemary Radford Ruether, *Sexism and God Talk: Toward a Feminist Theology* (Boston, MA: Beacon Press, 1983), 18–19.
3. For a summary of the place of religion in studies of Internet communication by Communication scholars, see Heidi Campbell, "Making Space for Religion in Internet Studies," *The Information Society* 21, no. 4 (2005): 309–315.

4. Cf. Kam Ming Wong, "Christians Outside the Church: An Ecclesiological Critique of Virtual Church," *Heythrop Journal* 49, no. 5 (2008): 822–840.
5. See, for example, Teresa Delgado, "This is My Body . . . Given for You: Theological Anthropology Latinamente," in *Frontiers in Catholic Feminist Theology: Shoulder to Shoulder,* ed. Susan Abraham and Elena Procario-Foley (Minneapolis, MN: Fortress Press, 2009), 25–47.
6. Sandra Schneiders, *The Revelatory Text: Interpreting the New Testament as Sacred Scripture* (Collegeville, MN: Liturgical Press, 1999).
7. See, for example, Roberto S. Goizueta, *Caminemos con Jesus: A Hispanic/Latino Theology of Accompaniment* (Maryknoll, NY: Orbis, 1995); and Orlando O. Espín, *The Faith of the People: Theological Reflections on Popular Catholicism* (Maryknoll, NY: Orbis, 1997).
8. See Ada María Isasi-Díaz, *En la Lucha: Elaborating a* Mujerista *Theology* (Minneapolis, MN: Fortress Press, 2004), 80–103.
9. Graham, *Transforming Practice,* 140.
10. Graham, *Transforming Practice,* 156.
11. The Paulists founded a Catholic press in the mid-19th century, operated a radio station in the 1930s, and pioneered religious television programming in the 1960s and 1970s. The author was formerly a member of this congregation.
12. For a more complete narrative on the origins of BustedHalo, see Michael Hayes and Brett C. Hoover, "Virtual Church for Young Adults," *The Way* 45, no. 2 (2006). I am also grateful to Barbara Wheeler, BustedHalo.com's current editor-in-chief, for allowing herself to be interviewed about BustedHalo's current state.
13. Older Catholics, notably, associated the name with Catholic guilt.
14. The unique visitor information comes from Paulist Young Adult Ministries' Report to the Paulists, January 2004. The Facebook information comes from current BustedHalo editor-in-chief Barbara Wheeler.
15. Quote from email to BustedHalo, Paulist Young Adult Ministries' Report to the Paulist Community, January 2004.
16. BustedHalo has also received criticism from conservative Catholic media for including left-of-center perspectives. See Jonathan V. Last, "God on the Internet," *First Things* (December 2005); and Paulist Young Adult Ministries Report to the Paulists, January 2004.
17. Gerardo Martí and Gladys Ganiel, *The Deconstructed Church* (New York: Oxford University Press, 2014).
18. Pete Ward, *Liquid Church* (Peabody, MA: Hendrickson Publishers, 2002), 2.
19. Ward, *Liquid Church,* 16.
20. Ward's understanding of Bauman's concept focuses more attention on the positive outcomes of this process, especially for well-educated, highly mobile young professionals. But liquid modernity seems a decidedly mixed blessing for those dispossessed by the movement of global capital and industry, such as economic migrants from the Global South and Western factory workers made redundant.
21. Peter Berger, Grace Davie, and Effie Fokas, *Religious America, Secular Europe? A Theme and Variations* (Burlington, VT: Ashgate, 2008), 27.
22. Natalie K. Watson, *Introducing Feminist Ecclesiology* (Cleveland, OH: Pilgrim Press, 2002), 2.
23. Rosemary Radford Ruether, *Women-Church: Theology and Practice of Feminist Liturgical Communities* (San Francisco, CA: Harper & Row, 1985), 33.
24. Cf. Robert A. Ludwig, *Reconstructing Catholicism: For a New Generation* (New York: Crossroad, 1996); Tom Beaudoin, *Virtual Faith: The Irreverent Spiritual Quest of Generation X* (San Francisco, CA: Jossey-Bass, 1998); Dean Hoge, William D. Dinges, Mary Johnson, and Juan L. Gonzales, Jr., *Young Adult Catholics: Religion in the Culture of Choice* (Notre Dame, IN: University of Notre Dame Press, 2001).

25. Graham, *Transforming Practice,* 9.
26. Quoted in Hayes and Hoover, "Viritual Church," 10.
27. Graham, *Transforming Practice,* 9.
28. Susan Abraham, "Justice as the Mark of Catholic Feminist Ecclesiology," in *Frontiers in Catholic Feminist Ecclesiology,* ed. Susan Abraham and Elena Procario-Foley (Minneapolis, MN: Fortress, 2009), 211.
29. Hayes and Hoover, "Virtual Church," 12.
30. Congregation for the Doctrine of the Faith, *Dominus Iesus,* 16–17.
31. Natalie K. Wilson, *Introducing Feminist Ecclesiology,* 2.
32. Susan Abraham, "Justice as the Mark of Catholic Feminist Ecclesiology," 194.
33. Elisabeth Schüssler Fiorenza, *In Memory of Her: A Feminist Theological Reconstruction of Christian Origins* (New York: Crossroad, 1983), 285–342; and Schüssler Fiorenza, *Discipleship of Equals: A Critical Feminist Ekklesia-logy of Liberation* (New York: Crossroad, 1993).
34. Letty Russell, *Church in the Round: Feminist Interpretation of the Church* (Louisville, KY: Westminster/John Knox, 1993).
35. Veli-Matti Kärkkäinen, "Ecclesiology," in *Global Dictionary of Theology: A Resource for the Worldwide Church,* ed. William A. Dyrness and Veli-Matti Kärkäinen (Downers Grove, IL: Intervarsity Press, 2008), 258.
36. Ward, *Liquid Church,* 41–42.
37. Pete Ward, *Participation and Mediation: A Practical Theology for the Liquid Church* (London: SCM Press, 2008), 24–25, 187; and Ward, *Liquid Church,* 49–55.
38. See, for example, Catherine Mowry LaCugna, *God for Us: The Trinity and Christian Life* (New York: HarperCollins, 1991), 270–278; and Elizabeth Johnson, *She Who Is: The Mystery of God in Feminist Theological Discourse* (New York: Crossroad, 1992), 220–222.
39. Kam Ming Wong, "Christians Outside the Church," 837.
40. Kam Ming Wong, "Christians Outside the Church," 836.
41. Johannes Baptist Metz, "Messianic or 'Bourgeois' Religion," in *Christianity and the Bourgeoisie,* ed. Johannes Metz (New York: Seabury, 1979), 61–73.
42. See, for example, Sallie McFague, *The Body of God* (Philadelphia: Westminster Press, 1993); Susan A. Ross, *Extravagant Affections: A Feminist Sacramental Theology* (New York: Continuum, 1998); Kelly Brown Douglas, *Sexuality and the Black Church: A Womanist Perspective* (Maryknoll, NY: Orbis, 1999); and Nancy Pineda-Madrid, *Suffering and Salvation in Ciudad Juárez* (Minneapolis, MN: Fortress Press, 2011).
43. Christine E. Gudorf, *Body, Self, and Pleasure: Reconstructing Christian Sexual Ethics* (Cleveland, OH: Pilgrim Press, 1994), 205–218.
44. See, for example, Elizabeth A. Johnson, "Imaging God, Embodying Christ: Women as a Sign of the Times," in *The Church Women Want: Catholic Women in Dialogue,* ed. Elizabeth A. Johnson (New York: Crossroad, 2002), 45–59; Elisabeth Moltmann-Wendel, *I Am My Body: A Theology of Embodiment,* trans. John Bowden (New York: Continuum, 1995), xii–xv; and Teresa Delgado, "This Is My Body," 33.
45. See, for example, Eleazar S. Fernandez, *Reimagining the Human: Theological Anthropology in Response to Systemic Evil* (St. Louis: Chalice Press, 2003), 11–15. See also Delgado, "This Is My Body," 36.
46. G. M. Chen, "Why Do Women Write Personal Blogs?" *Computers in Human Behavior* 28, no. 1 (2012) 171–172; and Megan Garber, "The Digital (Gender) Divide: Women Are More Likely Than Men to Have a Blog (and a Facebook Profile)," *The Atlantic* (April 27, 2012), www.theatlantic.com/technology/archive/2012/04/the-digital-gender-divide-women-are-more-likely-than-men-to-have-a-blog-and-a-facebook-profile/256466/.
47. See Jessica L. Beyer, "Women's (Dis)Embodied Engagement with Male-Dominated Online Communities," in *Cyberfeminism 2.0,* ed. Radhika Gajjala and Yeon

Ju Oh (New York: Peter Lang, 2012), 153–170; and Sarah Neely, "Making Bodies Visible: Post-feminism and the Pornographication of Online Identities," in *Transgression 2.0: Media, Culture, and the Politics of a Digital Age*, ed. Ted Gournelos and David J. Gunkel (New York: Continuum, 2012), 101–117.

48. Gary A. Mann, "Em-bodied Spirit/In-spired Matter: Against Tech-Gnosticism," in *Broken and Whole: Essays on the Body and Religion*, ed. Maureen A. Tilley and Susan A. Ross, The Annual Publication of the College Theology Society, vol. 39 (Lanham, MD: University Press of America, 1993), 120.

49. Mann, "Em-bodied Spirit/In-spired Matter," 120.

50. Elisabeth Moltmann-Wendel, *I Am My Body: A Theology of Embodiment*, trans. John Bowden (New York: Continuum, 1995), 37.

51. Abraham, "Justice as the Mark," 195–197.

52. Susan A. Ross, *Extravagant Affections: A Feminist Sacramental Theology* (New York: Continuum, 1998), 57–59.

53. Abraham, "Justice as the Mark," 196; and Ross, *Extravagant Affections,* 34–35.

54. Natalie K. Watson, *Introducing Feminist Ecclesiology*, 78–100.

55. Radhika Gajjala and Yeon Ju Oh, "Cyberfeminism 2.0: Where Have All the Cyberfeminists Gone?" in *Cyberfeminism 2.0,* ed. Radhika Gajjala and Yeon Ju Oh (New York: Peter Lang, 2012), 1.

56. Gajjala and Oh, "Cyberfeminism 2.0," 1.

57. Ward, *Liquid Church,* 42.

58. Nancy Dallavalle, "Toward a Theology that Is Catholic and Feminist: Some Basic Issues," *Modern Theology* 14, no. 4 (1998): 548.

59. See, for example, Ron Austin, *In a New Light: Spirituality and the Media Arts* (Grand Rapids, MI: Eerdmans, 2007), 3–20.

60. Kam Ming Wong, "Christians Outside the Church," 834–840.

61. Graham, *Transforming Practice,* 9.

62. Dallavalle, "Catholic and Feminist," 548.

63. See, for example, Heidi Beirich, "Federation for American Immigration Reform's Hate Filled Track Record," *Intelligence Report*, Winter 2007, Issue 128.

64. Graham, *Transforming Practice,* 129.

11 From Telephone to Live Broadcast

Becoming a Brick-and-Mortar Synagogue without Walls

Bracha Yael

For more than two thousand years, the synagogue has housed the Jewish community and with it the responsibility to meet the spiritual, intellectual, and emotional needs of its members. Community is central to Judaism; as pioneer Jewish Feminist theologian Judith Plaskow says, "Relationship with God is mediated through community and expresses itself in community."[1] It is at the heart of the covenantal relationship between God and the people.

Historically, physical presence has been the cornerstone of synagogue life: either you're present and in community or you're outside of it. Although the synagogue community will venture out at times, perhaps to bring food to a sick person or sit with a grieving family, it largely remains within the confines of its walls. So, if you are unable to be physically present due to isolation, illness, distance, travel, or any other reason, you are denied the opportunity of community. Today, however, technology enables us to remove the now-artificial limits of synagogue life, to step beyond the physicality of its foundation, and grant anyone—anywhere—access to a vibrant spiritual community. Brick-and-mortar synagogues represent what community once was and not what it is becoming.

The demand for an alternative to the traditional model is evident in the burgeoning virtual synagogue movement. Rabbi Laura Baum, the spiritual leader of OurJewishCommunity.org, founded in 2008 and the world's largest online synagogue, contends that a virtual synagogue can meet the needs of its members as well as or better than a brick-and-mortar one. She told the CNN Religion Blog on October 4, 2010: "There's a persistent myth that community is something that only happens in person, that relationships and memberships must be defined in geographic terms. The reality is that relationships built and maintained online, using tools like Facebook, Twitter and Skype, are increasingly common and can even be stronger than physical connections." If her assertion is true, brick-and-mortar synagogues must join religion's technology and social media revolution to remain relevant in the 21st century.

If brick-and-mortar synagogues embrace this technological imperative, they can foster a powerful synergy between the bedrock of a physical community experience and the flexibility of a virtual one. Combined, the physical and virtual community can give better comfort for the ill and emotionally pained;

bring families and friends together in new creative ways; and deliver information and thought to a far-larger audience.

There can be conflicts between the use of technology and Jewish *halachah* (Jewish law), especially in Orthodox Judaism. On *Shabbat* (the Jewish Sabbath) and holiday services, the Orthodox strictly prohibit the use of technology in the sanctuary, even microphones. That's not to say they've eschewed its use in other settings, however. For instance, every Friday afternoon, one Orthodox Jewish secondary school teacher tweets a reminder to his students to turn off their mobile phones for Shabbat; and Chabad.org, the Internet arm of the very Orthodox Chabad-Lubavitcher movement, has become one of the most comprehensive Jewish websites in North America.

For the most part, the liberal branches of Judaism have little difficulty with the use of technology in Jewish worship. The concept of informed choice has and will make Liberal Judaism more open to bringing technology into the sanctuary. Already, The Union of Reform Judaism (URJ), the largest Jewish organization in North America, and the umbrella organization of the Reform Movement, gives financial, informational, and technical support to its synagogues for increasing the role of technology to serve its members.

The Los Angeles congregation Beth Chayim Chadashim (BCC) provides a useful illustration of new uses of technology in synagogue life and the impacts—some expected, some surprising—its use can have on the very concept of community. Founded in 1972, BCC is the first known LGBT synagogue in the world, and the first such religious institution—Jewish, Christian, or other—recognized by a mainstream religious movement; BCC was accepted as a member of the URJ in 1974. Its contributions include the creation of one of the first gender-neutral prayer books, the first Jewish response to AIDS (*Nechama*), "queering" traditional texts, and as we'll see, becoming an innovator in the realm of "virtual" community.

The origins, values, and development of BCC's initial foray into technology began with a project called the Telephone Minyan, a low tech, peer-to-peer, remote site program. The Telephone Minyan evolved into a much more ambitious implementation of technology called BCC Live, a high-tech, clergy-driven, interactive on- and offsite program. The Telephone Minyan and BCC Live, although always expected to bring benefits to the BCC community, reached far beyond, transforming BCC's brick-and-mortar home into a synagogue without walls.

This is the second time that I've examined BCC to explore synagogue issues. In 2000, I wrote my master's thesis on the impact of HIV/AIDs on LGBT religious institutions.[2] As a BCC member since 1996, with that study and now again, I've had access to valuable information through sources like internal correspondence, records, clergy, and other members. However, insider advantages can bring the danger of a skewed perspective. This is especially true in this case study, because I've been an active player and advocate for technology in the synagogue. Although I may not have fully overcome my own biases, I've tried to mitigate them by interweaving other people's experiences, recollections, and personal archives with institutional source materials to provide a broader, more nuanced perspective than my own.

BCC and the Telephone Minyan

In 2005, five homebound or nearly homebound BCC members—two gay men and three lesbian women (including myself)—organized a weekly conference call to provide support to each other and to study Torah (Bible). All five of us had recently been stricken with various debilitating illnesses. Although BCC's compassionate response to AIDS in the 1980s left it with a strong ethos of *Bikkur Cholim* (caring for the sick), in the mid-2000s there was no mechanism in place to bridge our ongoing confinement and the synagogue's brick-and-mortar-centric community. We knew that if we wanted a way to transcend our isolation and find connection to our spiritual tradition, then we'd have to invent it for ourselves. And so we invented the Telephone Minyan.

We chose the name for two reasons. "Telephone" was an obvious choice because that was how we "met" to study, pray, and share. It was simple, cheap, easily accessible, and interactive. We found a free conference call service and provided free calling cards to cover personal carrier fees to anyone who needed help with their phone bill. For the participants' comfort and practicality, we decided not to use video chat or other video technologies. Respectful of energy levels, events were kept to a maximum of one hour and held during the day when most felt at their strongest. All activities were free (minimal costs were underwritten mainly by the participants), did not require Temple membership, and were mostly peer led, primarily by me.

We chose the word "Minyan" because it is the basic unit of Jewish community.[3] Traditionally, halachah defines a *Minyan* as the physical gathering of ten or more Jewish men. It's the foundation of communal worship and certain prayers (maybe the most notable, the Mourner's *Kaddish*) cannot be recited without one. Due to its central significance in Jewish spiritual life, one of the earliest demands of Jewish feminists in the 1970s was for women to be counted toward a Minyan. Rabbi Rachel Adler argued in her groundbreaking 1971 essay "The Jew Who Wasn't There" that women would be "peripheral Jews" until they were included in a Minyan.[4] Even though we didn't fit the halachic criterion for a Minyan even in liberal Judaism—we had neither the required minimum nor physical presence—we self-identified as such. We were "not breaking away from the community, but struggling to become full members of it."[5] Like Adler, Plaskow, and other Jewish feminists, the importance of community, full access to religious life, and the ability to re-interpret halachah and develop new rituals underlay the origins of the Telephone Minyan and, by extension, BCC Live.[6]

The Telephone Minyan started down its path with the practice that has connected Jews together for centuries: weekly Torah study. Although Torah can be broadly defined as any Jewish learning, strictly defined it is the five books of Moses (commonly known as Genesis, Exodus, Leviticus, Numbers, and

Deuteronomy). Jews from all over the world study a portion of Torah each week, so that by year's end its reading has been completed, all to start anew. One Minyan member says his attraction to Torah is the continuity of this cycle. He explains, "Although we read the five books over and over again, it always feels relevant at that moment." For him and others, Torah never begins or ends but is always present. Simply providing the *mitzvah* (commandment or good deed) of Torah study to an otherwise-isolated group via the simplest technology was a moving achievement.

Over time, the Telephone Minyan grew, as more people through BCC correspondence, word of mouth, and search engine inquiries sought its benefits. Whereas chronic illness drove the interest of the five founders, the motivations of these new participants varied widely, including living at a distance, business or vacation travel, recent retirement, non-traditional work schedules, and recuperation from temporary illness or surgery. Quickly, it was clear that Torah study alone no longer addressed the needs of this larger, diverse group. As a result, special Shabbat, High Holy Days (*Rosh HaShanah* and *Yom Kippur*) and *Yom HaShoah* (Holocaust Remembrance Day) services were added, along with study sessions not related to Torah and discussions on various aspects of Jewish life.

These new offerings were designed to meet the pressing needs of the Telephone Minyan's shifting composition. For example, after a series of deaths occurred in the lives of several participants, the group conducted a two-part study session about Jewish perspectives on loss and mourning. Another response to the changing wishes of the group was the addition of a Yom HaShoah service. Many had relatives who had perished in the Holocaust, one person's parents were survivors, and another was a survivor herself. Probably the most significant addition, though, was the Yom Kippur service, allowing us to observe the holiest day on the Jewish calendar in community.

Jews, even the most alienated, find a strong emotional and spiritual connection to this annual day of internal and communal reflection. The prospect of being physically unable to attend services or observe the traditional fast can be gut wrenching. For example, a long-time BCC member suddenly came down with the flu on Yom Kippur. After fifty plus years of faithfully attending Yom Kippur services, he couldn't imagine not being "there." The Telephone Minyan service—along with its specially prepared Yom Kippur prayer book created from the writings, prayers, and poems submitted by its participants—gave him an alternative way to be present in community on this most sacred day.

The Yom Kippur fast is another crucial element that marks the day. Some seek solace for their incapacity to perform it. The Telephone Minyan tries to provide comfort for those people through the recitation of the prayer "Yom Kippur for the One Who Cannot Fast" by Rabbi Simkha Y. Weintraub.[7] In it, the individual declares the day's unique importance, acknowledges the fast's centrality to it, and includes accepting the reality that illness will prevent him or her from its observance. The prayer also relieves the person's anxiety at being apart from people and tradition because of being unable to observe the fast.

As seen here, personal circumstances can cause people to feel cut off. Long periods of isolation due to illness can have a profound impact on one's social circle. One member who was homebound for two years says, "Before I got ill I had a lot more friends. But, people move away. Or drift away because you're not as exciting as you once were." The Telephone Minyan helped her re-establish a social network: "I developed meaningful friendships with people I had never met before. It gave me a way to connect with BCC and also a way for BCC members to connect back during my recuperation." She fondly recalls, "People remembered me and called to see how I was. I wasn't forgotten." For BCC, the Telephone Minyan was the first step on the path toward accepting the responsibility to make use of new technology in order to provide a substantial virtual space for those who needed it.

BCC's next innovation was to connect offsite participants with actual onsite services and events in real time. With limited resources and some apprehension over its use, BCC cautiously inched its way toward the introduction of technology into the sanctuary. A non-BCC member who is an active Telephone Minyan participant donated funds to buy a conference phone with two lavaliere microphones for the clergy. The spaceship-looking phone was placed on the *bima* (altar). It was unsightly and provided telephone-only access to the regular Friday night Shabbat services, but it was a start. Further, we found it appealed to a greater cross-section of people, such as a closeted gay couple in Mexico City, a Las Vegas-to-Los Angeles Friday night commuter, a vacationer in New York, and so on. For the first time, people could enjoy the rabbi's *drash* (sermon) or the cantor's melodies outside the sanctuary.

Also, they could experience the full force of community in a way never before. The following story shows this well. After two years battling lung cancer, a BCC member's father died at sunset Friday night in his Florida home surrounded by her, her partner, also a BCC member, and other loved ones. They received what she calls a "long distance hug" from the congregation later that night when they called into Shabbat services. In a September 5, 2012, email, she remembers that evening,

> On loudspeaker setting that little phone delivered all the sounds of the sanctuary directly into my father's house, where we had made it to the end of a very long, very difficult, but strangely exhilarating day. I recognized this feeling from having been with my mother and, six years later, my youngest brother, when they died, also of cancer, also in their homes. But this was the first time I had access, immediately after a death, to such direct communication and connection with my community. I felt embraced and supported, comforted by the words and the music, the feeling of home.
>
> At the end of the service came Kaddish and I knew that it was not appropriate to say this prayer before my father was buried. But Rabbi Edwards, with characteristic gentleness, had let the congregation know that he had died just hours earlier and that [we] were participating via phone in the service. Again, a special feeling of being held, now as mourners, by the rabbi, the congregation, and our Jewish traditions.

With simple, even crude, technology, the Friday night service finally had transcended sanctuary walls.

The *bima* conference phone though had its detractors. A few congregants in the sanctuary found the contraption an intrusion into their spiritual space, especially since it was on the *bima*. Some scoffed at the idea and seriously questioned its ability to provide a satisfying spiritual experience. Others who attempted to call in became exasperated when at times they could barely hear the rabbi or cantor over the ambient noise in the sanctuary. Despite its short-comings, however, the experiment suggested that a brick-and-mortar syna-gogue could use technology to expand community. Its promise even caught the eye of the URJ, which awarded BCC a $5,000 "Incubator Grant" to further its movement into technological community-building innovation just as BCC was moving into a new building.

Planning provided by the URJ grant persuaded BCC to allocate space and budget for a higher-quality audio system in its new building. Moreover, the sanctuary was designed to include live stream audio and video technology, with elements such as a cubbyhole set high into the back wall of the sanctuary for the remotely controlled movable camera, and a special alcove for the com-puter, camera joystick, and sound system. The phones were wired directly into the sound system, so the "low tech" conference phone option is still available without need for the unsightly *bima* phone.

BCC titled its new high-tech community-builder "BCC Live." Under the program, as of 2012 all Shabbat services and some lectures and classes are available in real time both visually by computer and aurally via telephone. All video is archived, with edited versions (usually the *drash*) available on BCC's Ustream and YouTube channels and on its website. In addition, any lifecycle event can be streamed. Amazingly, this is all accomplished by volunteers. Like the Telephone Minyan, it is free, accessible to anyone, and largely self-funded by enthusiasts.

BCC Live again shows that technology enables a brick-and-mortar syna-gogue to have an ongoing significant relationship with its members, no matter their current location. One member declares, "I'm a wonderful case study of how technology has helped me stay connected with BCC!" Here's one of the many examples he gives: "I flew into Kennedy airport on a Friday, rushed to my mother's bed side, spent hours at the hospital with her, drove to Long Island to stay with my brother, who I don't fight with but I'm not comfort-able with, visited with my family, collapsed into bed, and then turned on my computer to be with BCC, my chosen family." For him, that night, the live broadcast was not merely a means to watch the service, but, instead, a powerful source of "real comfort" during this difficult period.

Live streaming provides creative opportunities to relieve the suffering of others. For instance, one Friday night before the healing prayer, BCC Rabbi Lisa Edwards took a moment to give words of comfort to a congregant in an isolation room at the City of Hope, a comprehensive cancer center in Los Angeles. While the healing prayer was being chanted, friends of the latter sur-prised him by turning around and holding up to the camera signs that together read, "We love you," punctuated with a big red heart. Through technology, this literally isolated man was able to make a virtual physical and spiritual connection with friends and community.

BCC fosters an atmosphere that encourages interaction between physical and virtual attendees. Early in the service, the clergy greet all offsite participants and encourage those onsite to do the same. As mentioned above, congregants give well wishes to viewers who are ill at home or in the hospital, and also acknowledge any mourners. The broadcast operator "chats" online with viewers, and during the final song of the evening, many turn to the camera and sing, clap, or dance so everyone can feel included in the community's Shabbat celebration. At the conclusion of the service, while congregants bustle off to the *oneg* room (social hall), Rabbi Edwards takes time to say a last quiet goodbye to those not physically there.

Some BCC members and followers have found rituals to interweave their home Shabbat observance with the Friday night broadcasts. One couple allows their young son to stay up late one night a week, Friday night, so the whole family can watch the service together. Outside of Shabbat dinner, another couple prefers that their two pre-school daughters follow their usual weekly routine. After the girls have finished their evening prayers and gone to sleep, one of the parents takes some personal time to observe Shabbat in her own creative way. She draws a warm bath, lights candles, and places her laptop safely nearby. She says, "I feel a strong spiritual connection to BCC when I see my friends and hear my favorite melodies." And, there are couples who regularly "attend" services "together" despite being in different cities. One couple talks on the telephone while they watch, so they can share the experience more fully. Yet another member strengthens his connection to BCC by lighting candles, chanting *Kiddush* (blessing over the wine) and *HaMotzi* (blessing over the bread) at the same time as he sees BCC members doing so on his computer screen.

While some have joyfully developed their own "ritual reenactments" around the broadcasts, others have wondered for themselves what the appropriate decorum is for the evening.[8] "Is it okay if I recline while watching?" "Should I stand up and be seated where it is customary to do so?" As technology expands communal worship into alternative spaces be they home, hotel, hospital room, etc., Jewish denominations, congregations, and individuals will grapple with these and other contemporary questions of *halachah* and custom. Hopefully, any guidelines set forth will honor those who've found their own ways to merge their brick-and-mortar community with their own spiritual space.

Not everyone has embraced the concept of virtual community. Some are dubious that introducing technology into the sanctuary is correct. Others have a general "discomfort" knowing the service they are attending is being streamed, especially with the possibility they might appear on the broadcast. This is a legitimate concern, because even though there is a "no film" area in the sanctuary, it's difficult to guarantee someone won't be captured on film. Also, broadcasting begs the question, "Why would people come to synagogue when they can just watch it at home?" Although regular attendees admit from time to time they'll just feel lazy and stay home, they generally consider the streamed services to be a supplement and not a replacement of the physical synagogue experience. Since those who were unable to attend before due to illness, distance, travel, and so forth can now do so through virtual means, it can even be argued that actual overall "attendance" has risen when the number of viewers is added to the number physically in attendance. Another common concern is that paid membership will decline because people can watch services for free. What other synagogues have discovered and BCC confirms, is that the option of virtual attendance actually helps with membership retention. This positive effect results because live and archived services and events provide more options for people to remain engaged and committed to their community.

Doubting the effectiveness of off-site participation, one member believes there is no *kavanah* (intention or direction of the heart) unless one is "physically present." Others, who have an overall positive attitude toward broadcasting services, may still see serious limitations. One congregant explains, "BCC Live helps me feel more connected to the *experience* of BCC than the *community* of BCC. I need that social part after the service to really feel connected." For her, "Community is a place where there are roots," so she questions how totally virtual communities can sustain themselves. The proliferation of virtual synagogues suggests that they can be a vibrant option to expand the traditional synagogue model. Nevertheless, a synagogue like BCC presents the best of both worlds: a choice between the concreteness of a physical presence and the fluidness of a virtual one.

Even though broadcasting life cycle events was not an original aim of BCC Live, it has become one of its most popular unforeseen benefits. Scattered families and friends frequently "gather together" from across town, the nation, and even the world for Bar and Bat Mitzvahs, anniversaries, weddings, cancer-free rituals, memorials, and so forth. Broadcasting enables congregants to be with their synagogue family during their own important occasions. A lovely example occurred when a BCC couple were in Frankfurt, Germany, to be married in proximity with the bride's family, yet celebrated their *auf ruf*—Jewish custom for the congregation to offer a special blessing to the wedding couple on the Sabbath before their wedding—"at" BCC. During BCC's Friday night service, while the couple watched from their hotel room early on Saturday morning, clergy and congregants turned toward the camera for the blessing and a rousing *Mazel Tov*. After the festivities ended, the couple quickly "chatted" back their appreciation, which was happily shared with the congregation. When the bride returned to Los Angeles, she was surprised by the number of people who said how special it was for them "to be there."

Although the couple's *auf ruf* presented no technological or *halachic* challenges, their wedding the next evening was a different story. As an interfaith couple, they could not find a rabbi in Germany that would marry them. They ended up flying in a rabbi from England to perform the ceremony. For ease of family and friends (mostly not Jewish), they chose to have the wedding on Saturday night. However, since Judaism forbids weddings (and funerals) on

Shabbat, they had to schedule it late, after sundown. As the date approached, the bride, who had developed a strong connection to BCC, realized that the ceremony would be much more "personal" if her rabbi, Rabbi Edwards, was "there in some way."

Technology made the solution simple but *halachically* problematic. Incorporating technology into Jewish life cycle events may present little difficulty in liberal Judaism, but in this case the time difference between Germany (Saturday night) and Los Angeles (Shabbat morning) created a challenge: although Skype technology might make it technically workable for Rabbi Edwards to co-officiate at the wedding, *halachah* prevented it.

Historically, rabbis have been given latitude to determine what is best for their community, provided it's reasoned within the spirit of Jewish law. Since the wedding plans were in place before the couple knew BCC well, and they had been careful to schedule the wedding after Shabbat, Rabbi Edwards wanted to find a suitable compromise. Because it was Shabbat in Los Angeles, she would not co-officiate at the wedding. However, since she'd married couples after sundown on Saturday night before, she judged it acceptable to participate in the *Havdalah* (service marking the end of Shabbat). The couple's *aufruf* reveals how easily a virtual bridge brings people into community. Their wedding shows that if synagogues are to remain an integral part of Jewish lives, they must embrace technological opportunities and the demands for re-interpreting laws and customs that accompany them.

In addition to Jewish worship and life cycle events, the synagogue provides a place for study and contemplation. For its part, BCC has played a pioneering role in the spread of feminist and queer Jewish thought. Its clergy and members have authored or have been the subject of books, articles, plays, and films. They've put a face on the LGBT Jewish community through political rallies, interfaith services, media appearances, university courses, and public lectures. Furthermore, they've promoted the important work of other original thinkers. For example, in the 2000s, BCC hosted a series of classes by lesbian rabbi and *halachic* scholar Benay Lappe on Talmudic attitudes toward sexual and gender identity. Soon thereafter, Rabbi Steven Greenberg, the first openly gay Orthodox rabbi, lectured at BCC on his groundbreaking book *Wrestling with God and Men: Homosexuality in the Jewish Tradition*. And now in this second decade of the 21st century, BCC has taken advantage of technology to expand its influential sphere far beyond the in-person limitations that had formerly denied interested people the rewards of studying at BCC.

The appetite for technological access to what goes on in a synagogue building is illustrated by the reception of a remarkable *drash* delivered at BCC by Rabbi Adler in May 2012. In it, she addressed the critical questions that arise from Leviticus 18:22 and 20:13, which forbid "a man to lie with a male as one lies with a woman," namely: "What do we do with texts that won't let people live?" and, "How can we understand such texts and take away their destructive powers?" Although Rabbi Adler's *drash* covered some common ground (she even cites Lappe and Greenberg's BCC appearances), it had a broader and swifter impact inside and outside of BCC because of the new broadcast and distribution capabilities; in fact, the YouTube video of her sermon received over 800 hits in the two weeks following its delivery. Of course, Rabbi Adler's being a widely respected scholar and people's significant interest in the topic were crucial components to its success. But without BCC's expanded means of communication playing a role, the possibility of reaching a much greater audience would not have existed. Many of those who watched her *drash*, either live or archived, used social media such as Facebook or email to share it further. The URJ highlighted it on their website, as did Hebrew Union College (HUC), the Reform Movement's seminary. BCC featured it on its website, FaceBook, and Twitter pages, and in its email correspondence and e-newsletter. Collectively, these sources and networks gave, and continue to give, multiple search engine opportunities for those interested in LGBT Jewish issues—a potentially exponential expansion.

Innovators at BCC, through the establishment of the Telephone Minyan and then BCC Live, have built, sustained, and intertwined a communal physical and virtual presence accessible far beyond the synagogue building itself. Both innovations were and continue to be guided by the feminist values of equality, access, inclusion, and responsiveness. They show that technology's success depends on "why and how," not on "what" is used. A simple landline telephone or a high-tech live broadcast can be equally potent if both aim to extend community beyond its previous borders. No doubt as more synagogues embrace technology, more inventive and appropriate designs will be developed to broadcast their activities.

Clearly, technology can bring new religious opportunities as well as conflicts and questions. Skype may make it possible for people to be "together" anywhere in the world; but, what should we do with the potential conflicts between secular and sacred time? What is appropriate worship behavior for those at home or elsewhere—should it merely follow those in the sanctuary or can individuals create their own rituals and observances? These questions seek thoughtful consideration by various Jewish denominations, congregations, and individuals.

Finally and most importantly, the BCC story reveals that some people require a physical space to meet their spiritual and social needs, while others—due to illness, distance, travel, and other reasons—need a dynamic virtual space. The powerful synergy generated when a brick-and-mortar religious institution expands itself by means of a virtual alternative highlights the potential for religion to develop a powerful and relevant Jewish voice in the 21st century.

Notes

1. Judith Plaskow, *Standing Again at Sinai: Judaism from a Feminist Perspective* (San Francisco, CA: Harper & Row, 1990), xix.
2. Jeannette Vance (aka Bracha Yael), "The Impact of AIDS/HIV Disease on LGBT Religious Institutions: A Comparative Study of the Metropolitan Community

Church of Los Angeles and Beth Chayim Chadashim" (Master's Thesis, Claremont Graduate University, 2000).

3. Rachel Adler, "The Jew Who Wasn't There: Halakhah and the Jewish Woman," in *On Being a Jewish Feminist: A Reader*, edited by Susannah Heschel (New York: Schocken Books, 1983), 13.
4. Adler, "The Jew Who Wasn't There," 13.
5. Susannah Heschel, introduction to *On Being a Jewish Feminist: A Reader*, edited by Susannah Heschel (New York: Schocken Books, 1983), xv. Heschel discusses the intentions of second-wave Jewish feminists.
6. A sampling of other Jewish feminists' views in this area: Lori Hope Lefkovitz and Rona Shapiro, "The Politics and Aesthetics of Jewish Women's Spirituality," in *New Jewish Feminism: Probing the Past, Forging the Future*, edited by Elyse Goldstein (Woodstock, VT: Jewish Lights Publishing, 2009); Elyse Goldstein, "The Pink Tallit: Women's Rituals as Imitative or Inventive?" *Jewish Feminism: Probing the Past, Forging the Future*, edited by Elyse Goldstein (Woodstock, VT: Jewish Lights Publishing, 2009); Gail Shulman, "A Feminist Path to Judaism," in *On Being a Jewish Feminist: A Reader*, edited by Susannah Heschel (New York: Schocken Books, 1983).
7. Rabbi Simkha Y. Weintraub, "Yom Kippur for the One Who Cannot Fast," www.ritualwell.org/ritual/meditation-yom-kippur-one-who-cannot-fast.
8. Claire R. Satloff, "History, Fiction and the Tradition" in *On Being a Jewish Feminist: A Reader*, ed. Susannah Heschel (New York: Schocken Books, 1983), 189.

12 Creating "Open-Source" Community

Just Hospitality or Cyberspace Ivory Tower?

Kate M. Ott

Feminist theo-ethical discourse has from its beginning been concerned with how communities "ought to be," and, perhaps more importantly, how we go about getting there. In other words, feminist scholars did not just put forth a theological vision or an ethical ideal, but also raised concerns about the process of achieving said vision. Thus, the method was as important as the outcome. From the beginning, feminist scholars in the academic study of religion were focused on practices that differed from many of their male peers. For example, they did more than work to support each others' publications, they collaborated on texts and published together, and they created new spaces of publication that expanded the canon of "appropriate" topics and style.

My own mentor, Letty Russell, was a foundational scholar in feminist and liberation theologies. She, and her partner Shannon Clarkson, worked to change the academic landscape by developing an international feminist doctorate of ministry program and supporting a variety of global women's theological initiatives through the World Council of Churches.[1] I spent a good deal of time with her in various capacities, learning how feminist theological communities could be structured differently from the dominant social, academic, and church paradigms. She was not perfect, and neither were the initiatives, as none of us are. However, it is these experiences that deeply shape my theo-ethical imagination. As I work with feminist scholars of religion to develop communities via new media, I find great similarity between Russell's theo-ethical concept/practice of just hospitality and the technological method/practice of open source. In comparing and contrasting them, we may just gain some clues into 21st-century 2.0 feminist community building in the academy.

In the last two decades, scholars in media studies and religious studies made a shift from a technology-as-medium focus to considering technology as social meaning, or how humans are mediated and created in relationship to technology.[2] This is a movement away from a concentration on the tools or processes of technology to considering the social context.[3] An example of this shift is the work of Heidi A. Campbell. She developed the religious-social shaping of technology (or RSST) framework based on the sociological framework SST (social shaping of technology). In SST, technology is presented as a product of the interplay between different technical and social factors in both design and use. Thus, it is a social process—neither human nor the device or program is solely determinative. Campbell writes,

> A unique element of the religious-social shaping of technology is that it seeks to explore in more detail how spiritual, moral and theological codes of practice guide technological negotiation . . . [It] involves asking questions about how technologies are conceived of, as well as used, in light of a religious community's beliefs, moral codes, and historical traditions of engagement with other forms of media technology.[4]

The discussion in this chapter falls into the category of religious–social shaping of technology or the shift to a value-centered approach rather than a technical-centered approach. Such an approach suggests that one cannot view technology as a morally neutral tool, but rather as an interactive, mutually constitutive relationship. In other words, what I am most interested in is how we engage the values and opportunities of such systems, and thus how the technologies reinforce, disrupt, and transform communities and individuals interacting with them. I am reminded of Wayne Meeks's statement in *The Origins of Christian Morality*, "Making morals means making community."[5] Thus, our histories, practices, and future visions of how things ought to be create a community structure. From my perspective, the praxes of just hospitality and open source create communities that share a remarkably similar moral structure.

In a sense, then, this chapter is an exploration of how two praxes, one from technology and one from theology, come into conversation.[6] I present both in a descriptive, rather than evaluative, manner. Discussions of how feminist theology/ethics and technology intersect are relatively new and, thus, more time (and space) is needed prior to presenting an evaluation. For example, a fuller, long-term study of how various feminist religious studies blogs, microblogs, Facebook groups, and Wiki sites develop out of and provide new theological and ethical insights is a project for the coming decade. Right now, they are still nascent. Specifically, I address how strategies from "open source" technology intersect with the theo-ethical concept of "just hospitality" to raise questions about promotion of access, diversity, and peer production, which I would argue are foundational feminist academic concerns. In particular, recent shifts in new media raises distinct issues regarding academic standards of knowledge production that may have a deep impact on the current configuration of the academy. The final question of this chapter is whether or not this impact can be shaped toward a feminist model of community and what underlying values are needed to do so. I might sum up my inquiry in this way: Can we imagine how open-source technology can bring more just hospitality to the academic endeavor of knowledge production?

Defining Open Source

"Open source" originates as a term in technological development most closely associated with software creation, meaning a program including source code, that is freely distributed and accessible. Since open-source systems and products are in the public domain, there is greater access and availability. Open source is non-restrictive of future use and development. That means, all future iterations must also be open source. This built-in requirement perpetuates the values and practices of open-source development. Often, in the creation stages, peer evaluation is built into the production process rather than as gatekeepers at a final stage. It is not always the case that the full source code (or blueprint) of the product is available, but in most cases it is or can be accessed within certain parameters. The movement to open-source code, especially given the rise of the Internet, allowed for collaboration in production that promotes variation, assistance with patches, and unanticipated end products.[7] This is counter to the centralized development and restrictive copyright practices of commercial companies.

Some common examples of open-source software or systems we use are OpenOffice, an alternative to Microsoft Office products or the Mozilla Firefox browser, an alternative to Internet Explorer or Safari. Then there is Moodle, the course management system, an alternative for Blackboard or Classes V.2. There are the social media services like Twitter, Facebook, or Wordpress. Open source applies to other areas of technology related to hardware and operating systems, such as Google and Android products. In a broader sense of the term, open source is a model or methodology that can be applied to government, activism, media, military/law enforcement intelligence gathering, healthcare, and education.[8] Consider new forms of journalism. Open-source journalism relies on user-generated content, where those seeing the story or participating in the event gather and collate to present a story. This does not mean it is free of fact; it does, however, provide a level of subjectivity that traditional journalism has not admitted. In most cases, open-source systems have standards to maintain the integrity of their story or "product." The community itself determines the authenticity of the story via comment structures or product ratings. Wikipedia is a prime example of open-source production of knowledge. It creates the platform for individuals to voluntarily contribute information (user generated) and is rated based on community-developed standards for providing reference and supporting materials. It promotes an endless diversity of growth and contributions, while still maintaining community-derived and -maintained limits. In contrast to what many people think, open source is not without standards of conduct and fact checking or licensing structures when it comes to software. What is possible via such a methodology is collaborative, diverse, and mutually enhancing idea generation, production, and implementation with a built-in feedback loop.

"Open source" is a term coined in the Internet era, but it is truly a historical practice. The basic idea is that information, including its production and source(s), once shared in a public domain can be modified, re-purposed, or built on by others. Consider sharing recipes or even the oral traditions that later become our biblical texts. This doesn't mean that it is all opinion, but recipes, like the biblical narrative, required a number of hands and voices to alter and arrange it prior to its current form. When considering religious traditions, Midrash might be a closer analogy to open-source development than anything my Christian community has to offer.

Open-source praxis creates a space where humans become "produsers" (producer + user) and "prosumers" (producer + consumer) of technology, and information more generally, I would argue.[9] It is an explicitly interactive and co-constitutive process between technology and humans. For many of us, we are not developing source code for an updated version of the Firefox browser or Wordpress weblog. However, we are using many of these products, such as Google-based systems that run on Android, YouTube, Twitter, and Facebook. Pauline Hope Cheong and Charles Ess suggest in the introduction to their new volume on *Digital Media, Social Media and Culture: Perspectives, Practices and Futures*,

> Very clearly, digital media facilitate and mediate social relations, including people's notions of relationship, patterns of belonging, and community—and in doing so, digital media thus immediately intersect with, and significantly impact, central religious concerns with (re)establishing right relationship or harmony in these various communities.[10]

In other words, we may be shifting our values around storytelling, product development, access, or information sharing. Have you ever been upset when you could not access the correct page on a Google book posting, due to limited copyright? Shouldn't all writing be shared and free? What about your book? How do we approach writing differently given new platforms and social media avenues? Ever wonder why a colleague's well-thought-out and intriguing blog with 2,000 hits is considered a lower standard of scholarship than a published book that sells less than 100 copies? These questions require us to revisit the ethical values embedded in the technology we use, the standards we expect, and our response to its limitations. In other words, how is our interaction with open-source technology changing or deepening our values?

Defining Just Hospitality

I have no doubt that social media not only provides new modes of interaction, but also shapes those relationships in new ways. The values on which any technology is produced affect how it shapes us and can be reshaped by us. For Russell, hospitality is a necessary Christian practice—not something that only some of us have a talent for or are called to do. She might even say it is pervasive and inescapable, much like new media.[11] There is a co-constitutive experience with both technology and hospitality. Russell suggests we have to be specific about practices of hospitality. She defines the praxis of just hospitality as, "God's welcome, embodied in our actions as we reach across difference to participate with God in bringing justice and healing to our world in crisis." Thus, "hospitality suggests how people of a covenant should relate to their neighbors" but we need justice as part of hospitality to ensure that power is shared and that difference is valued.[12] Open source holds similar tenets born out of technology development, not theological community. And, thus, it may provide a translatable ethical vision for technological development and engagement that promotes feminist liberation values.

The theo-ethical vision of just hospitality has at its core: vulnerability, relational difference, and partnership. Vulnerability is necessary to the practice of just hospitality. Being open to the stranger means that one risks some level of safety and privacy. By virtue of definition, being open and welcoming—especially of strangers—suggests a level of trust expressed through vulnerability. When one enters into a moment of hospitality, one is connected to others in a new way. This produces an opportunity to recognize difference.

As a practice of just hospitality, relational difference calls for a balance of sameness and difference through authentic unity. That is to say, in every relationship there will be some level of sameness, but that must not be used to erase real differences in order to provide a false unity or unity-in-tension.[13] It is much easier to reduce conflict and disagreements if we focus on what makes us the same. What makes us different usually involves recognition of power differences. Instead, Russell suggests in response to knowledge of the "other," we should focus on difference. Then, there is an opportunity to be called to partnership as we see how forms of oppression have used difference to divide us. This partnership is marked by advocacy for others and creation of community.[14] The praxis of just hospitality "sees the struggle for justice as part and parcel of welcoming the stranger," as opposed to hospitality as an act of charity devoid of awareness of larger social forces causing oppression and justice as a broad-scale re-visioning of social structures without concerns for how human relationships are harmed or healed.[15] In other words, just hospitality requires an awareness of the personal and the social situations in which we live and are called to welcome others.

Russell uses the biblical narratives of the Tower of Babel and Pentecost to make her point regarding difference. The Tower of Babel (Genesis 11:1–9) is biblical narrative in the Hebrew Scriptures where God destroys the tower being built by the people as a show of their power. It is often considered an account of the fall of the nations, with the resulting confusion of their language and their dispersal across the earth.[16] God's action is often seen as a consequence (or punishment) for human pride and lust for power. It is the story of a community requiring conformity and sameness as a means to ultimate power. It is a closed system. In response, God creates difference (via language and location).[17] The Pentecost (Acts 2: 1–21) narrative offers a different scenario. The diverse languages of the people gathered no longer divide; instead, they are able to understand each other.[18] This might be seen as a reversal of the Tower of Babel story.[19] However, Russell states, "We need to look again at the Pentecost message of unity in light of our understanding that the confusion of tongues at Babel was God's gift of difference. If difference is a gift that helps to prevent domination, surely it is not something to be overcome." The narrative of Pentecost teaches us about a "very different kind of world from the one envisioned by the builders at Babel, and in it the unity comes, not by building a tower of domination or uniformity, but through communication."[20]

If God creates the gift of difference as a means to preventing domination and oppression, then we need a system of community that promotes an understanding of differences, not an erasure of them. At Pentecost, it is the Holy Spirit that is said to bring the gift of hearing to the people. In this text, the "spirit does not so much create the structures and procedures, but rather breaks open structures that confine and separate people so that they can welcome difference and the challenges and opportunities for new understanding that difference brings."[21] Not to take the analogy too far, but there is a way in which Pentecost is an open-source event. It does not seek to erase the original or be proprietary, but promotes understanding and engagement, calling forth new things, new community. This occurs and recurs, as Russell suggests, through the praxis of just hospitality.

Values of Open Source and Just Hospitality

At their core, I suggest that open source and just hospitality are feminist praxis. That is to say, they value inclusion, encourage difference, and promote shared knowledge in an effort to minimize (if not eliminate) closed systems of power and structures of hierarchy. Just hospitality is about the practice of welcoming, creating a more open and inclusive circle. Open-source practice is based on inviting an ever-widening circle of people to participate in creation and development. In this process, open-source projects include different agendas and approaches working in chorus (or cacophony). A metaphor used by proponents of open-source software development is the bazaar.[22] A scene that mimics the settings of just hospitality where strangers are welcomed in their difference, unaware of the outcome—consider the newsroom or kitchen (often the same location) of the Catholic Worker.

Both just hospitality and open source are intentional about promoting shared knowledge in these spaces of welcome and difference. In fact, it is because of the inclusive and diverse nature of the communities that there is knowledge to be shared. Toward what end? Russell suggests that out of the practice of inclusion/welcome and valuing difference, one has no ethical alternative but to seek greater justice and advocate on behalf of one another. Open-source praxis might not be seen internally as having such lofty social aims. Yet, by definition, any open-source development must continue as such available in the public domain and accessible to all. In addition, it may not discriminate against person or groups or against fields of endeavor.[23] In this way, both just hospitality and open source, within their own spheres, push against closed systems of power and structures of hierarchy by operating with values of inclusion, difference, and shared knowledge.

21st-Century 2.0 Feminist Academic Community

How do the praxes of open source and just hospitality shape new social media, the feminist academic community, and knowledge production? Feminist scholars of religion have over time, I would argue, lived out just hospitality in certain aspects of their academic community. Examples include things like starting groups and enacting policies so that women both topically and physically would be represented in departments, at annual meetings of professional societies, and in publications.[24] In particular, the very presence of feminist scholars changed methods of knowledge production in the academy by insisting on use of personal experience as a source, collaborative projects, and a diversity of conversation partners. Feminist scholars and scholarship became a site of reflexive critique addressing internal divisions related to racism, classism, heterosexism, nationalism, and so on.[25] Yet, in many other ways, hierarchical and closed systems of power have remained, including status of senior and junior scholars (not to mention adjuncts), publish-or-perish tenure tracks, banking systems of teaching, and secretive peer-review structures. Many of these rely on a particular notion of how one evaluates knowledge production.

It is in relation to knowledge production that I believe open-source praxis will shift the academy (probably kicking and screaming) toward greater realization of a feminist, liberation praxis of just hospitality. Open source, like just hospitality, suggests a praxis that is inclusive (radically so), built on recognizing and encouraging difference, and dependent on shared knowledge for its continuation. It further debunks the notion that knowledge is objective; and if not completely objective, able to be objectively judged by a small cohort of self-appointed individuals. Knowledge is shifted to a communal creation rather than something one gains over time and bestows on others. In "Open Standards, Open Minds and Ownership of Ideas in Education," Barbara Iverson points out,

> The jarring and liberating explosion of digital technology in our world has upset historic intellectual structures . . . collaboration, appropriation, mixing, and re-mixing the work of others into new expressions, statements, narratives, and representations of ideas are part of authorship, creativity and the work our students will do.[26]

In open source, knowledge production is no longer only about creating a new, unique entity (if it ever was; that may just be what was rewarded). Knowledge production includes at least four aspects: creativity (new idea, not just in organization, but in structure/theory), collation (which is new in the sense of organization, not development), improvement/addition (which is taking the original source and repurposing, patching, etc.), and access (providing avenues and translations). Each of these aspects is valued and necessary in an open-source model. In fact, collation, improvement/addition, and access are not only crucial, but they *are* knowledge production in an open-source value system.

Scholarship Production

This has significant implications for current practices of copyright, tenure systems based on publication of single-author print books, and the assumptions of authority embedded in both. For example, the notion of open source, where user-generated content like a blog serves as knowledge production, raises particular questions for the academy. What is the review process? How can you make a well-crafted argument in 600 words? Is a link really a citation?[27] Behind these questions are issues of authorship standards or discipline specificity that begin to erode when we produce knowledge in an open-source format. It also begs the question of how current print publication systems are expensive, untimely, and restricted by overly proprietary copyright laws. While copyright law may have moved into a far too proprietary realm to support the intellectual expansiveness of the Internet, we may still need some level of copyright. Within the definition of open source is recognition of the integrity of the author's source code, not to mention open-source supporters like Creative Commons, who seek to "provide legal and technical infrastructure that maximizes digital creativity, sharing, and innovation" rather than restrict it.[28] We are on a course that requires that we change our academic values (and evaluation) of collaboration, hierarchy, and ownership of ideas. When we as scholars use digital open-source media, we begin to see how open source is a technological embodiment of just hospitality—full of vulnerability, encounters with relational difference, and sustained through partnership. There is a way in which the technology and our use of it may further shift feminist academic communities toward the practice of values that are deeply rooted in our traditions.

Networking

Technologies have allowed, even encouraged us to build spaces for network and conversation, to meet the stranger and test differences. These spaces are not only text based or single dimensional (e.g., I put my information out, you read it, you react), but they often also contain visuals and data-gathering aspects (like Facebook's "Where I've Been" application). In fact, they can also share aspects of our embodied selves in a live manner, like Skype video-calling. Digital technologies and social network technologies, in particular, are not going to completely replace in-person, embodied community, especially when it comes to feminist community, due to its commitment to the embodied nature of personhood as a relational aspect of who we are. However, technologies allow us to build on in-person communities that will expose us to greater difference and provide opportunities to understand new people and ideas (much like Pentecost). Chapter 4 in this volume is an example of how this has worked for a feminist blogging community.

The academy currently lives in a hybrid state of open-source and closed-source networks. There is a push to expand to be more open source or develop what some have named "intellectual commons."[29] This is happening through the online networks of scholars made possible because of social networking (much of which is open source). Additionally, some larger universities have already opened up their courses to non-matriculating students, such as through the Connexions Project at Rice University or OpenCourseWare project at MIT. None of these institutions have closed their doors to matriculating students or stopped paying their professors. They have simply allowed for a co-existence of open-source intellectual commons and the already closed system of the university. One lesson to be learned here is that these two objectives are not mutually destructive. Keeping just hospitality in mind, the meeting of the stranger in their difference does not tend toward assimilation or erasure, but rather toward partnership. I have serious reservations whether an intellectual commons can survive in a capitalist structure, but certainly it has resonance in a liberal arts model of learning.

Teaching

Beginning with a smaller space, how might our classrooms become an intellectual commons, further debunking a banking method of education built on hierarchy and ownership as well as combating a new consumerist student model? Open-source teaching changes the traditional notion of one person being the teacher. We might choose to have colleagues Skype into our classes so we can learn not only from a written text, but also from the embodied, interactive engagement with a person. This expands the classroom space and the teaching role. Students may generate learning materials or collaborate virtually on projects. For example, I asked the students in my Christian Ethics class to text, call, Facebook post/message, or email friends and family to ask about definitions of ethics. They then collated in real time the comments they received on a shared online word processing document. This exercise expanded the classroom conversation and invited a new group of people to "be students." At the same time, it offered an opportunity for the classroom students to be teachers and produce knowledge—in this case, about how we define ethics. In the process, they began to prioritize and categorize particular sources; they recognized and valued the difference that was born out of an opening of the classroom and intentional invitation to be collaborative and inclusive. The pedagogical model of partnership and valuing difference requires vulnerability on the part of the teacher who traditionally holds authority. A classroom that practices just hospitality models an open-source space.

As more journals go to online, open-access formats and networks of people join together for the sole purpose of producing knowledge, the liberal arts will have to step outside its peer-reviewed print journal standards and single-author book requirements, definitions of service as an embodied bureaucratic activity, and closed-classroom system. We need new criteria for accessing the open-source academic profession of online, user-generated publishing, network development, and facilitation of intellectual commons.[30] The impulse will be to use the same criteria we have, with little tweaks to fit a new medium. That will be a mistake. We need to stop trying to fit the square peg (or cloud) of open-source knowledge production and dissemination into the round hole (or paper copy) of current academic standards. Only then can we imagine the possibilities of how knowledge itself is and will be different in the future.

I do not hold technology up as a cure all for any issue. There are certainly positive benefits and negative outcomes to these changes. In fact, I have tried to stress that the moral values upon which a technology functions and is engaged *matter*. In Russell's work on just hospitality, she does not suggest that such praxis is without risk or without limitation. There is vulnerability implicit in the opening of any door or system. And, of course, there is always a question of capacity that is set by personal limits, social structural limits, and, in the case of just hospitality, limits of the theological tradition.[31] The real question is whether we have the will to try to live into or beyond those limits and vulnerabilities. Can we imagine how open-source technology can bring more just hospitality to the academic endeavor of knowledge production? Will it be more authentic and communal or contribute to devaluation and disembodied dialogue?[32] Will we work to overcome limited access based on economic stratification of hardware costs and Internet access or geopolitical limitations on information as social control? As a feminist scholar committed to intellectual commons that empower the "stranger" or least among us, open source offers a technology-based praxis that may become as deeply rooted as the theological tradition of just hospitality.

Notes

1. See Chapter 1 in particular, but also narratives throughout the text that discuss collaborations with international women's theology groups in Letty M. Russell, *Just Hospitality: God's Welcome in a World of Difference*, ed. J. Shannon Clarkson and Kate M. Ott (Louisville, KY: Westminster John Knox, 2009). Also, visit the nascent site for the International Feminist DMin program at https://sites.google.com/site/feministdmin/.
2. Heidi A. Campbell, *When Religion Meets New Media* (New York: Routledge, 2010), 42.
3. Noreen Herzfeld, *Technology and Religion: Remaining Human in a Co-Created World* (West Conshohocken, PA: Templeton Press, 2009), 8.
4. Campbell, 59.
5. Wayne A. Meeks, *The Origins of Christian Morality: The First Two Centuries* (New Haven, CT: Yale University, 1993), 5. Meeks uses this theory throughout the text to justify his historical ethnographic approach to understanding the morality of early Christians and also proposes it as a final thesis at the end of the book.
6. I'm specifically using the word *praxis* here to denote the combination of a theoretical basis and lived practice that just hospitality and open source are by definition.
7. The Open Source Initiative was started in 1998 to promote the open source definition and develop community standards, specifically a licensing structure for open

source product development. "Open Source Initiative," http://opensource.org/docs/definition.html.

8. "Open Source," http://en.wikipedia.org/wiki/Open_source. Wikipedia is an example of open-source server software that creates the platform for individuals to voluntarily contribute information (user-generated) and is rated based on community-developed standards for providing reference and supporting materials.

9. For a discussion related to religious communities and history of the terms see, Peter Fischer-Nielsen and Stefan Gelfgren, "Conclusion: Religion in a Digital Age: future Developments and Research Directions," in *Digital Media, Social Media and Culture: Perspectives, Practices and Futures,* ed. Pauline Hope Cheong, Peter Fisher-Neilsen, Stefan Gelfgren, and Charles Ess (New York: Peter Lang Publishing, 2012), 296–298.

10. Pauline Hope Cheong and Charles Ess, "Introduction: Religion 2.0? Relational and Hybridizing Pathways in Religion, Social Media, and Culture," in *Digital Media, Social Media and Culture: Perspectives, Practices and Futures,* ed. Pauline Hope Cheong, Peter Fisher-Neilsen, Stefan Gelfgren, and Charles Ess (New York: Peter Lang Publishing, 2012), 12. Here, digital media is defined as computer-mediated communication affiliated with Web 2.0, such as social media including social networking sites (e.g., Facebook), blogs and microblogs (e.g., Twitter), user-generated content (e.g., YouTube), and virtual worlds/games (e.g., Second Life). See pages 1–3 for further explanation.

11. Russell, 19.

12. Russell, 43.

13. Russell, 63–69.

14. Russell, see Chapter 4, "Reframing a Theology of Hospitality," especially 77–101.

15. Russell, 106–107.

16. Russell, 55.

17. José Miguez Bonino, "Genesis 11:1–9: A Latin American Perspective," in *Return to Babel: Global Perspectives on the Bible*, ed. Priscilla Pope-Levison and John R. Levison (Louisville, KY: Westminster John Knox Press, 1999), 15. See also, Walter Wink, *Engaging the Powers: Discernment and Resistance in a World of Domination* (Minneapolis, MN: Fortress Press, 1992).

18. Peter Gomes, "Beyond the Human Point of View," Address to the Covenant Network General Assembly Luncheon delivered on June 21, 1999. Accessed on February 21, 2013, at http://covnetpres.org/2011/03/good-words-from-the-author-of-the-good-book/.

19. I admit that this can be read as placing a Christian scriptural event as the antidote for a Hebrew scriptural event, which makes it appear that Christianity is a corrective to Hebraic scriptural models of community. This is only one scriptural example. I do think Russell or I are using this as an example that suggests we have something to learn about a response to difference that sees it as an asset not a detriment to community regardless of its scriptural placement. Russell and the biblical scholars she quotes in this section would argue that Babel is also a story meant to signal a positive response to difference as God's gift.

20. Russell, 60.

21. Russell, 61. See also, Justo L. González, "Reading from My Bicultural Place: Acts 6:1–7," in *Reading from this Place: Social Location and Biblical Interpretation in the United States*, ed. Fernando F. Segovia and Mary Ann Tolbert (Minneapolis, MN: Fortress Press, 1995), 1:146.

22. The term was coined by Eric S. Raymond in an essay later reprinted as *The Cathedral & the Bazaar: Musings on Linux and Open Source by an Accidental Revolutionary* (Sebastopol, CA: O'Reilly Media, 1999).

23. The Open Source Definition, accessed on August 21, 2012, http://opensource.org/docs/osd.

24. For an example, see the Status on Women in the Profession Group of the American Academy of Religion, www.aarweb.org/About_AAR/Committees/Status_of_Women_in_the_Profession/default.asp.

25. For discussion on the early conversations related to theory and practice of feminist scholars in religion, see *Feminist Theological Ethics: A Reader*, ed. Lois K. Daly (Louisville, KY: Westminster John Knox, 1994); and "Roundtable Discussion on Feminist Methodology," *Journal of Feminist Studies in Religion* 1, no. 2 (Fall 1985): 73–88. Specific to issues of (trans)nationalism see, Nami Kim, "Transformative 'Moves' to Join: A Transnational Feminist Pedagogical Practice," in *Faith, Feminism and Scholarship: The Next Generation,* ed. Melanie L. Harris and Kate M. Ott (New York: Palgrave Macmillan, 2011).

26. Barbara K. Iverson, "Open Standards, Open Minds, and Ownership of Ideas in Education: Navigating Hazards Between the Pirate Bay and Hollywood," paper presented at ICERI 2009 Madrid, Spain, accessed August 21, 2012, http://colum. academia.edu/BarbaraIverson/Papers/129903/OPEN_STANDARDS_OPEN_MINDS_AND_OWNERSHIP_OF_IDEAS_IN_EDUCATION_NAVIGATING_HAZARDS_BETWEEN_THE_PIRATE_BAY_AND_HOLLYWOOD.

27. I have to admit that even in writing this article I have had the impulse to embed links rather than footnotes, not to mention the multimedia contribution of a YouTube video explaining the benefits of open-source development. In my opinion, this would offer greater diversity to the communication method, interest for the reader, and depth of sources.

28. See "Creative Commons Mission," http://creativecommons.org/about and "Open Source Definition," http://opensource.org/docs/osd.

29. Iverson, Section 3.1 "The Public, the Commons, and Open Source."

30. Many institutions and individuals have already been working on issues related to digital technologies and scholarship in tenure and promotion. The following are a sampling of helpful resources: Anatoliy Gruzd1, Kathleen Staves, and Amanda Wilk, "Tenure and Promotion in the Age of Online Social Media," in *Proceedings of the American Society for Information Science and Technology* 48, no. 1 (2011): 1–9. There are numerous articles on the topic at HASTAC—Humanities, Arts, Science, and Technology Advanced Collaboratory at www.hastac.org.

31. Russell, 116.

32. Herzfeld, 68. See specifically the discussion in Chapter 3, "Cyberspace on Our Minds."

13 The Mormon "Ordain Women" Movement

The Virtue of Virtual Activism

Margaret M. Toscano

Every year on March 17, the Mormon Church, or more officially the Church of Jesus Christ of Latter-Day Saints (aka LDS), celebrates the birthday of the Female Relief Society, the Church's worldwide organization for its women members begun in 1842. On March 17, 2013, a few dozen Mormon women and men launched a new website named "Ordain Women: Mormon Women Seeking Equality and Ordination to the Priesthood," located at www.ordainwomen. org. Originally at the top of the home page, there was a picture of three pretty, young, white women who looked to be in their early twenties; their smiling faces were close together, suggesting sisterhood. Today, a collage-like rectangle of ninety-six mini-portraits graces the home page of OrdainWomen.org.[1] They are still mostly white women, though they give the impression of more diversity, since their ages range from early twenties to late sixties, and since men and some people of color are now included. Some of the pictures show women or men alone, others with family groups and couples, or mothers and fathers with their children. Under this colorful patchwork, the following words announce the purpose of the site:

> Ordain Women aspires to create a space for Mormon women to articulate issues of gender inequality they may be hesitant to raise alone. As a group we intend to put ourselves in the public eye and call attention to the need for the ordination of Mormon women to the priesthood.

Scrolling down, the observer finds the same photographs as above, but enlarged now. Click on each picture, and up comes a profile where the person identifies herself or himself, using some variation of the formula, "I am a Mormon woman or man who does such and such and who likes such and such. And I believe that women should be ordained to the priesthood." Sometimes, the statement ends with this declaration, and sometimes, people list the reasons for their belief.

On the first day of its launching, OrdainWomen.org had thousands of hits, which have now reached the 100,000s. On the corresponding Facebook page, however, only 711 people have given Ordain Women a "Like" sign.[2] While supporters may appear to be a small group in comparison to the 14 million

LDS Church members worldwide, it is a significant number for a grassroots movement like this. As a Mormon feminist who has publicly advocated for the ordination of women since 1984, this is the first time I have seen more than a handful of people willing to state publicly their belief that women should be ordained. In the past, women's ordination has always been the dividing issue among Mormon feminists.[3] All Mormon feminists want women to have more voice in the Church, more decision-making power, more visible authority and equality, and more recognition of their spiritual gifts. Very few have ever expressed a desire to be ordained into the priesthood leadership structure of the Church, though more have claimed a private, spiritual priesthood.[4] This essay explores the tensions underlying the "Ordain Women" movement in Mormon culture. On the one hand, the Internet is instrumental to the forming, structuring, and momentum of this new activist group. But, in spite of the advantages online connections and social media give to such groups, the Mormon "Ordain Women" movement faces enormous obstacles, due both to the hierarchical and conservative structure of the LDS Church, and also to cultural norms and expectations that infiltrate the collective psyche of Mormon people. Scholars such as Heidi A. Campbell have documented the ways online religion reflects broader "cultural changes at work in religion in general society," including "shifting authority."[5] While Mormon discussions online also reveal a shift toward individual self-authorization among many members, still these same members always show some discomfort in pitting themselves against Church leaders, who continue to assert that priesthood ordination is for men only.[6]

The founders of the Ordain Women movement did not expect as much positive reaction to their website as they received; neither did they expect it to take on a life of its own.[7] They saw it as the first step in a series of activist tactics to bring pressure on the LDS Church to ordain women. The organizers' original plan was for a group of women to stage some kind of a demonstration about women's ordination on April 6, 2013, at the semi-annual general priesthood meeting, for men only, held in Salt Lake City at Church headquarters.[8] The goal was to draw media attention to the event so that LDS leaders would recognize that many Mormon women are not happy with their present status. But all of this was pre-empted by the Ordain Women website itself. The twenty-four brave women and men who first posted their testimonies had placed their Church membership and status on the line because of their deep spiritual convictions about the need for women's ordination.[9] Others quickly responded through online blogs and social media, with some expressing their support of the movement on various Mormon blogs, and others submitting their own personal profiles for OrdainWomen.org. To stage a 1960s-type protest after this seemed a betrayal of the religious sensibilities of those who had pledged allegiance to the movement because Mormons as a group are uncomfortable with making demands on Church leaders. Instead, on April 6, 2013, at the same time as mainstream male members were attending the Church's priesthood session in downtown Salt Lake, the Ordain Women movement held their own priesthood meeting across town at the University of Utah, where

Kate Kelly explained why she had started the movement, and others articulated their reasons for believing in ordination. About one hundred supporters participated in the lively, often emotional, meeting, which received national media attention and stimulated immediate online buzz in the widespread Mormon blogosphere.[10]

This shift in tactics demonstrates the virtue of virtual activism. I use the word "virtue" here in the broadest sense of its meaning: something that has merit, potency, and excellence. And I am playing with the contrast between the word's Latin root, meaning manly courage, and its common modern context, referring to female chastity or modesty. In the case of the Mormon Ordain Women movement, the more indirect "womanly" approach online had more power to rally supporters than would a direct confrontation with male priesthood leaders in person, because most active LDS Church members would have interpreted such an action as disrespectful and a sign of disbelief in the basic tenets of the faith. I am not arguing here that certain approaches or qualities are gender essentialist, in fact, quite the opposite. I am using traditional uses of language to help us reconsider the meaning of terms such as "active" and "passive," or "real" and "virtual," in a 21st-century context when people spend most of their waking hours in the virtual reality of social media, in what looks like a passive state.[11] And yet, virtual interaction online provides the most vital and active point of connection among people on a daily basis in today's world, while the Internet also fuels activist movements toward social justice.[12] Movement in the virtual world crosses over to movement in the "real" world, because people connect in "real" time online, because online connections lead to face-to-face interaction, and because our perceptions of reality are daily formed and reformed by online activity. The virtual has become real.[13]

The online community created by OrdainWomen.org is a group geared for activism. It aims to make changes in the LDS Church. And, so far, it has been more successful in gaining support for women's ordination than past Mormon feminist groups.[14] In part, this is due to the power of the Internet, though I do not believe that is the main cause. What we are observing in Mormon culture is part of a larger sea change in worldwide attitudes about equality and personal empowerment. I like to believe that the work of feminism in the past fifty years has created a different set of expectations for younger women, even those who would never call themselves feminists.[15] They expect equal opportunities and treatment as their due in a way that their mothers and grandmothers never did at their age. For Mormon women, this results in a dissonance between their experiences in everyday secular culture and what happens to them in their LDS Church lives, where, they are told, ultimate truth rests. Danielle Miller Mooney described such a contrast as the beginning of her Mormon feminist awakening.[16] In 2007 while she was at Wellesley College, Danielle was listening on TV to a live speech by a high female leader in the LDS Church about the central role of motherhood and homemaking for women. Because she felt "like I was listening to a song that was off-key," Danielle began her search on the Internet. Here, she found online groups, such as Feminist Mormon Housewives, where people can explore their hardest questions in a forum where others understand the tensions they feel between their faith and their experiences, and between their deep Mormon identity and their feelings of estrangement from their religious community, which begins to happen as they question Church policies about gender inequality and other social and intellectual issues.

The Internet may not be the primary cause of Mormon feminist activism, but it is now the major catalyst for feminist identification, both personal and group, that also stimulates the desire to take action. The Internet also shapes the way in which activism happens and is perceived. Of course, it has become somewhat of a cliché to tout the benefits of the Internet for social interaction of all kinds, including social activism since the advent of the Arab Spring.[17] Nevertheless, it is important to reiterate how the Internet facilitates and encourages the growth of communities necessary to build the coalition and mutual support needed to ask for change from a powerful hierarchy. Resources available through the Internet, such as open blogs and closed Facebook groups, are the chief tool Mormon feminist leaders use for disseminating their messages and organizing actions, many of which are in virtual time and space. The Internet creates not only a mechanism but also an environment where activism can thrive, especially in a religious culture such as Mormonism. It does this in several ways, which are common effects of technology. First, there is the ease of connection. Because almost anyone has access to the Internet, people who would not otherwise connect can connect, whether they live near or far. Mormon feminist and intellectual publications and forums that provide support to questioning Mormons have been around since the 1960s.[18] But in the past, people might not have known about such resources unless they met someone who passed on this information, in part because there are taboos on certain topics in mainstream Mormon culture. Second, the anonymity of the Internet makes people feel safe, so that they can express their deepest doubts online. On one level, this sense of security is an illusion, but in general there is real safety for discussing religious issues.[19] Third, and perhaps most importantly, the Internet creates a virtual community that is based on shared experiences and feelings that create powerful bonds and group courage. The model of social media has infiltrated all aspects of communication on the Internet. Though the Internet has facilitated activism by making information available that otherwise might be hard to find, still for most people these days it is not facts that persuade but feelings and personal connections.[20]

It is the Internet that made it possible for Kate Kelly to connect with Lorie Winder and Hannah Wheelwright, which has been fortunate since they each have talents and resources that facilitated the formation of Ordain Women.[21] Kate, an active member of the LDS Church and a human rights attorney, became frustrated about gender inequality in her Church and decided she wanted to do something about it. As she talked to her college friend, Ashley Sanders, about her feelings, she became convinced that nothing short of priesthood ordination could solve the problem of women's second-class status in the LDS Church. Kate contacted John Dehlin, because he is the founder of the very popular and visible online group Mormon Stories (mormonstories.org), which helps people through crises of faith. John told Kate that if she was interested in women's ordination, the person she needed to contact was Lorie Winder.

Though Lorie has been advocating women's ordination since 1985, she became especially discouraged in 2012 about the lack of movement on the issue. So she decided to take action—through online communities. She first wrote a blog for the feminist Mormon group Exponent II, which she called "Sacred Disobedience," praising the Roman Catholic Women Priests movement and calling for action from Mormon women.[22] Then Lorie organized a Mormon–Catholic dialogue on women's ordination at Claremont Graduate School to set up a coalition between these two faith groups.[23] And finally, she coordinated the "All Are Alike Unto God" website that calls for LDS Church leaders to pray about the possibility of women's ordination and to work on other ways to create gender equality in the Church.[24] Signers of this online document were hoping that the radical request for ordination would at least lead to more moderate changes that will "foster a more equitable religious community," such as including women in leadership councils, giving them more control over their own organizations, and including more stories and images of girls and women in Church publications.[25]

Lorie, who is well-connected with the widespread Mormon feminist community, online and in person, made it possible for Kate to connect with other women who were willing to participate, especially by submitting profiles for the website.[26] Because Lorie also has editorial skills and knowledge of past feminist writings, she wrote the FAQs, helped shape the tone of the group, and collected resources for the website. Hannah Wheelwright, a graduate of the Church-owned Brigham Young University, became a crucial player too. She was already online as part of the Young Mormon Feminists blog, which connected her to what was at first a secret discussion group before the March 17 launch of Ordain Women. But Hannah's intelligence and courageous conviction about women's ordination quickly put her in the spotlight as a spokesperson for the group, along with Lorie and Kate.[27]

It was Kate who kept insisting that the Ordain Women group had to be bold, even confrontational, to bring the ordination issue into the spotlight. She had the idea for the website as the first step toward other actions that would make the media, and therefore Church leaders, take note. The way Kate decided to structure the website is a crucial part of the tactic that has made the Ordain Women movement effective. The look of the website, including the personal testimonials, strikes a familiar chord with LDS Church members. A few years ago, the Church started the "I am a Mormon" campaign on its official website, www.lds.org, which carries a series of profiles of a wide variety of people from different ethnic and racial backgrounds, with a range of professions, hobbies, and interests. The purpose of the campaign is fairly easy to guess: to show outsiders that Mormons are both a very diverse people and also very normal. Obviously, the LDS Church is trying hard to dispel the notion that Mormons are a cult; they want to be perceived as mainstream Americans and Christians. The

Ordain Women website speaks in a similar language to persuade fellow Mormons that its members are not a bunch of radical feminists out to destroy the Church. They do this by speaking in another familiar Mormon discourse, the discourse of testimony. They bear witness that they have a spiritual testimony that women should be ordained, implying that they believe this in the same way they believe other tenets of their faith. The testimonies given by Mormons on both the Church's website and the Ordain Women's site are related to what researchers call life stories or storied identities, which have been shown to be powerful sources for social and political activism.[28]

Another important strategy of the launch of the Ordain Women movement was to get media coverage of both the website and the April 6 action. This, of course, is a traditional activist technique, both to get the message out there and to put pressure on the organizations you want to change. Movements like Ordain Women have a new advantage now in 2013, not available in the past, because newspaper stories and TV and radio coverage stay online for people to continue to access after a live event is over, whenever people Google a topic like "Mormon women and priesthood." Moreover, people have the ability to add their online comments and interact with other comments on the webpage where the story is covered, even months after the story first appears. The Ordain Women website gives links to all the major news coverage about their April 6 launch, to encourage people to look at the stories and to remind viewers that their cause has national importance. The *Boston Globe*, the *Daily Beast/ Newsweek*, and the *Wall Street Journal* were the national presses that covered the March launch and April event, highlighting Mormon feminism as much as the ordination movement itself.[29] Locally in Salt Lake City, Fox 13 did three shows covering the Ordain Women movement, while ABC 4 News ran two stories before and during the April 6 event.[30] Importantly, all the TV coverage highlighted the website as much as the live interviews with organizers. Each news story focused on the pictures of people with online profiles, which emphasized the vitality of the movement on the Internet. The way the TV stations interspersed live taping with photos of the online website shows the complexity of virtual reality, even in what seems like more conventional media.

The LDS Church's three carefully crafted replies on the question of women's ordination show that their public relations department has been paying attention to online activity since Ordain Women's beginning on March 17.[31] The Church released a video, along with an official transcript, on April 5, one day before the already-announced Ordain Women launch meeting. In this video, Ruth Todd, the Church's Public Affairs Department senior manager, interviewed the general presidents of the three female organizations of the Church. First, Todd directed the conversation around the roles these three women play on leadership councils in the Church, emphasizing how the male leaders in the Church value their opinions and are concerned about the women of the Church. Then, Todd turned the discussion toward their relationship to priesthood, asking them a direct question that obviously referred to the Ordain Women movement, but significantly not by name: "Some women are concerned that they don't hold the priesthood and feel like they're not equal. What do you say to them?" Relief Society President Linda Burton answered that most women in the Church are happy with the blessings of the priesthood and don't desire the authority, because they understand that women and men have "complementary roles and are happy with that." She concluded that equality is not sameness.[32]

Similar language has been used by the Church in its other responses to the ordination question. On March 24, the Church released its first official statement: "It is the doctrine of the Church that men and women are equal. The Church follows the pattern set by the Savior when it comes to priesthood ordination." By April 5, the Church's website carried a more-detailed explanation of their position against women's ordination, stating that their view is divinely inspired and can only be changed by revelation through a prophet.[33] They quote the words of the previous prophet and president of the Church, Gordon B. Hinckley: "Women do not hold the priesthood because the Lord has put it that way. It is part of His program. Women have a very prominent place in this Church. Men hold the priesthood offices of the Church." Then, almost in response to the testimonies of women and men on the Ordain Women website, about 700 people answered the questions the Church's website asks: "Why don't women hold the priesthood in The Church of Jesus Christ of Latter-day Saints? How do women lead?" All of the members who responded follow typical Church answers to these questions: It is God's way. The prophets have given us the answers. Women have motherhood. Women are more spiritual than men so they don't need the priesthood. Women do have leadership in the Church, through the female auxiliaries; and women's gifts and leadership is just as important as men's. "I am a strong, independent woman and I have never felt unequal in the Church."[34] This last woman's statement demonstrates how much the Internet encourages discourse among people who are nevertheless not speaking directly to each other, or even admitting that they are aware of each other. The Ordain Women movement is a critique of LDS practice and culture, while this LDS Church webpage, which gives an open invitation to members, only reflects the views of those who are critical of women who want the priesthood.[35]

In an April 11 *Daily Beast* article, Patrick Mason, the chair of Mormon studies at Claremont Graduate School, explained the central challenge faced by the Ordain Women movement,

> Church leadership doesn't react in accordance with public opinion. "It's not going to scramble because of this website . . . Mormons care a lot about cohesion and unity . . . They're tolerant of people with different views, but not when those people are outspoken and especially not when people are perceived as criticizing the leaders of the church."[36]

Mason's statement is borne out by the 700 people responding on the Church's website about the question of why women don't hold priesthood in the LDS Church. But, ironically, the Church does react on their website indirectly to dissenting members, with an expected reinforcement of the status quo. Similar conservative statements can be found in the responses from the general public in all the online reports of the Ordain Women movement, especially in forums such as Fox News 13 and ABC Channel 4 in Salt Lake.

However, a middle ground between advocates of Ordain Women and the Church's online forum can be found in the Mormon blogosphere, sometimes called the blogernacle.[37] While there are also many private, conservative blogs (such as FAIR), there are a number of others that represent thousands of progressive, and sometimes moderately progressive, Mormons.[38] Here, the issue of women's priesthood ordination has been passionately debated since the Ordain Women website went up on March 17. For example, on March 22 on a site called Times and Seasons, Alison Moore Smith posted a blog entitled "Dumb Reasons for Exclusively Male Priesthood," where she uses humor to undercut the typical reasons given to exclude women from ordination. Alison ends her post by saying that while she supports Ordain Women's goals, she has not submitted a profile, because she doesn't feel it is her place to "call" for ordination, which she sees as demanding leaders to change.[39] Many Mormons seem to feel that demanding is a form of criticism of leaders, which is taboo, as noted by Mason. This is the major cultural obstacle faced by supporters of Ordain Women.

The most popular Mormon feminist blog is *Feminist Mormon Housewives*, started by Lisa Butterworth in 2004.[40] But even here, the perma-bloggers, which include both men and women, disagree about the issue of women's ordination, showing how charged the issue is for Mormon feminists, as well as for mainstream Mormons. Still, there is an important difference between the discussions on this site and those on the Church's website. On the private feminist sites, the assumption is that it is okay to disagree, with each other and even with Church leaders. Significantly though, the spring of 2013 is the first time the priesthood issue has been debated on *Feminist Mormon Housewives*. The high visibility of the Ordain Women site broke the unspoken taboo and made it acceptable to discuss this most controversial of feminist topics. In a March 21, 2013, post, the perma-bloggers expressed their views about women's ordination. The two men both support it without question; three women do as well. But eight women are ambivalent, most arguing that while they don't see a good reason against it, they also either don't want it for themselves or resist receiving priesthood from men. Lisa states another difficulty: "Men can favor women's ordination without fear of being labeled dangerous power-grubbers. The ladies, not so much."[41]

Joanna ends this discussion by emphasizing what is at stake,

> Last summer, on a national television program about Mormonism, in explaining Mormon feminism, I stated that for some Mormon feminists, equality in church participation and decision-making is an issue, while for others ordination is a pressing spiritual concern. The next day, strangers stopped me in the airport and told me how furious their friends and relatives were with me; others called for my excommunication on blogs and

Twitter. Just for stating the fact that some Mormon women do care about ordination. Which is a fact.

The last voice in this post is Joanna Brooks of "Ask Mormon Girl" fame, who writes for *Religion Dispatches* and became a high-profile spokesperson on Mormon issues during "The Mormon Moment" in the presidential campaign of Mitt Romney. Though Joanna herself has mixed feelings on the issue of women's ordination, the fact that someone of her importance in social media is willing to discuss the issue has changed the discourse significantly.[42]

The *Exponent II* blog, another important Mormon feminist site, is unique because many of the perma-bloggers here have taken a strong pro-ordination stance, both by posting their profiles on the Ordain Women site and also arguing strongly for women's ordination on their own website.[43] Though *Exponent II* does not usually get the traffic of *Feminist Mormon Housewives*, the one post that drew the most responses was written by a guest blogger, Catherine Worthington: "Why a Self-Proclaimed Feminist Is Uncomfortable with the Recent Push for the Ordination of Women." This post elicited a spirited exchange because so many *Exponent II* women and men publicly support women's ordination.[44] One of the differences between exchanges on feminist sites like this and other more-public exchanges on news websites is the desire to have a civil discussion, which, of course, is controlled by the webmasters.

My brief overview of the discussions taking place on Mormon blog sites is only a small window into this large and widespread online community. While it is true that many of the same people respond regularly, covering the same ground again and again, the nature of Internet discussions is such that the repetition itself becomes a mechanism for the ongoing inclusion of new voices and possible converts for one's causes. It is hard to get an accurate statistical count of how many online Mormons favor women's ordination.[45] While most people seem torn or ambivalent, still most also believe that people should have the freedom to discuss the issues, which itself is a step forward in Mormon culture. While Mormons are hesitant to disagree face to face, they will argue passionately online. The Internet has created a new sensibility among younger Mormons, who expect the right to express their opinions online, even when they also express apprehension about what this means for their LDS membership.

Not only has modern technology through the Internet made more honest and complex interaction among Mormons possible, but it has also been a mechanism for more interfaith dialogue. Lorie Winder has continued with her work to bring Mormon and Catholic women together in mutual support on the ordination question. Using the Mormon Ordain Women movement as her base, Lorie has made common cause with the Catholic Women's Ordination Conference to put together the next action to promote women's ordination. In order to build a wider coalition, the organizers decided to make their goal broader, focusing on justice and equitable inclusion for women in all religious groups. They announced that "Roman Catholic, Mormon, Muslim, Jewish and Evangelical women will mark National Women's Equality Day on Monday, August 26 [2013], by joining with women of other faiths in a nation-wide fast for gender justice and the equitable inclusion of women in their religious traditions," culminating in an interfaith prayer service at St. Stephen's Episcopal Church in Washington, DC.[46] The press release also included an option for those who could not attend the event. They were "encouraged to participate through Equal in Faith's Facebook event page. Organizers invite all who join them in fasting to post a personal statement of support on the event page and donate the money they would have spent on food to an organization of their choice that supports gender equity in religion." The Internet made it possible for women to feel connected to the real-time event with their active participation online. Thus, virtual participation itself became reality.

The impulse for the Mormon Ordain Women movement did not start on the Internet. It started with Kate Kelly's desire to do something activist in person because she was upset about the everyday inequality she had been experiencing in her local LDS congregations for years. But the Internet made it possible for her to connect with other key organizers, who added momentum and clarity to her original idea. Social media groups have been the means for the organization's growth by facilitating discussions, by making people aware of resources they hadn't heard about before, by drawing in people who weren't aware that others were pro-ordination, and by creating group cohesion and courage. The number of supporters for the Mormon Ordain Women movement is still not large by any count in comparison to LDS Church membership. But ongoing work on the Internet may eventually bring in more people. The fact that discussions about women's ordination are happening is a huge step forward for a culture that likes to avoid controversy. It is no coincidence that some such as Libby Boss, a Mormon feminist who blogs on *Exponent II*, hopes that we are seeing the beginning of a "Mormon Spring."[47] Like democratic movements across the globe, the "Mormon Spring" is being fueled by the power of the Internet to bring people together and to give them the sense of their power as a group, which is more than any one individual can exert. As stated on its home page: "Ordain Women aspires to create a space for Mormon women to articulate issues of gender inequality they may be hesitant to raise alone." While I am skeptical about the LDS Church changing its policy on women's ordination any time soon, the movement I see happening on the Internet gives me hope that change may happen in the next few decades, because there is virtue in virtual activism. Sean Cubitt, a scholar of technology and cultural politics, argues that the real power of the virtual world is its ongoing power "to produce change, and to produce the capacity to produce more change" because the virtual world always thrusts us into the future with its potential for something different, a new world that we first have to be able to imagine.[48] We are currently seeing this kind of virtual imagining in the Mormon Ordain Women movement.

Postscript

Kate Kelly was excommunicated from the LDS Church on June 23, 2014, "for conduct contrary to the laws and order of the Church," according to the letter sent to her by the leaders of her Virginia congregation. They informed her that she would not be readmitted unless she demonstrated "over a period of time" that she has "stopped teachings and actions that undermine the Church, its leaders, and the doctrine of the priesthood." In particular, the leaders cite both the "protest during General Conference" of the LDS Church (April 5, 2014), where approximately four hundred women congregated to ask for admission to the all-male priesthood meeting, and also the Ordain Women website that seeks to persuade people to join the movement for women's ordination. Kate and the other leaders of Ordain Women have announced that they do not plan to take down the website or stop advocating for women's equality in Mormonism.[49]

Notes

1. On August 25, 2013, there were 108 profiles posted in the individual spaces below the collage. According to Kate Kelly, at least thirty more people have submitted profiles in support of the movement's goal of women's ordination.
2. This is as of August 25, 2013.
3. See *Women and Authority: Re-Emerging Mormon Feminism*, ed. Maxine Hanks (Salt Lake City, UT: Signature Books, 1992), for past debates on the issue of women's ordination. For a discussion of women's resistance within the LDS Church, see my "Are Boys More Important than Girls? The Continuing Conflict of Gender Difference and Equality in Mormonism," *Sunstone Magazine* 146 (June 2007): 19–29.
4. Women's priesthood ordination is made more crucial in the LDS Church because the Mormon priesthood structure is based on a lay priesthood where all active boys and men are ordained. What this means is that grown women have less practical and religious authority than their twelve-year-old sons. Male priesthood councils control all resources—monetary, doctrinal, and organizational.
5. Heidi A. Campbell, "Understanding the Relationship between Religion Online and Offline in a Networked Society," *Journal of American Academy of Religion* 80, no. 1 (March 2012): 64–93. In addition to "shifting authority," Campbell also lists "networked community, storied identities, convergent practice, and a multisite reality" as the "five key traits of online religion."
6. Russell Ballard, one of the twelve apostles of the LDS Church, gave a talk to a large BYU Education Week crowd on August 20, 2013, about the reasons women don't need priesthood. The talk, which seems a response to the Ordain Women movement, again set the online blogs buzzing.
7. I have conducted phone interviews with both Kate Kelly (July 24, 2013) and Lorie Winder (July 22, 2013). In addition, I have been involved in a secret planning committee for Ordain Women, managed online through a Facebook private group.
8. April 6 is another important date for Mormons, since it commemorates the official organization of the Church of Jesus Christ of Latter-Day Saints in 1830.
9. Since other feminists like myself have been excommunicated for their public stance on women's ordination, the fear of losing one's Church membership is real. See my essay in *Transforming the Faiths of Our Fathers: Women Who Changed American Religion*, ed. Ann Braude (New York: Palgrave, 2004), 157–171.
10. The six main speakers were Kate Kelly, Lorie Winder, myself—Margaret Toscano—Mary Ellen Robertson, Debra Jenson, and Hannah Wheelwright. Later in the meeting, the floor was opened for many others to express their feelings. All seemed to be pro-ordination.
11. See Peter K. Fallon, *The Metaphysics of Media: Toward an End of Postmodern Cynicism and the Construction of a Virtuous Reality* (Scranton, PA: University

of Scranton Press, 2009). Like me, Fallon plays with the complexity of the term "virtual," exploring the philosophic and literary complexity of the "real" in ways I cannot in my limited space.

12. See Sue Curry Jansen, Jefferson Pooley, and Lora Taub-Pervizpour, eds., *Media and Social Justice* (New York: Palgrave, 2011).

13. For an overview of the literature on the relationship between the virtual and the real and its connection to the "politics of resistance," see Ian Saunders, "Virtual Cultures," *Year's Work in Critical and Cultural Theory* 15, no. 1 (2007): 128–145.

14. Mormon feminist groups have always been hesitant to make demands or even call for changes. As one of the founding members of the Mormon Women's Forum in 1988, I remember endless discussions about how to state our purpose, which in the end made no demands because some were concerned about losing supporters if we seemed too critical of the Church. And yet, in the spring of 1989, the forum sponsored a debate about women's priesthood ordination. There were speakers on both sides of the issue at this meeting where 600 people attended (http://66.147.24 4.239/~girlsgo6/mormonwomensforum/).

15. I certainly do not believe that feminism's goals have been reached. For an exploration of this problem, see Yvonne Tasker and Diane Negra, eds., *Interrogating Post-Feminism: Gender and the Politics of Popular Culture* (Durham, NC: Duke University Press, 2007).

16. Danielle's account is reported by Lisa Wangsness in her April 5, 2013, *Boston Globe* story on the Ordain Women movement (www.bostonglobe.com/metro/2013/04/05/ women-hope-for-mormon-spring/kSchzSqQDRRKAQtvfi8hhL/story.html).

17. See, for example, Melissa Y. Lerner, "Connecting the Actual with the Virtual: The Internet and Social Movement Theory in the Muslim World—The Cases of Iran and Egypt," *Journal of Muslim Minority Affairs* 30, no. 4 (December 2010): 555–574.

18. The two major groups with publications are *Dialogue, a Journal of Mormon Thought* (www.dialoguejournal.com/), and *Sunstone*, both a magazine and an annual cycle of symposia (www.sunstonemagazine.com/).

19. In her post "Mormons Advocate for Women's Ordination" on *Feminism and Religion* (blog), Caroline Kline describes the fear and doubt she felt about coming out publicly with her belief that women should be ordained. Though she bravely used her real name, she likely would not have been so public without the support of the larger online group (http://feminismandreligion.com/2013/03/26/ mormons-advocate-for-womens-ordination-by-caroline-kline/).

20. The 1842 Nauvoo Relief Society Minutes are now available online, where Joseph Smith tells the women that he intends to make them "a kingdom of priests as in Enoch's day—as in Paul's day" (http://josephsmithpapers.org/paperSummary/ nauvoo-relief-society-minute-book). Hannah Wheelwright describes in her profile how reading this was instrumental in convincing her that women should be ordained.

21. Kimberly Baptista was important for Ordain Women's launch because she did much initial work to connect with the press, which was crucial for the group to get noticed and have an effect. But because of personal issues, she had to drop out before the Salt Lake event.

22. See www.the-exponent.com/sacred-disobedience-womens-call-to-ministry/.

23. The participants of this September 19, 2012, dialogue were: Claremont academics, Gina Messina-Dysert and Karen Jo Torjesen; Mormon feminist activists, Lorie Winder, myself—Margaret Toscano—and Mary Ellen Robertson; and Roman Catholics in the Women Priest movement and Ordination Conference, Victoria Rue, Christine Haider-Winnet, and Jennifer O'Malley (www.huffingtonpost.com/ karen-torjesen/catholics-and-mormons-new-sisterhood-in-struggle-for-womens-ordination_b_2114214.html).

24. On July 29, 2013, some 1,143 women and men had signed their names to this document, mostly from the USA, but also some from other countries around the world.

25. The website "All Are Alike Unto God" calls upon top LDS priesthood leaders to pray about women's ordination and in the interim to consider twenty-two changes to institutional policies that would create a more equitable Church for women (http://whatwomenknow.org/all_are_alike/).

26. Mormon feminist retreat groups, many started in the 1970s and 1980s, have been instrumental in cultivating feminist communities and writings, as well as mentoring new generations of women.

27. After the April 6 event, Hannah published an opinion piece in the Provo, Utah, *Daily Herald*, where she asks people to consider the possibility of women's ordination. While many predictably criticized her in online responses, many more thanked her and praised her courage for speaking out as a BYU student (www. heraldextra.com/news/opinion/utah-valley/essay-i-plead-for-consideration-regard ing-ordination-of-women/article_cbe0bd2b-cf49-5a4e-86ae-6a24ce6d96c4.html).

28. Campbell lists "storied identities" as one of the "five key traits" of "networked religion" (64). See also Helga Lenart-Cheng and Darija Walker, "Recent Trends in Using Life Stories for Social and Political Activism," *Biography: An Interdisciplinary Quarterly* 34, no. 1 (Winter 2011): 141–179.

29. See Lisa Wangsness, "Mormon Feminists Speak Out," in *The Boston Globe,* April 5, 2013, www.bostonglobe.com/metro/2013/04/05/women-hope-for-mormon-spring/ kSchzSqQDRRKAQtvfi8hhL/story.html; Nina Strochlic, "Mormon Women Face Off Over Right to Priesthood," in *The Daily Beast,* April 11, 2013, www.thedailybeast. com/content/witw/articles/2013/04/11/mormon-women-face-off-over-right-to-priesthood.html; Geoffrey A. Fowler, "Woman Takes Rare Lead Roal at Mormon Event," in *The Wall Street Journal,* April 6, 2013, http://online.wsj.com/article/SB1 0001424127887324600704578407020865769616.html?mod=googlenews_wsj.

30. See Ben Winslow, "Feminists Call for LDS Church to Give Women the Priesthood," March 21, 2013, http://fox13now.com/2013/03/21/feminists-call-for-lds-to-give-women-priesthood/; Brittany Green-Miner and Todd Tanner, "Mormon Group Pushes for Women to Get the Priesthood," April 3, 2013, http://fox13now. com/2013/04/03/mormon-group-pushes-for-women-to-get-the-priesthood/; and Mark Green, "Group Advocating Ordaining LDS Women to Priesthood Launch Event," April 6, 2013, http://fox13now.com/2013/04/06/group-advocating-ordaining-lds-women-to-priesthood-hold-launch-event/. Also see "Group Pushing to Ordain LDS Women," April 3, 2013, www.abc4.com/mostpopular/story/Group-pushing-to-ordain-LDS-women/U66p73-Ko0GYTXT2-ITrqw.cspx; "LDS Women Group Want Priesthood," April 6, 2013, www.abc4.com/news/local/story/LDS-women-group-wants-priesthood/zVcJ9PZDmUmudtiTKZdyJg.cspx.

31. The Church's public relations arm is visible on www.mormonnewsroom.org.

32. See "Top Mormon Women Leaders Provide Their Insight into Church Leadership," April 5, 2013, www.mormonnewsroom.org/article/women-leaders-insights-church-leadership.

33. The Church has three linked sites: www.lds.org, www.mormon.org, and www.mor monnewsroom.org.

34. See http://mormon.org/faq/women-in-the-church.

35. One wonders whether the Church's PR department censored comments, or there was simply self-censorship.

36. See Strochlic, "Mormon Women Face Off over Right to Priesthood," www.the dailybeast.com/content/witw/articles/2013/04/11/mormon-women-face-off-over-right-to-priesthood.html.

37. The analogy is to the Church's tabernacle in SLC, a pioneer building constructed in 1875 that served as the main gathering place for church meetings until the recent conference center was completed in 2000.

38. *FAIR: Defending Mormonism* = *Foundation for Apologetic Information and Research* (http://fairlds.org). *Times and Seasons* (http://timesandseasons.org/) and *By Common Consent* (http://bycommonconsent.com/) are two of the most important and more progressive sites that have been dominated more by men's voices than women's. Interestingly, on both sites men have presented strong arguments for women's ordination.

39. See Allison Moore Smith, "Dumb Reasons for Exclusively Male Priesthood," March 22, 2103, http://timesandseasons.org/index.php/2013/03/dumb-reasons-for-exclusively-male-priesthood/.

40. The emergence of *Feminist Mormon Housewives* in 2004 (www.feministmormon housewives.org/), and the *Exponent II* blog (www.the-exponent.com/), in 2005 have completely reinvigorated Mormon feminism. *Feminist Mormon Housewives* often gets 5,000 hits a day.

41. See "Thoughts on the Ordination of Women? Our Diversity of Views," *Feminist Mormon Housewives* (blog), March 21, 2013, www.feministmormonhousewives. org/2013/03/thoughts-on-the-ordination-of-women-our-diversity-of-views/.

42. Joanna's regular blog is *Ask a Mormon Girl* (http://askmormongirl.com/). She did a series of blogs on women and priesthood ordination from August 2012 to August 2013.

43. April Bennett deserves mention. One of the *Exponent II* perma-bloggers, she has written blog after blog answering objections to common objections to women's ordination and posting helpful links and persuasive information. Jana Riess is another high-profile Mormon woman and author who has taken a strong stand for women's ordination on her Flunking Sainthood blog (http://janariess.religionnews. com/).

44. See Catherine Worthington, "Why a Self-Proclaimed Feminist Is Uncomfortable with the Recent Push for the Ordination of Women," *The Exponent II* (blog), May 9, 2013, www.the-exponent.com/guest-post-why-a-self-proclaimed-feminist-is-uncom fortable-with-the-recent-push-for-the-ordination-of-women-2/.

45. Probably the most scientific survey was done by the Faith Matters Survey in 2006, where 90 percent of Mormon women are said to be against women's ordination, while 52 percent of Mormon men are said to be against it (reported in *American Grace: How Religion Divides and Unites Us*, by Robert D. Putnam and David E. Campbell, Simon & Schuster, 2010, 244). Recent informal polls are likely inaccurate because of self-selected demographics. For example, in the *Exponent II* blog survey, 90.52 percent said they would be pleased with women's ordination, while 9.48 percent said they would be upset (out of 306 votes).

46. For the Facebook announcement, see www.facebook.com/events/548948465 166297/.

47. Quoted in Wangsness, *Boston Globe*, April 5, 2013.

48. Sean Cubitt, "Virtual Dialectics and Technological Aesthetics," Cultural Politics 4, no. 2 (2008): 133–154.

49. "Letter to Kathleen Marie Kelly from the Church of the Latter Day Saints," June 22, 2013, www.deseretnews.com/media/pdf/1365030.pdf.

14 Experimenting with Feminist Pedagogy and Technology in the Classroom

Grace Yia-Hei Kao

Teachers who employ feminist pedagogy believe in creating more egalitarian and collaborative learning environments wherein student perspectives on the course material count as genuine contributions to knowledge. Before actualizing their commitments in the classroom, however, feminist teachers must grapple with several theoretical and practical questions, including how to maximize student empowerment while maintaining classroom order. While drawing upon the scholarly literature on feminist pedagogy and using my Fall 2011 Feminist Ethics class as a case study, I discuss how my experimental use of two technology-reliant assignments either enhanced or impeded my course objectives and pedagogical goals. The first was a weekly blogging assignment on the then-newly created blogsite *Feminism and Religion*. The second was the use of a wiki as a learning tool for students to master difficult concepts and terms in feminist ethics. In the first section of this article, I provide a working definition of feminism and outline what I take to be several features of feminist pedagogy. In the second section, I explain the context in which I attempted to apply feminist pedagogical principles through these assignments. In the third section, I show how certain feminist pedagogical principles were either actualized or frustrated as students completed the work for the class. I conclude with some reflections on feminist pedagogy as well as some tips for maximizing the use of technology for feminist pedagogical ends.

What Is Feminism and Feminist Pedagogy?

Before we can understand what "feminist pedagogy" is and what those who employ it hope to accomplish, a word should be said about "feminism" itself. The most meaningful definitions to me have also been the simplest; these include Judith Butler's notion of feminism as committed to the "social transformation of gender relations" and bell hooks's characterization of feminism as a movement to "end sexism, sexist exploitation, and oppression."[1] As successive waves of feminist scholarship have made clear, the best feminist analysis today is an intersectional one—it examines the operations of gender alongside of race, class, sexuality, age, religion, and so forth. For this and other reasons, the descriptor "feminist" today is often understood to cover a broad array of "progressive, radical, or liberationist ideologies."[2] I should add that among my students and in the literature on feminism, an internal debate exists about whether men committed to the reformation of patriarchal institutions should call themselves "feminists" or more properly "feminist allies," the larger question being whether being a woman is an essential feature of being a feminist (my view is that it is not).

Like "feminism," "feminist pedagogy" has been understood to encompass a variety of tenets. While Robin Crabtree and David Sapp provide a useful formal definition, "a set of classroom practices, teaching strategies, approaches to content, and relationships grounded in critical pedagogical and feminist theory,"[3] the actual content of this pedagogy remains to be explained. According to Frinde Maher, radical feminist teachers are those today who are "centrally concerned with unpacking complex relations of privilege and oppression, and thus fundamentally reworking the structural as well as representational terms of inclusion that feminist teaching promises."[4] Juanita Johnson-Bailey and Ming-Yeh Lee contend that feminist pedagogy entails a distinctive teaching style that is "nonauthoritative and nurturing" as it "employs a political framework that attends to or encourages consciousness raising, activism, and a caring and safe environment.[5] To be sure, not every feminist teacher affirms the desideratum of classroom "safety." Such rhetoric has been challenged especially by women of color as either poorly reflecting the reality of their presence in the classroom when they are minorities in majority white institutions or undermining the role that "difficulty," not safe and "cozy, good feeling[s]," may play in students' intellectual development.[6]

Without discounting the afore-mentioned definitions, I find much to commend in Laura Larson's identification of four common characteristics of feminist pedagogy that are employed in higher education environments. According to her, feminist pedagogy,

1.   utilizes "personal experience as legitimate sites of knowledge"
2.   uses "theoretical frameworks" to analyze those experiences "for the purpose of understanding how larger socioeconomic systems and dominant narrative shape our realities"
3.   attends to "process" as well as "content" in the classroom to provide an environment that is "inclusive, egalitarian, and empowering for all students"
4.   identifies "strategies for individual and collective action to change oppressive behaviors and the larger systems behind them."[7]

Larson's first and third points merit further consideration. What grounds this first point about the role of personal experience for many feminist teachers is the movement's well-known mantra that "the personal is political," and the insight that one's social location invariably shapes one's perspectives. These convictions accordingly lead to calls for more self-disclosure than is typical in non-feminist classrooms.

Feminist pedagogues commonly link Larson's third point, the creation of "inclusive, egalitarian, and empowering" classrooms, to attempts to reduce social hierarchies, including between instructor and students. As Larson herself notes, such strategies can include placing chairs in a circle rather than in rows facing the teacher, using student moderators or facilitators during discussion, minimizing the lecture format of instruction, and using a combination of small and large group activities. As I shall discuss in the next section, they can also include invitations to students to design their own assignments and to participate, in whole or in part, in the grading process. Feminist teachers who seek to complicate traditional instructor–student hierarchies are essentially democratizing notions of authority and expertise in the classroom, and perhaps also, in the words of Martha Copp and Sherryl Klein, encouraging the students to see the instructor–student relationship as a state of only "temporary inequality" as students grow in confidence, knowledge, and responsibility.[8]

Admittedly, the degree to which feminist teachers ought to kenotically empty themselves of their authority is a matter of some debate. The feminist movement's "ambivalence toward the exercise of power" is itself echoed in the discourse on feminist pedagogy, as some theorists contend that "acting as a mediator or facilitator (i.e., a nurturer) will empower students," while others argue that teachers "cannot responsibly ignore the regulatory aspects of pedagogy" by ignoring or downplaying their power.[9] An additional reservation about yielding power to students is that such a technique may not serve the best interests of faculty who might already be professionally marginalized (on account of their gender, race, age, rank, etc.) and who might already be encountering resistance inside and outside of the classroom about their rightful teaching authority.[10]

These and other concerns lead me ultimately to affirm the idea that feminist pedagogy resists generalization. There may be an overlapping consensus of commitments among teachers who employ feminist pedagogy as discussed, but what may be best for any given feminist teacher to implement in any given classroom setting may depend more on particular cultural factors and how her colleagues and students react to her embodied self than by feminist pedagogical principles considered in the abstract.[11]

Setting the Context

I taught Feminist Ethics for the first time in Fall 2011 to twenty-five graduate students at a progressive Christian seminary on the West Coast. My institution is women and feminist friendly: most faculty and students subscribe to feminist/womanist ideals of women's dignity, equality, and leadership in their religious institutions and beyond. The students in my course were pursuing either MA, MDiv, and PhD degrees in religion, ethics, and/or women's studies, were in their first to third years of coursework, and had varying levels of background in these subjects. As is common in Women's Studies courses, the class was female dominated: only five (20 percent) students were male. While the majority of the students identified as Protestant or Catholic in some fashion, there was one Mormon, two Jewish, two Unitarian, one Muslim, one Buddhist/ Christian, and four atheist students. The class was diverse in other ways: one-third of the students were persons of color (three African Americans, three Asian international students who spoke English as a Second Language, one Persian/Indian American, and one Hispanic), three students were "out" (two lesbians and one gay man) and five students were several decades older than their twenty-to-thirty-year-old classmates.

While I employed several techniques to facilitate the creation of a feminist classroom, the one that most differentiated this class from (my and my students') others was my invitation to the students to co-construct the syllabus with me. Instead of handing them on the first day of class a comprehensive syllabus detailing all readings, assignments, and classroom policies, I explained that only several aspects of the course were non-negotiable, as these were tied to institutional requirements: (1) the booklist (since books had already been pre-ordered due to a Department of Education requirement), (2) the time/day/ duration of our class meetings, (3) the stipulation that course assignments and grading had to differ for students depending on the number of units for which they had enrolled, and (4) the requirement that everyone receive a final letter grade. The class was otherwise given free reign to determine almost everything else: the manner in which they would be evaluated (*which* assignments they would complete, *how* they would be graded, and *who* would be doing the grading), how they as a class would address me, and the parameters for class etiquette. The skeletal draft syllabus I distributed on the first day of class included sample topics with readings for the remaining weeks of the course (with a proviso that these, too, could be modified), boilerplate information about our institutional policies for students with disabilities and plagiarism, and a list of provisional student learning objectives. It left blank spaces under headings for the remainder: assignments, grading, policy on late work, class etiquette. In two groups, one for students enrolled in the course for three units (MAs and MDiv students), and the other for those students taking the course for four units (all doctoral students and a few MAs), the students spent time at the end of the first class and the beginning of the second discussing with one another the work they would do. A finalized syllabus, incorporating all changes and the different assignments and grading schemes for both groups, was reached shortly after the second course, as were collective decisions about class etiquette and how the students would address me in class (they chose the traditional route of my honorific title, Dr. or Professor Kao, not the more informal address of my first name, in part because nearly all other professors are addressed formally at our school and they did not want to signal to outsiders any lack of respect to me).

As I suspected would be the case, the process of co-constructing the syllabus met with mixed reactions. Several three-unit and four-unit students eagerly embraced the opportunity to take charge, commenting publicly and in private emails to me that they had never before been invited to provide so much input into a class at its outset. Others were either less enthusiastic or even wary about the process for one of the following reasons: (1) they felt the pressure of their schedules and just wanted to plug assignments and due dates into their calendars; (2) they were first-year graduate students and didn't really know what the "normal" was to which I was inviting them to disrupt; or (3) they were advanced graduate students who wanted to learn in a less experimental classroom because they wanted me, the "expert," to certify their competence in the traditional way.[12] According to student self-reports, 100 percent of the students who had enrolled in the course did so either because of the course subject (feminist ethics) or because of the instructor (me), or both. Not everyone, however, voiced excitement about my announcement on the first day of the kind of pedagogy I would be employing, especially because what drew some of the students to enroll was precisely the very structured and organized way I ordinarily teach.

It is worth underscoring that even some of those who self-identified as feminist reported feeling unsettled by the messy, time-intensive process of deliberating with others about the assignments that would either best meet the goals of the course or were the ones that they otherwise wished to complete. While my reflections on the syllabus-construction phase of the class exceed what can be provided here, I have sketched its basic contours to set the context for what is more properly the focus of this essay—the two technology-heavy assignments that we collectively adopted as a class. Put differently, the full significance of the use of technology in those assignments can best be understood against the backdrop of a course that was constituted and explicitly identified as an experiment in feminist pedagogy.

Experimenting with Technology

Blogging

Unlike most other assignments that the students determined on their own, I actively encouraged both three-unit and four-unit students to incorporate blogging on *Feminism and Religion* as one of the ways that they would be assessed in the course.[13] In making my "plug" for blogging, I was well aware that I was using my authority as a teacher (and, thus, the students' desire to please me) as a way to motivate the students to respond to my suggestion.

As Nicole Seymour has noted, there is not much discussion in the feminist pedagogy literature on *how* exactly the feminist classroom is initiated—"via group consensus? Through the syllabus? In class discussion? By the teacher's open goal-setting?"[14] In turn, teachers who "initiate" the feminist classroom, by far the most common course of events, cannot properly characterize themselves as "react[ing] against hierarchical set-ups," because the result itself will have stemmed "from a normal hierarchical set-up," as it was in my Fall 2011 Feminist Ethics course.[15]

When inquiring about the students' agency and observing that the desire for feminist pedagogy usually stems from the instructor herself, Seymour ponders the following,

> If they [the students] clearly understood what feminist pedagogy strives to offer students, would they develop such a desire? If not, how can instructors/ theorists reconcile lack of student investment in a feminist classroom with a choice to nonetheless implement a feminist classroom? If the "ultimate good" is invoked in such a reconciliation—as it often, somewhat silently, seems to be—how do instructors/theorists grapple with the paternalistic undertones of such a concept?[16]

Seymour's concern applies equally to my choice to initiate the creation of a feminist classroom through the syllabus co-construction process and to the encouragement I gave my students to select blogging to further that end. Because my Confucian heritage, years of teaching experience, and predilection for efficiency makes me more comfortable with the responsible exercise of hierarchical power than many of my feminist colleagues might be with the same, I experienced no pangs of conscience about the "paternalism" involved in those decisions. I had simply concluded that an exciting way for me to teach feminist *ethics* would be through an explicit adoption of more feminist *pedagogy* than I had previously used in my other courses. As I will explain further below, I also believed that blogging on *Feminism and Religion* would be a thoroughly feminist endeavor and, thus, a valuable learning experience for all.

Before commenting on whether my hopes for the blogging assignment were realized in the course, let me first say how the students came to "choose" blogging and what we collectively agreed would be the assignment.

First, I explained to the course that I had recently agreed to blog regularly on *Feminism and Religion* even though I had not yet (on the first day of class) ever blogged before—either on that blogsite or anywhere else. I had told the class that I had recently been pondering the pedagogical possibilities of social media and that I was excited about exploring the intersection of feminism and religion in a public and highly accessible forum that was designed for *everyone*—not just scholars of religion, feminist theorists, or other academic specialists. Second, I explained that I had made arrangements with one of the co-founders of *Feminism and Religion* for the class to blog weekly on their site and that two of the co-founders would be helping us with the mechanics of blogging: how to write in a style appropriate for blogs, how to attach photos and hyperlinks, and how to post or comment anonymously. Third, I had arranged for another regular contributor of the blog, herself a perma-blogger on a Mormon feminist blog and a student enrolled in the course, to explain on the first day of class why she blogs and what for her is particularly feminist about blogging. That student made a number of powerful points. I include below the ones that resonated most with me:

1. Blogs are a genre that privileges personal experience.

2. Blogs are usually dialogical in form and break down traditional barriers between those who write and those who read: readers can instantly connect with the authors by responding *via* comments, thus shifting the author's role from writer to reader and back to writer as she responds.
3. Blogs are non-elitist in inviting the public-at-large to enter into conversation about various topics. One doesn't have to pay tuition or be pursuing an advanced educational degree to participate in blogging.
4. Blogs authored by women allow us to document our own history; when scholars in successive generations pursue research on what women in the early part of the 21st century thought about feminism and religion, they can use these blogs as primary sources.

While some of my students ran their own blogsites or were regular contributors on others, approximately half of the class had never previously blogged. Regardless of past experience, almost everyone demonstrated either excitement or at least willingness to give it a try as an ongoing class assignment. Because a handful of students still expressed discomfort with the idea on the second day of class,[17] provisions were made for anyone to either blog or comment *anonymously* on *Feminism and Religion* or to avoid posting anything publicly at all by just submitting what they would have posted on the class-restricted discussion board on the course website on our course management system (Sakai) that was only available for class participants.

The mutually agreed-on directions for the blogging assignment on the final syllabus read as follows,

> All students will submit *one* primary post (on prearranged rotation either on Saturday or Sunday) either on the *Feminism and Religion* blog or on Sakai. All students will also be responsible for commenting on any *seven* different primary posts/comment threads as well as replying (at least once) to the comments on your primary post that you will undoubtedly receive from others. More instructions will be provided in class and in the relevant handouts; please remember that there is an option for students to post and comment anonymously on the blog. For the most part, you will be assessed for completion so long as you meet baseline criteria (i.e., you follow the guidelines and etiquette, show evidence of thoughtfulness, connect your post and comments to themes of the course, etc.).

Four-unit students agreed that their primary post would be worth fifteen points or 7.5 percent of their final grade and that their eight comments (seven on the posts of others, one on their own) would be worth eight points or 4 percent of their final grade.[18] The three-unit students agreed to the same grade/percentage point breakdown for blogging, though they did so in the context of a schedule of different assignments.[19]

In light of the greater enrollment size relative to the number of weeks in the course, we ended up posting two blogs each week on the blogsite. Students submitted their completed entries to both Gina Messina-Dysert, one of the co-founders of the blog, and me, and then Gina uploaded them thereafter. She also categorized all of our blogs under the label "feminist ethics class dialogue project" and included introductory text about our class at the beginning of each entry. I "advertised" for these blogs on my Facebook status updates as well as on the Facebook "walls" of my educational institutions; many students did similarly in addition to using their Twitter accounts. While not required to do so, most students connected the subject of their blog to either the previous or following week's reading. Since scholars have noted that women students especially struggle with the notion that "their experiences might contribute to the class's understanding of a text," the fact that most students seamlessly wove together personal narrative with textual analysis was something to behold.

From my vantage point, the class blogging assignment achieved several other feminist pedagogical ends. First, some have argued, "a feminist classroom should be a place where students are free to express their innermost thoughts and to openly reflect on their personal experiences while using those reflections as a way to connect with the course content."[20] This is exactly what my students created—both during class discussions and especially as they blogged and commented upon their classmates' entries. To provide some examples, a Mormon wrote powerfully about applying the implications of Carol Gilligan's findings to her religious context, a lesbian "Jewnitarian" (Jewish + Unitarian) explained her disavowal of lesbian separatism, a Muslim woman recounted the reasons that led her to found an interfaith nonprofit called "I am Jerusalem," and a Christian white woman wrote about her rejection of Southern belle culture and its underlying conservative sexual ethics. The blogging genre not only *encouraged* thoughtful reflections on personal experience, but it also ended up *validating* them as my students received many affirmations of what they had just written, sometimes within minutes or hours of first posting them.

Second, feminist pedagogy has commonly been characterized as attempting to "break down barriers and create new democratic spaces."[21] Through the power of the Internet and social media networking, the blog achieved those ends. It allowed students to carry on conversations with one another outside of the formal classroom structure and unmediated by any need for them to raise their hand and be called on to speak. Second, it instantly connected students in my class to students and scholars elsewhere and to interested members of the general public, including the students' extended networks of friends and family and persons who might not otherwise have been drawn to the intersection of feminism and religion. Put differently, people who do not have the luxury of a graduate school education or otherwise might not have access to what the likes of Nel Noddings, Margaret Farley, Ada Maria Isasi-Diaz, Martha Nussbaum, and Audre Lord taught and wrote, were able to read digestible bits of their scholarship through my students' highly accessible blogs.

So understood, the blog was not simply an assignment that students completed for a grade; it itself could be conceptualized as a service we as a class rendered to scholarship and to the wider community. A female student's blog about the deep role that Mary Daly played in her self-discovery and awakening as a feminist led to an opportunity for the editorial board of *Feminism and Religion* to set the record straight about a common, but unfortunate, misperception about her that had become the paradigmatic case about the racism of second-wave white feminists.[22] In another case, my Burmese male student's blog entitled "Karai Kasang: Rebirthing the Non-Patriarchal Image of God in Kachin Culture" was reposted with permission on globaltheology.org because of their interest in highlighting non-Western perspectives and his beautiful rewriting of the Lord's Prayer in a feminist and Kachin/Burmese manner.

Third, the blogging assignment allowed for a diminishment of my teaching authority. To be sure, I was still the one who assigned the grades (the students rejected the opportunity to grade one another), but the "real" judge of each student's submission was one another as well as the public-at-large. In addition, because I had been transparent with my students, they knew that I was learning more about the genre alongside of many of them. In short, they knew that my disclaiming of expertise about blogging was not simply false modesty.

These points notwithstanding, feminist teachers who might wish to assign blogging in their courses should be aware of certain risks. One concern is for the younger twenty-year-old students who have grown up under the omnipresence of reality TV and social media sites and, thus, who may not always appreciate the value of discretion. A second concern is for students of any age who are still maturing in their thought and, thus, whose interests may not be served best if their initial explorations of a topic are permanently recorded on the Internet for all to see. To use examples drawn from my class, a talented male doctoral student entitled his blog "I don't think I'm a feminist ethicist." While it was a thoughtful entry that generated serious discussion about the distinctiveness of feminist ethics, another colleague of mine and I were concerned about the possibility of the post, even by the title alone, "haunting" him in future job searches or in the perceptions that strangers might form of him (i.e., that he wasn't committed to feminist *ideals*). After thinking the matter over, we asked *Feminism and Religion* to delete the blog from their website at the end of the class and they complied with our request. In another case, a Christian woman who was currently working with young children in a school setting wisely anticipated that there might be unpleasant consequences for her if either school administrators or parents discovered her blog, which is why she posted her "Finding My Voice Through Vagina Monologues" entry anonymously. In a third case, another talented male doctoral student of mine decided to use the blogging assignment to disclose that he is a survivor of intimate partner rape. He told me that he was aware that many people would be shocked by his admission, but that he and his wife were ready for it. In debriefing with him, I had to make sure that he knew that his grade on the blog didn't depend on either shock value or the level of personal exposure and that, unfortunately, we live in a world where people still believe that sexual aggression by a woman against a man is either technically impossible or in fact something to be desired. I count his blog and the online and in-person discussions it generated as one of the most powerful events that transpired in the course. But I am well aware that the experience could have easily gone the other way for this student. To conclude, then, we instructors not only need to understand these risks—but we also need to convey them to our students.

Overall, I am pleased with our experimental class blogging assignment on *Feminism and Religion*. It not only increased traffic to the blogsite (itself a worthy goal), but it also helped to contribute to our creation of a feminist classroom. Out of nineteen student evaluations, nine students wrote "blogging" on the questions either which assignment was "most helpful" or "what were the especially strong points of the course?" One student commented that blogging "contributed to exploring my own objectives," another that "blogging was exciting," and still a third that "the blogs gave us instant feedback on our work from our community." In fact, I received the *highest* number of positive comments about blogging: positive write-in comments about the small papers, particularly the extensive feedback I gave on them, came in second place (eight students), and "feminist pedagogy" came in third (six students).

Wiki

The second assignment that would have been impossible for the students to do without the appropriate technology was the wiki. Recall that my students were not deciding in a vacuum the assignments they would complete, for I had provided on the first day of class a tentative list of student learning objectives, with the proviso that the objectives themselves could be modified.[23] Learning objective #2 read as follows: "By the end of the course, students will be able to comprehend the meaning of key terms in feminist ethics." While the four-unit students elected to fulfill this objective by completing a standard final fifteen- to twenty-page term paper, the three-unit students were more creative—they wanted to use the wiki feature on our recently installed course-management software to achieve this same outcome.

How had the students come up with this alternative plan? In conversations I overhead, the three-unit students indicated that they understood that the learning objective of mastering key terms was more commonly assessed through timed or take-home exams, as it has been in my other ethics courses. The handful of students who proposed the wiki idea were able to convince their classmates that it would be even better than an exam, for three primary reasons:

1. The wiki would not induce in them the same test-taking anxiety as exams generally do.
2. The prospect of progressively defining terms through the wiki would better meet the feminist pedagogical objectives of student-centered learning and collaboration.
3. The wiki, because unfamiliar to many and otherwise unconventional as a graded assignment for a graduate-level course, would be more fun and accordingly add to the experimental character of the course.

I had never previously heard of the idea of using wikis for graded assignments and was unfamiliar with the wiki feature on Sakai, for our institution had just that semester adopted a limited version (rsmart). Nevertheless, I was intrigued by the prospect of students actively participating in the construction of knowledge, wanted to empower them in their choice of an unconventional assignment, and assumed that it would not be too difficult for any of us to learn how to use the wiki feature.

As negotiated by the students and me, the instructions for the wiki assignment on the finalized syllabus read as follows,

> All 3-unit students will create together a wiki on Sakai wherein they will provide definitions of helpful or must-know terms in feminist ethics. Each student will be responsible for generating one *novel* term with a minimum of a 4–5 sentence description and then making 3 other substantial (not just grammatical) edits on the terms defined initially by others. You will be deciding on your own *which* terms should be included (so there is obviously an incentive for each student to post her initial definition on the sooner rather than later end). You will also be assessed qualitatively here (but need not fear that you will automatically "lose points" if classmates contest what you have written by making corrections).

Each student's original contribution/definition of one term would be worth ten points or 5 percent of their final grade, and their three different edits of the terms of others would be worth nine points or 4.5 percent of their grade. As in the case of blogging, the students elected not to grade one another explicitly (i.e., in the assigning of the points), although they were obviously going to be evaluating one another's work through the editing process.

Pedagogically speaking, I was curious to see *which* terms the students as a whole would choose to define (i.e., would they be the same ones that I as the instructor would have selected?) and *how* the revisions would proceed—would students be as, more, or less demanding than I would normally be if were doing the edits myself? Truth be told, I was fairly certain that a more traditional timed or take-home exam would provide me with a more accurate assessment of each student's knowledge of key terms—the stated goal of student learning objective #2. However, I also understood that the wiki held the potential of realizing other feminist pedagogical ends, including the creation of a space for truly student-centered and collaborative learning, since students would be selecting their own key terms and successively refining the original contributions of others.[24] So understood, the wiki would help facilitate a feminist pedagogical goal of breaking down strict instructor-student hierarchy, since student peers (not the instructor) would be providing immediate and qualitative feedback. To enhance peer- (not instructor-) evaluation desideratum, while the directions on the syllabus note that the instructor would grade work on the wiki qualitatively, I ultimately gave everyone full credit so long as they followed all directions and demonstrated evidence of adequate effort.

Approximately one month into the course, a few students began working on the wiki and immediately encountered technical problems. Some students were accidentally deleting the previous work of others when either making their own first-time contribution to the wiki or editing terms already posted. For a few days, neither the technology RA assigned to the course, nor the newly appointed head of online learning for our institution could effectively figure out a way to prevent this problem from recurring (in part because we were working on a limited version of Sakai), leading to frustrating experiences for all involved. After we were able to troubleshoot the problem successfully, something else wonderful happened pedagogically. One of the students who had already posted her term on the wiki took the initiative to put together a very user-friendly, step-by-step tutorial on how to use the wiki in ways that would preserve the work of others. In essence, that student took the mantle of the authority figure in voluntarily assuming the responsibility for showing her classmates how to do the assignment correctly. That incident was the clearest moment in the course where my feminist pedagogical hope of democratizing expertise in the room had been realized!

The Sakai wiki became especially active in the last four to six weeks or so of the course. To give an example of the kinds of terms and definitions discussed, a white woman who blogged about intercultural understanding provided the following (initial) definition of *mujerista/mujerista theology*,

> Mujerista, derived from the Spanish word *mujer* (woman), is a term coined by Catholic theologian and ethicist Ada Maria Isasi-Diaz in the 1980s. It refers to a person who makes a preferential option for Latina women in their communal struggle for liberation from multiple oppressions of sexism, racism, and classism. Mujerista theology is a liberative praxis, which takes into account ethics, theology, and faith of women as they live out their daily lives. Further it demands that Latinas determine their own future.
>
> (Derived from Isasi-Diaz's definition of the terms on
> her webpage at Drew University where she is a
> professor of ethics and theology)

To use another example, an "out" white lesbian in her forties provided the following initial definition of "lesbian,"

> Lesbian: A woman identified primarily with women as one's potential or actual beloved. Given that sexuality is fluid, there is not an assumption that one is always a lesbian, just as there is no assumption that one is always heterosexual. A lesbian is not defined primarily by her sexual preference, but rather her choice of whom to love as a life partner and/or spouse. This modern definition of lesbian does not require or ask for a female-centered or separatist world, but instead one where equality is the norm. Terms such as "butch" and "femme" are appropriate when self-owned by the lesbians

in question, though many lesbians of the younger generation will not iden-tify in this manner, feeling, instead, that it perpetuates the perception that there is a male and female in all intimate relationships.

Other terms included androcentric/androcentrism, autokoenony, compas-sionate respect, ecofeminism, feminist bioethics, feminist intercultural theology, heteropatriarchy, separatism, womanist/womanism, feminist pedagogy, and gyn/ecology.

In breaking the mold of choosing to define terms that might appear on a standard feminist ethics exam, one student told me that she had been inspired by Mary Daly's clever neologisms and thereafter coined her own term "womb-an"—"A woman of the world. She has the freedom and ability to do, say, and make decisions appropriate for her own body. Her body is hers, her choices are her own." Her classmates' editorial comments were mixed: some liked and expanded on the definition's thrust of reproductive freedom. Others articulated concern about the equation of "woman" with "womb," sensing that the over-identification of women with their bodies (in general and in term the "womb-an") was precisely part of the problem.

In the nineteen student evaluations I received in the course, all students with the exception of two rated student learning objective #2 as a 5 on a scale of 1–5 (with 5 being the best) in how well the course fulfilled the objective (the other two had given it a score of 4). Nevertheless, the most common answer to the question "which readings or assignments were least helpful" was the Sakai wiki, with close to half of the three-unit students (six total) indicating something to that effect. One student wrote in that the Sakai wiki "felt like a slog at the end of the term." Another student noted that the Sakai felt "more like a 'to-do' rather than something interesting." A third student had these keen insights to make, "I don't think this ended up being as dynamic as we hoped. It was hard to figure out and we didn't have very many words."

This last comment is worth unpacking. Even prior to reading the student evaluations, I, too, would have said that the least successful assignment in the course was the wiki. As previously indicated, I did not believe that the wiki would be the best way for me to assess each student's mastery of key terms and concepts in feminist ethics, but was willing to compromise on fulfilling that pedagogical objective for the possibility of meeting others. However, though the wiki held all of the promise of student-centered, collaborative learning and the maximum creative potential, we were indeed hampered by our technologi-cal inabilities to use the feature with ease. Still, even if we had not experienced those early technical difficulties, I suspect that the sentiment that the wiki felt like just another thing they had to do would probably still have remained. Why? To decrease the pressure of grades, the three-unit students were very intentional about wanting to do lots of mini-assignments for a few points each instead of having to do only a few assignments that would be weighted heavily. As I knew from years of teaching experience at the start of the course, how-ever, what the students might gain from minimizing the stress of grades per each assignment would be offset, in whole or in part, by the multiple assignments that they would inevitably have to complete, particularly when the stress of preparing for multiple final exams and papers in other courses would compound their ability to finish all of the course requirements in mine.

I would be remiss if I did not also comment about the possible gendered nature of the wiki in contributing to class dissatisfaction about it. In conducting research for this chapter, I was reminded of several widely publicized stories in the news media of the gender gap in Wikipedia. For example, in a series of "room for debate" articles in the *New York Times* on February 2, 2011, nine discussants attempted to explain why approximately 85 percent of all contributors on Wikipedia are men, and the significance of that number. While various theories were proposed, Susan C. Herrig, a professor of information science and linguistics at Indiana University, offered that it might have to do with the gendered nature of the genre. In her piece entitled "A Difference of Communication Styles," Herdig noted that Wikipedia "doesn't allow for the non-assertive style preferred by many women," but instead "enforces a 'neutral point of view' policy, which favors a more masculine style of communication—just the facts, ma'am." While it is certainly beyond the scope of this chapter to argue for gendered differences in communication (whether innate or socially constructed), Herrig's observation about Wikipedia nonetheless prompted me to re-read the types of definitions offered by my students. Though not explicitly instructed to do so, everyone—including the author of "womb-an"—provided very neutral-sounding, dictionary-like definitions. It is likely that they were familiar with the genre of wikis and thus attempted to emulate its style. When we keep in mind that the class was 80 percent female, it is possible that the wiki's flat and dry tone contributed to several of my students' lack of excitement about it.

Conclusion

The success or lack thereof of the wiki assignment can be appreciated best when examined in contrast with the blogging assignment. Even though the Saki wiki was an entirely student-generated idea, approximately half of the students who participated in it voted it as the least successful assignment, leading me to conclude that some of the very students who were excited about this "alternative" pedagogy may actually have come to resent it. In contrast, while the blogging assignment was initiated and advocated by me, the instructor, it was ranked by close to half of the class in those same anonymous student evaluations as one of the most helpful or strongest points of the course. The juxtaposition of these two experiences reveals that "having a choice" in the design of class assignments is no guarantee of student satisfaction. It also reaffirms to me the idea that instructors do have important roles to play in shepherding students toward assignments that will meet course objectives and other goals. So, while it remains helpful to think of teachers who employ feminist pedagogy more as "facilitators of this radical process" than absolute "authority figures,"[25] the responsibility for managing the class and troubleshooting any and all problems that arise should still rest more on the instructor than the students we otherwise hope to empower.

Although feminist pedagogues have described the ideal feminist classroom as "places not of stability, but, by nature, in constant flux," this flux was not always easy to handle.[26] My students were juggling difficult course content on top of their other professional and personal responsibilities, not to mention dealing with their classmates in a much more intense way as per the requirements of a feminist classroom. When we factor in having to complete assignments of a type many of them had never done before, such as the blogs and the wiki, it is not surprising to me that the students reported on the last day of class that they felt like they had endured so much.

In her own work on feminist teachers, Nicole Seymour has concluded that "feminist pedagogy [is] a form of feminist ethics."[27] I am heartened to know that the conviction with which I experimentally organized my class is shared by at least one other fellow traveler.

Notes

1. Judith Butler, "The Question of Social Transformation," in *Undoing Gender,* ed. Judith Butler, 204–231 (New York: Routledge, 2004), 204. bell hooks, *Feminism Is for Everybody: Passionate Politics.* (Cambridge, MA: South End Press, 2000), 1.
2. Nicole Seymour, "The Interests of Full Disclosure: Agenda-Setting and the Practical Initiation of the Feminist Classroom," *Feminist Teacher* 17, no. 3 (2007): 187–203, 187.
3. Robbin D. Crabtree and David Alan Sapp, "Theoretical, Political, and Pedagogical Challenges in the Feminist Classroom: Our Struggles to Walk the Walk," *College Teaching* 51, no. 4 (2003): 131–140, 131.
4. Frinde Maher, "Twisted Privileges: Terms of Inclusion in Feminist Teacher," *Radical Teacher* 83 (2008): 5–9, 5.
5. Juanita Johnson-Bailey and Ming-Yeh Lee, "Women of Color in the Academy: Where's Our Authority in the Classroom?" *Feminist Teacher* 15, no. 2 (2005): 111–122 at 111 and 113–114.
6. For the first critique, see Kyoko Kishimoto and Mumbi Mwangi, "Critiquing the Rhetoric of 'Safety' in Feminist Pedagogy: Women of Color Offering an Account of Ourselves," *Feminist Teacher* 19, no. 2(2009): 87–102. For the second, see bell hooks, *Teaching to Transgress: Education as the Practice of Freedom* (New York: Routledge, 1994), 154.
7. Larson is clear to note that these are not fixed tenets, for feminist pedagogy must adapt to be effective since teaching never occurs in a vacuum of "fixed social and political conditions" (136). See her "The Necessity of Feminist Pedagogy in a Climate of Political Backlash," *Equity & Excellence in Education* 38, no. 2 (2005): 135–144.
8. Martha Copp and Sherryl Kleinman, "Practicing What We Teach: Feminist Strategies for Teaching about Sexism," *Feminist Teacher* 18, no. 2 (2008): 101–124 on 102, with citation omitted.
9. Ellen Carillo, "Feminist" Teaching/Teaching "Feminism," *Feminist Teacher* 18, no. 1 (2007): 28–40 at 33.
10. See, for example Crabbtree and Sapp, 134–135; and Kishimoto & Mwangi, "Critiquing the Rhetoric of 'Safety' in Feminist Pedagogy."

11. Bailey and Lee, "Women of Color in the Academy,"114.
12. While I understand that many women of color encounter resistance to their authority and leadership in the classroom, I do not believe that my being one of the two youngest faculty members and an Asian American woman was a key factor in some students' initial resistance to the process of creating the syllabus. The "model minority" myth is devastating to our community as a whole, but it actually works in my favor, as per the "Connie Chung" effect (i.e., perception of second-generation Asian American women as smart, articulate, and cultured). Moreover, since our institution is small, my students knew of my "pedigree" (i.e., education at elite colleges), my reputation as a "good" but "tough teacher," and the fact that I had been selected by the students to receive our institution's inaugural faculty teaching award the previous year.
13. The other assignment that I more or less required from them was a short paper to be completed within the first four weeks of class. I did so for two primary reasons: (1) my institution had been encouraging all faculty to institute some sort of graded assignment within the first six weeks of class, (2) I myself wanted to get a feel for the writing abilities of my students so I could be sure to provide additional help to those who might need it in assignments later to come.
14. Seymour, "The Interests of Full Disclosure," 187.
15. Seymour, 195.
16. Seymour, 190.
17. I should add that one of those three resisters ended up writing the most popular blog of the class (as measured by the number of views and comments), and told me later that she was embarrassed by her earlier recalcitrance. The other two submitted blog-like entries for our class eyes' only with no incident.
18. In addition to blogging, four-unit students would be writing one short paper in the first month of class on the ethics of care (10 percent), making one 15–20 presentation about a feminist organization or an issue of special importance to women (15 percent), writing a final term paper and all that entailed (submitting a prospectus beforehand, giving feedback on the prospecti of their peers, 57.5 percent) and actively participating in class (6 percent).
19. More specifically, they too would be writing a short paper on the ethics of care (10 percent) and would be assessed by their active participation in class (7.5 percent). But the three-unit students proposed to do a group wiki as one of their assignments (11 percent) as will be discussed in the next section, and then decided that each student in their cohort could choose two out of three of the following options for the remaining 60 percent of their grade: (1) make a 15–20 in-class presentation; (2) write a 10–15-page final paper and all that entailed; or (3) write three 2–4-page response papers (see note #19 for details of options #1 and #2).
20. Bailey and Lee, "Women of Color in the Academy," 115.
21. Crabtree and Sapp, "Theoretical, Political, and Pedagogical Challenges in the Feminist Classroom," 132.
22. Contrary to what Audre Lorde herself had represented for years, Mary Daly had in fact responded to Lorde's critique of her work—a fact confirmed by Audre Lorde's discovery of Daly's letter in Lorde's paper, with Daly's name written in the bottom corner in Lorde's handwriting. For more details, see Gina Messina Dysert's blog, "Mary Daly's Letter to Audre Lord," October 5, 2011, http://feminismandreligion.com/2011/10/05/mary-daly's-letter-to-audre-lorde/.
23. To be clear, every instructor at our institution must specify a series of "student learning objectives," though it is up to the discretion of each instructor to determine what these will be. The students accepted what I had proposed as they were, with no additions or revisions.
24. This is not to suggest that collaborative learning cannot take place in more traditional assignments, for students often study together in small groups prior to taking

tests. However, in contrast to traditional exams wherein individual performance is generally evaluated only once by authority figures (teaching assistants and/or instructors), each student's identification and definition of a key term in the wiki would be evaluated successively by multiple peers as their classmates offered their own corrections or other modifications of the initial contribution.

25. Ibid.
26. Larson, "The Necessity of Feminist Pedagogy in a Climate of Political Backlash," 143.
27. Seymour, "The Interests of Full Disclosure," 200.

Part III

Embodiment and Technology

15 Inter-cendent Bodies

A Study of Cyborgs, Relational Theo/alogy, and Multiple Embodiment in 21st-Century Gaming

Sara M. Frykenberg

July 26th, 2011, 10:43 a.m.:

> The Lady Sheogorath has not forsaken thee! She is instead, looking for amber matrices in the Shivering Isles . . . wondering why she can't get her minions to do this while she lazes about and watches dances provided for her entertainment . . . or [better yet] summon Haskil just because she feels like it.

I posted this message on Facebook after completing the main quest for the *Shivering Isles* expansion pack to Bethesda and 2K Games' 2006 *Elder Scrolls IV: Oblivion*. I hesitate to use the word "complete," however, when describing any game-play related to *Oblivion*. The *Elder Scrolls* is a massive gaming franchise, incorporating five games and several game expansions and is currently working toward the launch of *The Elder Scrolls Online* a MMORPG (Massively Multiplayer Online Role Playing Game).[1] Hailed for its immensity, diversity, and complexity, *Oblivion* won the Spike Video Games Award for Game of the Year in 2006. A critic from VGPub reviewed the game saying, "If Morrowind [Elder Scrolls III] defines the non-linear RPG genre, Oblivion adds clarity to that definition."[2] The game's main quest is only a small fragment of the gaming experience: side quests and repeat options keep gamers interested for much longer.

The *Shivering Isles* expansion pack adds even greater diversity to the non-linear adventure, allowing players to enter into "The Land of Madness": the realm of the Daedric Lord Sheogorath, the "god" of madness. Daedra are supernatural beings, who like the children of the Babylonian goddess Tiamat, were born from the blood spilt in a battle between primordial deities.[3] Players are eventually asked to assume the role of Lord or Lady Sheogorath to maintain balance in the Daedric cosmology. The player becomes the mad god or goddess, earning the reverence of the deity's minions and gaining the ability to manipulate weather in the Land of Madness. All of which means very little in terms of actual game play, since I still have to find my own amber matrices and other precious alloys in order to upgrade and build new armor.

I shared this success on Facebook and received the obligatory "you go girl" from fellow gamers. More surprisingly and to my delight, my non-gaming friends also "liked" the fantasy goddess image provided by the *Oblivion*-inspired post. I was proud of this new identity because it was both earned and something I chose to become. First, I chose my character's image: her body shape, racial identity, and profession(s), as well as specific coloring for her skin, hair, tattoos, and clothing. I also decided how I would proceed in this quest by joining one faction rather than another and by selecting particular strategies in my ever-changing role. I even had to choose to accept the role of goddess. However, I also had to reach certain proficiency within the game and defeat a specified series of quests in order to be given the option for goddess-hood at all—the game itself limits the choices I am allowed to make. Posting my achievement on Facebook, I then expanded this identity, opening very different dialogues in different communities. Overall, my post highlights several aspects of my relational experience: (1) my relationship to the game itself, (2) a conversation between gamers sharing the experience of a common gaming platform, (3) a social relationship to power and deification, and (4) my existential relationship to Facebook; not to mention my relationship to technology, race, class, gender, sexuality, economy, and economic reproduction, as well as the physical and non-physical aspects of experience.

My identity is constructed in multiple physical, discursive, and cyber realities, as the post illustrates. Humankind is no longer simply living on the boarders of cyber-reality in the technological world of the 21st century. We[4] human cyber-technology users may already be the cyborgs that Donna Haraway describes as "the offspring of implosions of subjects and objects and of the natural and artificial."[5] The gamer-player/ gamer-avatar identity is more like kin to this implosive identity: a different figuration that involves simultaneous embodiments and inter-be-ing. The question is what does this mean for feminist cosmology in the cyber-technology-using world? How do we begin to articulate the kind of embodiment created by technologically mediated social realities and the social reality of video games in particular?

It is my contention that when we consider video games through the lens of feminist theology and process philosophy, we will find that these are "real" spaces where living (part)icipants interact to form important aspects of identity. The embodiment of the gamer-player/ gamer-avatar is inter-cendent. It is both like and unlike a god/dess, sliding between divinity and distinctively non-divine characteristics in a parody of power and limitation. And it is this parody that makes video gaming particularly significant when considering feminism, religion, and technology in the 21st century. The gamer-player/ gamer-avatar's ability to mock and mimic, to embody and simultaneously, question the validity of an embodiment, gives it a transformative potential often overlooked by feminist theorists.

Feminist Cosmology and Digital Technology

Video gaming, both console gaming and online gaming, is an interesting example of the intersectional or existentially in-between space suggested by many feminist relational theologians and thealogians. Both video gaming and feminist process theology and thealogy suggest that "I" am not the static and stable reality that I imagine myself to be. Carol Christ's Harshornian-inspired process and feminist philosophy of religion[6] suggest that be-ings are always liminal, which is to say, never in one, static place and always engaged in an in-between way. "Change is:" change is an intrinsic part of human and creaturely identity because of life's inherent relationality and relationship to temporal, limited space. "Touch [also] is." We are affected by and affecting other creatures.[7]

Christ asserts, "to a greater or lesser degree, all individuals, including human beings, other animals, cells, atoms, and particles of atoms, exercise creative freedom."[8] Her definition here expands upon more narrow definitions of life, or more accurately, definitions of *significant* life, given in classical Christian theology in order to account for the "touch" inherent to relational cosmology. Using this cosmological understanding to describe cyber and digital realities, I suggest we add those elements or entities that Haraway calls cyborgs to Christ's list of creative agents. The "seed, chip, gene, data-base, bomb, fetus, race, brain, and ecosystem,"[9] to a greater or lesser degree, exercise creative freedom. The image created by Christ's thealogy is one of constant movement, genesis and interaction. An amalgam of particles swirls, perhaps harmoniously, perhaps agonistically, into one creation and then another, like the digital pixels of an RPG's changing landscape. The world is made up of multiple relationships and types of agents all affecting one another in a process worldview, just as it is in cyber-technologically created worlds.

If my identity is constantly changing, affected and affecting other be-ings, then it follows that my body is also constituted in multiple relationships. The physical body is "touched" by time, other physical bodies, emotional energy, thought, technology, etc. Emphasizing the body as an important place of knowledge, Christ's thealogy intentionally reinvests value and meaning into this partial, changeable, and limited form, simultaneously affirming its multiplicity.[10] On the one hand, she disclaims the idea that the body (and so female) is somehow less than spirit is wrong because it is "imperfect," or even evil. At the same time, Christ describes embodiment as an "irreducible continuum,"[11] between mind and body: a facet of being that is limited, relational, feeling, changing, physical, mental, and spiritual. Bodies change. Bodies pass away—but this isn't just "ok" or a burden we have to bear. On the contrary, Christ's work suggests that there is something about the body's limitation and changeable reality that is implicitly enjoyable.[12] The gamer-player/ gamer-avatar embodies this limited temporal enjoyment.

Video gaming can be understood as a highly visible form of relational embodiment, both because the gamer is engaged in a visually depicted cyber-reality and because while engaging that reality, the gamer is also physically present in a non-cyber world. The gamer's body is in-between in an obvious way. Online gamers play with other human beings or player characters (PCs) in virtual environments, interacting within chosen bodies (avatars) and with non-player characters (NPCs) generated by the computer. The gamer-player/

gamer-avatar is also physically engaged in both worlds, via keyboard, controller, and even the way in which some controllers are designed to shake or move in response to particular game stimulus.

Furthermore, the limitations of many games ensure that play time is extensive, but also temporary, and thoroughly enjoyable.[13] Psychological researcher's Przyblski and Ryan state, "Most players play because they find the activity itself to be interesting and enjoyable," noting, "conditions that enhance a person's sense of autonomy and competence support this intrinsic motivation, whereas factors that diminish perceived autonomy and competence undermine intrinsic motivation."[14] Successful agency motivates game play and impacts the enjoyment of a game. I like playing *Oblivion*. I perceive that I can do so successfully: a perception enhanced by my earned identity, Lady Sheogorath. Yet, this identity is only significant by virtue of its complex relationality to game play, community and the limitations of the game itself.

The relationality of the gamer-player/ gamer-avatar manifests in literally, more than one "place" at a time: in the physical space of Earth, the cyber or digital space created by humankind, as well as in the "place" of identity. Peculiarly relational, this embodiment constitutes the interconnection common to much feminist theo/alogy in a physical, psychological, and visual way. Illustrative, then, of the kind of in-between that relational theo/alogy describes, the gamer-player/ gamer-avatar may be capable of raising consciousness regarding feminist and relational cosmology. Like it or not, relational feminist theo/alogy plays out in video gaming worlds in such a way as to make inter-relationship an easily accessible[15] idea for those in the cyber-technology using world. One simply has to turn on the console and start playing.

However, video games also encapsulate the relational tension of being in-between in society that is largely oppressive. The "easy access" to a video game already assumes a social class and the global politics that give some nations access to a cyber-technology that is dependent on the labor and oppression of other nations. A literal product (of the gaming industry, Western capitalism, social constructs, etc.), the video game is created within what might be understood as an abusive cultural paradigm of domination within cyber-technology-using worlds. Video games' relational potential is mediated by their closeness (their close relationship) to an exploitative and oppressive dominant meaning system.

The Challenge of Social Media and Technology

The gamer is not on the fringe of embodying multiple and, perhaps, contradictory identities. They are already doing so; and therefore, I contend that the video gaming world is uniquely capable of illustrating and communicating the kind of liminal existence Christ's process philosophy describes. Yet video games are often criticized as juvenile, unreal fantasies that are, at best, a waste of time or a temporary escape, and, at worst, addictive mechanisms for the reproduction of societal oppression and violence. Many of these critiques are warranted.

Games like *Mass Effect* and *Call of Duty* often re/present the hyper-masculine apocalyptic[16] hero. Facing immanent danger, *Halo*'s Master Chief is clad in head-to-toe body armor. Norah Campbell describes this phenomenon in her article *Future Sex: Cyborg Bodies and the Politics of Meaning*. She states, "It is in computer games that the future masculine is most often presented, establishing the fantasy of armored impenetrability that is striking because of its overwhelming invariability."[17] Many video games, *invariably*, require that we embody masculinity as unmovable and ready for violence. The static and protected self is exaggerated in such images: a superlative representation that, ironically, may or may not be equipped to conquer or win in the "end of the world" scenario presented by the game. To complete quests, the seemingly untouchable hero will have to die many times. He or she must "level," or gain experience and corresponding power-ups to complete the game and even indi-vidual quests. The god-like body is more like a parody of god; because death-lessness in video games is only achieved through one's ability to die many, many times (or by contrast, the gamer-player's ability to cheat the system).

Campbell also suggests that cyborg re/presentations of the female or femi-nine tend to reify "a hegemonic gender dialectic."[18] Linda Eklund of Stock-holm University echoes this sentiment. In her study of eight Swedish female gamers playing *World of Warcraft* (WoW), an MMORPG by Blizzard Enter-tainment, Eklund suggests that the game was constructed with a heteronorma-tive bias. She writes, "in *WoW* our bodies are in a way performed for us. Their looks, hair, voice, body language have all been pre-programmed into a gender-stereotyped role clearly based on a heterosexual expectancy."[19] She goes onto describe character "/dance:" a common social function in MMORPG's. "The female dances are more enticing, sensual and in some instances purely sexual. Male characters' dances are more fun and even though many of them allude to sex with thrusting motions, it is so in an active way."[20] This herterosexual-ized behavior translates into player relationships, as well. Eklund explains that female characters that male characters perceive to be female online *and offline* are more likely to receive help, which study participants indicated was a useful tool in game play.[21] Furthermore, the study found that Eurocentric racial char-acteristics often motivated character selection. Eklund states that more overall players (not just those in the study) preferred "good-looking" avatars from the Alliance, one of the two factions to which players can belong—the *human* fac-tion, whereas they tended not to choose characters from the Hoard, ogre-like characters that are depicted as culturally "other" avatars with "coarser, tougher looking appearances."[22]

Admitting the racism, sexism, and heterosexism built into many games and "cyborg" images, both authors conclude that these techno-bodies also have a complicated potential to subvert such oppressive realities. Campbell's analysis suggests that technology muddles who we see as "other" altogether because of its ability to expose differences or diversity. She suggests that "otherness" is constituted by, "almost humans that use technology to threaten the Western border of traditional liberal humanness."[23] The multiplicity of difference itself, embodied in a gamer and exposed in technologically created spaces, becomes the threat Campbell refers to here.

The gamer-player creates an avatar from a variety of options in many RPGs. Selections may include race (human and non-human "races" are often available), profession, skin color, sex, astrological or mystical sign, body characteristics (height of cheek bones, eyebrow thickness and placement, lip shape, eye shape, etc.), tattoos, makeup, and even personality characteristics, among other choices. Avatar development is based solely on player choice and game construction, not the gamer-player's physical body. For example, a cis-gendered, Caucasian female might choose a male avatar that is a "dark elf," with green skin and white hair. The gamer-player/ gamer-avatar may embody difference, and, so, challenge expected standards because he, she, or they simply are what they also are not (while also not entirely *being* this chosen identity either). The gamer-player/ gamer-avatar is also both human and something other than human: human, a player, an avatar, and a part of the game program itself. Campbell's analysis suggests that this cyborg-ery challenges notions of a concrete and knowable "other." Gamers do not always know the supposed "real" identity of whom they are playing with. Therefore, arguably, cyber-technology *users* (or perhaps a better word for this is: interact-ers) too are a part of what is "other." The fear of technology is both an apocalyptic one, and one of the abject. It challenges the boundaries of who we are, while also evoking a fear of losing what it means to be human in the hybridization of the techno-biological world.

The potential for this disruption of categories is exemplified in a "technologized gaze" on the skin of the cyborg: "a gaze upon the female body that is both dispassionate and sexual."[24] Which is to say, as Campbell explains, we fetishize a hyper-sexualized female-cyborg, but this only precedes attention to her hyper-functionality.[25] Female avatar bodies (despite player choice and construction) usually fit into hyper-sexualized hetero-patriarchal fantasies. In fact, some games limit player choices to ensure that the archetypes are met. The Japanese game company Sting's 2007 *Dokapon Kingdom* limits female avatar selection (in Atlus's English release) to, "normal face," "sexy face," "selfish face," and "ditsy face."[26] However, the female avatar, fetishized as she is, is also extremely powerful. Her fantasy body is "hyper-functional": she is as prepared for the trials of the gaming environment as her armored male peers. Eklund's work elucidates this point further for video gaming.

Female characters and male characters have the same potential within *WoW*:[27] they can achieve the same levels and corresponding power despite traditional aesthetic gendering and female sexualization. In fact, Eklund's work suggests that there is not only an opportunity for the disruption of dominating meaning systems in video games, but there is also potential to create gender-queer *affirming* space. This occurs in those instances where the gamer-player/ gamer-avatar assumes those identities that he, she, or they (to borrow a gender-queer multiple identification from the LGBTQQIAA community) would be chastised for in the offline, out of game world.[28] The gamer-player/ gamer-avatar can be whom he, she, or they chose to be within limitation, embodying their own autonomy and even otherness. This is illustrated by the high regularity of gender swapping within games. Euklund notes, "there are more female avatars than female gamers" in *WoW*, and these female avatars "often have roles according to traditional roles of femininity."[29] In other words, many male players are performing cis-gendered femininity through their avatars. Furthermore, gender flopping is "normalized" in the game environment, even if only as an "aesthetic option."[30] Gamer-players do not expect gamer-avatars they meet to "match" the corresponding players. Another example of the slow disruption of the dominant meaning system can be seen in the 2012 release of *Guild Wars* 2, an MMORPG by ArenaNet. Character "/dance" in this game is distinctively more gender neutral and desexualized than in *WoW*, although the game does not escape a heavy racial and gendered aesthetic quality.

These disruptions might not be what one thinks of as the "justice-making" that theologians and thealogians such as Carol Christ, Carter Heyward, and Marjorie Suchocki describe as mutuality or shared well-being. However, it is my contention that they are a part of the work this justice making requires. The in-between-ness of video games captures the spirit of what Catherine Keller calls "counter-apocalypse." The disruption almost parallels oppression (it is in close relationship to it), but it also helps to alter the trajectory of meaning. The particular technological embodiment of the gamer-player/gamer-avatar, a multiple identity, has the potential to,

> [Provide] a shifting ground against which the refigurations and disfigurations of apocalypse may appear—toward the end of prefiguring a subjectivity, or intersubject, capable of entertaining their conceptual interaction.[31]

This identity is a fluid space in which we engage oppressive constructions of embodiment, while also gaining the active ability to refigure and disfigure this embodiment. It distorts the meaning system or expectation that is attached to oppressive symbols. The prefiguration Keller suggests above occurs as we change the very category human in the cyber-technology-using world. But critical to both counter-apocalypse and the potential impact of a gamer-player/ gamer-avatar's disruptive embodiment is that neither power is too far separated from the existent (oppressive) meaning system. If they were, they would be unable to "entertain [this system's] conceptual interaction." The gamer-player/ gamer-avatar is in close relationship with the abusive paradigms of society, but it is this closeness that gives the embodiment its transformative potential. The gamer-player/ gamer-avatar embodies the abuse paradigm while also embodying its "other." It is and is not: it is a representative and its negation.

Matters of Embodiment

The discourse of technology and body in many feminist circles often revolves around the members of what Donna Haraway calls her "menagerie of figurations,"[32] including the cyborg, the OncoMouse (who is a patented cyborg), the FemaleMan, the vampire, the primate, and the Modest_Witness, among others. As more and less than kin[33] to humanity, the cyborg and the other misfit toys, the gamer-player/ gamer-avatar shares commonalities with these figurations. For example, he, she or they share a common characteristic with the OncoMouse. The OncoMouse is "an invented animal that has been patented."[34] The gamer-player/ gamer-avatar similarly, has a complex relationship to patenting. Only particular parts of this in-between identity represent creative engineering that can be regulated and owned, such as the controller or other hardware, or particular aspects of game play. However, debates rage as to how appropriate these ownership laws are and whether or not anyone pays attention to them, particularly when patents seek to control techniques or the flow of ideas.[35] Furthermore, the human aspect of this player is a non-patented being engaging in what are created, scripted, and copyrighted categories of interaction.

Eklund's research highlights the scripted nature of video game play. She writes, "*WoW* is a game, created by Blizzard, who has created rules about who you can be and what you can do in the game."[36] On the one hand, this is very true. I can become a goddess when I play *Oblivion*; but I still have to build my own armor. Actually, I have to first collect the amber matrices that are used to build armor, then hand them over to the one particular non-player character who constructs light armor, and finally pay him[37] to build what I need. My abilities within the game are limited to the scope of its construction. On the other hand, this earned identification takes on new meaning in other relationships. Gaming often becomes an "internalized"[38] aspect of identity. That is to say, the identity I create within a game is significant to me. It becomes a part of how I see myself inside and outside of the gaming world. Overall, it is the gamer-player who ultimately gives video gaming its transformative potential in Eklund's view. She asserts that the game itself is "nothing but dead pixels"[39] without a human player. However, where Eklund considers gaming in terms of human autonomy, other theorists use Haraway's cyborg theories to suggest the video game itself is also a relational entity of some kind. Drawing from Christ's process thealogy, we might also say, the video game itself is in some sense alive. Author Seth Giddings suggests that the game and its corresponding components are actually all part(icipants) in the experience.[40]

Giddings states that, "human game players are *acted on* as much as they act, they must work out what the machine wants them to do (or what it will allow them to do) as well as engage with it imaginatively," concluding that, "neither agency or behavior can be restricted to the human participants here."[41] He situates the video gamer firmly in the realm of Haraway's cyborg, while paying his respects to the idea that to be a cyborg is to be a boundary crosser.[42] The mechanical and biological are connected and both influencing one another, and, significantly, resultant creations are neither fully human nor fully machine. Both the mechanical and biological have a stake in what happens within the world of video gaming.

Giddings also demonstrates the ways in which cyborg identity is tied to an overt relationship to temporality, change, and un-situated subjectivity. He states, "in the game 'I' is at once 'myself,' 'my avatar,' and 'myself and avatar;' a hybrid of human and technological identity."[43] I propose we add to this list, "I" is also a part of and yet separate from the games' part(icipants) themselves. Like human inter-actors, gamer-player/gamer-avatars, NPCs and/ or part(icipants) are all in relationship to one another. Giddings's response to this multiplicity of identification within the realm of the video game is to call for a new "microethology"[44] of gameplay that considers the various part(icipants), "without reinscribing humanist a priori distinctions between subject and object."[45] He critiques the theoretical bias for human autonomy in anthropological investigations of video gameplay, suggesting a research methodology capable of embracing the complex in-between identity of a cyborg or a gamer-player/gamer-avatar: microethology. He seems to suggest that we cannot give epistemological privilege to solely the human element in the cyber-technology using world. Therefore, the challenge of the video game to embodiment is that we cannot assume the human alone.

Haraway describes membership in her menagerie as being "a little bit like the Tarot card where you go in through different aspects. Not because you want to make some claim that this is the whole story but because it's an entry point."[46] I assert that the gamer-player/ gamer-avatar, as perhaps, *family* to her menagerie, also helps to tell a part of the story. It can be seen as another doorway to the exploration of this cyber-technological space of particularity, multiplicity, and in-betweenness. This particular form of embodiment could also be described as inter-cendent. It is neither transcendent of the physical world, nor is it totally situated within it. The gamer-player/ gamer-avatar is constructed and maintained by the rules of the game. Yet, he, she, they are also creatively autonomous within the game: choosing relationships, quests, appearance—and perhaps, even exploiting flaws within the game to gain a transcendent edge. The power of this particular kind of embodiment is what Haraway calls diffraction: "a narrative, graphic, psychological, spiritual, and political technology for making consequential meanings."[47] A mirror turns a quarter step. Instead of recreating what is in front of it, the looking glass avoids abusive re-genesis and the false homogeneity that dishonors inter-relationship. It redirects what we see.

Refraction is not an apocalypse of oppression or abusive paradigms. The embodiment of the gamer-player/gamer-avatar is not necessarily a safe space either;[48] it is often too close to abuse. But this in-between identity does use a kind of counter-power. It inter-cendently challenges the idea that humans are the center of the universe. He, she, and they are uniquely and apparently interrelational, representing relationship in diverse and playful creations and distortions. Video games and gamer-player/gamer-avatar embodiment can be transformative; and I would argue, video games are already starting to transform themselves.

Keller describes humankind as set upon suicidal self-"an/nihil/ation."[49] We are killing ourselves, recreating the nothingness or apocalypse after which we fashion our genesis.[50] Process theology tells us that we are in need of relationship, diffraction, and counter-power, a force that Keller calls: "capable of grounding, like lightning rods the theory, after-effects of apocalypse."[51] When handling lightning as a gamer-player/gamer-avatar in this Land of Madness, there is no body I want more than that of a Daedric goddess who's earned the right to manipulate the weather.

Notes

1. "Welcome to the Official The Elder Scrolls Online Community," October 15, 2012, www.elderscrollsonline.com/en/news/post/2012/10/15/welcome-to-the-official-the-elder-scrolls-online-community.
2. VG Pub, 2006, www.metacritic.com/game/xbox-360/the-eleder-scrolls-iv-oblivion/ciritc-reviews.
3. BoazMoerman, "Daedra," October 27, 2012, http://elderscrolls.wikia.com/wiki/Daedra.
4. "We" in this case refers to those human beings whose social location gives them direct access to (and often dependence on) technology. Many researchers, including Donna Haraway and Jenifer Gonzales, have recognized that this social location is often reliant on the subordination of other human beings or earth-creatures (often, even those who are responsible for assembling and distributing technological components they do not have the economic privilege to access).
5. Donna J. Haraway, *Modest_Witness@Second_Millennium: FemaleMan_Meets_OncoMouse* (New York: Routledge, 1997), 12.
6. Carol Christ, *She Who Changes* (New York: Palgrave MacMillian, 2003), 13. Christ very clearly situates her work in philosophy of religion, rather than theology or thealogy here, making her intention to describe reality in general explicit. Differentiating between theology and thealogy that "remains with a particular community," Christ's philosophy attempts to, "speak of meanings and values that are fundamental and basic in life."
7. Christ, *She Who Changes*. "Change is," and "Touch is," are names of book chapters in this text.
8. Ibid., 45.
9. Haraway, *Modest_Witness@Second_Millennium,* 12.
10. Christ, *She Who Changes*.
11. Ibid., 56.
12. Ibid. Christ discusses enjoyment and its relationship to body, women, and deity in the chapter "Life Is Meant to Be Enjoyed," 115–141.
13. Game-players who weighed in on the site www.gamefaqs.com estimated playing between 100 to 500 hours, playing *Oblivion* and each of its prequels. However, some players reported up to 3,500 to 5,000 hours of game play for these games.
14. Andrew Przybylski and Richard Ryan, "The Motivating Role of Violence in Video Games," *Personality and Social Psychology Bulletin* 35 (2009): 243, http://psp.sagepub.com/content/35/2/243, 244.
15. I am defining accessibility here in terms of what it takes to actually play a game in the "cyber-technology world": you push a button, point the controller, and play inter-relationship. However, I also would like to state here that accessibility to gaming technology itself is limited by social class and the global politics that mediate who and who does not have access to cyber-technology. This is an important justice issue. The cyborg is not a "better identity." It is simply one that illustrates particular relationships, and may be useful in a society that already preferences cyber-technology usage. The audience that this article hopes to reach is one that has access to and can be affected by video games.

16. I will clarify the video games' relationship to "apocalypse" later in the paper, using Catherine Keller's work on "counter-apocalypse."

17. Norah Campbell, "Future Sex: Cyborg Bodies and the Politics of Meaning," *Advertising and Society Review* 11, no. 1 (2010): 6.

18. Ibid.

19. Linda Eklund, "Doing Gender in Cyberspace: The Performance of Gender by Female World of Warcraft Players," *Convergence: The International Journal of Research into New Media Technologies* 17, no. 3 (2011): 336.

20. Ibid., 331–332.

21. Ibid., 332.

22. Ibid., 330.

23. Campbell, "Future Sex," 6.

24. Ibid., 10.

25. Ibid.

26. Male avatars in the game are given the choice of "normal face," "cool face," "mean face," and "enthused face."

27. Eklund, "Doing Gender in Cyberspace," 336. Eklund states, "[Study participants] underline the fact that female and male characters start off with the same conditions; there is no difference in game play or story for either sex. At the same time they mean that for gaming, sex has no influence on your level of mastery." The achievement components of *WoW* are not gender biased, which is itself a departure if not disruption of "offline" dominant meaning systems within Western patriarchal societies.

28. Ibid., 339.

29. Ibid., 327–328.

30. Ibid., 328.

31. Catherine Keller, *Apocalypse Now and Then* (Boston, MA: Beacon Press, 1996), 32–33.

32. Donna J. Haraway and T. N. Goodeve, *How Like a Leaf* (New York: Routledge, 2000), 135.

33. Haraway, *Modest_Witness@Second_Millennium*, 265. Haraway writes, "I believe that there will be no racial or sexual peace, no livable nature, until we learn to produce humanity through something more and less than kinship." It is my contention that the video gaming reality approaches this type of identification between human reproduction and its disruption by technology, like Haraway's other figurations.

34. Haraway, *How Like a Leaf*, 140.

35. Steve Chang and Ross Dannenberg, "The Ten Most Important Video Game Patents," *Gameasutra*. July 19, 2007, www.gamasutra.com/view/feature/130152/the_ten_most_important_video_game_php?page=1

36. Eklund, "Doing Gender in Cyberspace," 327.

37. The non-player character light armorer in the Land of Madness is physically male and non-human. The heavy armorer is physically female, also a non-human.

38. Eklund, "Doing Gender in Cyberspace," 326.

39. Ibid., 327.

40. Seth Giddings, "Events and Collusions: A Glossary for the Microethnography of Video Game Play," *Games and Culture* 4 (2009): 148.

41. Ibid., 151.

42. Ibid., 145.

43. Ibid., 146.

44. Ibid., 152. Giddings discusses ethology and ethnography in his piece; the former referring to the study of animal behavior, the later, human behavioral study. He advocates for a microethological view in order to avoid anthropocentrism in video game research.

45. Ibid., 155.

46. Haraway, *How Like a Leaf*, 138.
47. Ibid., 102.
48. I would argue, some games are "safe" places and actually designed to foster compassionate relationship between players. That Game Company's 2012 release *Journey* is a good example of this type of game.
49. Keller, *Apocalypse Now and Then*, 172.
50. Ibid.
51. Ibid., 32–33.

16 Broken Body, Virtual Body

Cyberfeminism and the Changing Goddess

Rachel Wagner and Sarah Scott

A woman, said Aristotle in *Generation of Animals*, is only produced through a "deviation," when "Nature has in a way strayed from the generic type." Other "monstrous" births, including ones with babies that look half-animal or appear with visible deformations, were for Aristotle more extreme forms of the same "deviation."[1] Womanhood, Rosi Braidotti argues, has been associated with the monstrous throughout history, such that misogyny in today's world "is not a hazard but rather the structural necessity of a system that can only represent 'otherness' as negativity."[2] Such "deviant" labeling can be seen today in the form of diagnostic assessments of feminine reproductive issues. Chronic pelvic pain is a "disorder." So is endometriosis, characterized by presumably "displaced" and "abnormal" tissue. The "inability" of a woman's body to produce eggs regularly is "ovarian failure." The term "hysterectomy" comes from the Greek *hystera*, for womb, such that a hysterectomy was an attempt to remove the womb in order to end "hysteria" and prompt a return to emotional stability.

Is it any wonder that one of the most important moves made by second-wave feminists was to represent the female body as an image of the divine Goddess? The self-conscious honoring of feminine bodily processes was a means of rejecting monstrous and damaging assessments of female embodiment and reclaiming a sense of connection with nature, with each other, with oneself. However, for the woman labeled as having "abnormal" uterine "dysfunction," it is hardly comforting to imagine the Goddess as a mother birthing the world, since images of the divine that rely on natural female functioning may be painful and alienating. This woman is considered "broken-bodied," and yet seeks, like all women, a sense of belonging in the larger community of feminist practice.

In the 1990s, when third-wave feminists were just beginning to critique what they saw as normalizing tendencies in first-wave feminism, some turned to the emerging realm of cyberspace for new feminist perspectives. For these "cyberfeminists," going online offered a means of combating misogyny by transcending gender entirely through "a merging of body and technology."[3] In claiming to overcome the body completely, they reversed the materiality of Goddess feminism, replacing it with a Platonism that left the body behind. And yet, Goddess religion and cyberfeminism *both* fail to comfort the broken-bodied woman whose body can neither be easily inhabited in its material form nor be symbolically transcended in digital space. With this woman in mind, we look here for analogs for a new kind of expression that depends neither upon the embodied fertility of the Goddess nor upon disembodied cyborgian entry into virtual reality. In doing so, we look to elements of first-wave and second-wave feminism for analogs, offering glimpses of a new perspective that makes room for reproductive difference while encouraging celebration of full womanhood.

Goddess Religion

Marianne Ferguson traces what she sees as evidence of the Mother Goddess throughout many strands of ancient religious practice, from stone female fig-ures of the Paleolithic age in Europe to the Asherah of ancient Canaanite tra-dition.[4] For some feminists, these discoveries justified a reimagining of the creation myth. Instead of being depicted as a male Father God, the Goddess is seen a fertile motherly force, as Monica Sjoo demonstrates in her retelling,

> In the beginning, life did not gestate within the body of any creature, but within the ocean womb containing all organic life. There were no special-ized sex organs; rather, a generalized female existence reproduced itself within the female body of the sea. Before more complex life forms could develop and move onto land, it was necessary to miniaturize the oceanic environment, to reproduce it on a small and mobile scale. Soft, moist eggs deposited on dry ground and exposed to air would die . . . In the course of evolution, the ocean—the protective and nourishing space, the amniotic fluids, even the lunar-tidal rhythm—was transferred into the individual female body.[5]

Sjoo's imagery draws heavily on the symbolism of fecundity, directly relat-ing creation to feminine reproduction. Merlin Stone, too, argues that worship of the divine feminine predates patriarchal father gods, and she looks to a time when the "image of the woman who had been their most ancient, their primal ancestor and that image thereby [was] Deified and revered as Divine Ances-tress."[6] The Goddess is often depicted "as a symbol for all the creative, life-giving powers of the universe."[7] But such rich imagery may not appeal to those women who will never be able to experience labor and birth, who deal with the daily pain of endometriosis, the grief of sterility, and the terror of ovarian cancer. For the broken-bodied woman, these myths may be just as alienating as patriarchal myths, since neither offers a space in which she can imagine herself in the image of the divine.

Carol P. Christ describes a summer solstice ritual in which women "simu-lated a birth canal and birthed each other into their circle."[8] Such a ritual is less than affirming for the woman whose ovaries have been removed, for the transsexual woman who will never have children, for the woman with chronic pelvic pain. Instead of promoting what Christ sees as a "mood" of positive joyful "affirmation of the female body and the life cycle expressed in it," such rituals call attention to the very elements of embodied identity that cause the broken-bodied woman suffering.[9] Just as womanist theologians found much of early white feminism lacking because it neglected the particularized experiences of black women, so too the broken-bodied woman may find Goddess feminism's celebration of fertility a bitter reminder of her own marginalized identity. Might the answer be to forgo materiality altogether and celebrate fluidity of identity in digital spaces, where gender is invisible?

Cyberfeminism

For cyberfeminists, the Internet is a site for hybridity, fluidity, and virtual performance of identity, creating discursive spaces that challenge preconceived binaries of gender. Energized by the possibilities for new performances of gender, cyberfeminists VNS Matrix announce to patriarchal producers of Internet technology in 1996: "We are the malignant accident which fell into your system while you were sleeping. And when you wake we will terminate your digital delusions, hijacking your impeccable software." The Internet is the place where "truth evaporates" and where "nothing is certain [because] [t]here are no maps."[10]

With hopes built on digital hybridity, Donna Haraway issued her famous manifesto: "I'd rather be a cyborg than a goddess."[11] Yvonne Volkart explains that whereas traditional feminism incorporates new technologies simply as "tools for women's liberation," cyberfeminism actively "promotes both the idea of becoming cyborgian and the pleasures involved in it." For Volkart, the new technologies were "no longer perceived as prosthesis and instruments for liberation which are separated from the body," but as a "merging of body and technology." The "technological body" *itself* became the site for liberation.[12] In cyberspace, "identity is a game" and draws from "a data base of possible representations, which you can remix as you like."[13] For cyberfeminists, fluidity represents freedom.

In their "Cyberfeminist Manifesto for the 21st Century," VNX Matrix declares: "We are the modern cunt . . . unbounded unleashed unforgiving . . . we believe in jouissance madness holiness and poetry / we are the virus of the new world disorder / rupturing the symbolic from within / saboteurs of big daddy mainframe . . . infiltrating disrupting disseminating / corrupting the discourse."[14] By enacting fluid identities in digital space, cyberfeminists saw a means to disrupt received gender binaries through transformative performance. Cyberfeminism, however, relies on one's ability to transcend the body, a kind of Platonism paradoxically rooted in a physical body that must cooperate by facilitating use of keyboards, computer screens, and other digital interfaces. Cyberfeminism relies on a body that willingly recedes as one immerses oneself into an online environment, but for the broken-bodied woman, real physicality intrudes on digital identity. Fluid virtuality is restrained by the body's own obstinate, painful reminder that the user is female.

Both Goddess traditions *and* cyberfeminism rely on an ideal image of the female against which real women must measure themselves. Within Goddess traditions, real women are invited to embrace their identities only insofar as they "naturally" blend in with Earth's cycles. Within cyberfeminism, real women can become liberated cyborgs only insofar as their physically determined bodies are replaced with new, virtual, fluid bodies with gender-streaming qualities. Neither of these options offers a means for the sterile woman or the woman in pain to identify herself with a larger system that is meaningful. For such women, the particularity of the body is a constant reminder that there is no escape to divine or virtual realms. New rituals, new forms of mythic liberation, are required. So if neither traditional Goddess religion nor newer cyberfeminist traditions can offer the broken-bodied woman a place, what other analogs exist for self-affirmation? The feminist and womanist traditions do offer some hints of what a new self-understanding might resemble for the broken-bodied woman. We consider here three sets of analogs drawn from existing traditions: audacity, hybridity, and eroticism.

Audacity

Audacity is one mode of embracing embodiment. We consider here three powerful examples of feminist audacity to see how audacious women have moved beyond external judgment to acceptance of themselves. In Princess Diana, in Crone-dom, in Womanist wisdom, we find powerful insights for acceptance and celebration of the embodied self.

Princess Diana

One of the most well-known examples of an audacious icon is Princess Diana. The values typically associated with her include "compassion, love, and recognition of the primacy of the common people, particularly those who are rejected by mainstream patriarchal society."[15] Indeed, Diana's name evokes the ideal of the "world folk deity Diana—goddess of light and dark, queen of the witches as well as the gender variant, the protector of the poor, the imprisoned, the sick, and the historical challenger of patriarchal hegemony."[16] Jane Caputi admires Princess Diana's "'whorish' character and 'witchy' pursuits," even though they "have been attacked by religious advocates of the chastened female sexuality."[17]

Diana fought relentlessly for social change, especially in regard to homelessness, AIDs, drug abuse, and landmine removal. Nonetheless, when the marriage with Prince Charles failed, Diana was castigated and stripped of her titles. Mary Daly argues that because of her audacity, Diana was "betrayed, mistreated, abused, chased by the paparazzi, and [finally] killed."[18] One life-giving audacious response to Diana's own audacity, says Caputi, would be to "[h]onor the queen within, naming, and claiming this powerful icon of power, transformation, and healing."[19] However, contemporary "female divinity" should not be confined to "illuminated lives" like Diana's, but should also be "recognized as most at home in the colonized, impoverished, exiled, caged, enslaved, raped, denigrated, and denied beings of the world—the gynocentric, the butch, the queer, the dark, the aged, the elemental, the common."[20] Diana is a goddess figure that even the broken-bodied woman can emulate through a refusal to let herself be defined by others, through the audacious embodiment of unexpected femininity, and through a commitment to social change.

Crone-dom

In Goddess traditions, womanhood is honored in the "triple goddess," described as "the triple aspect of youth, maturity, and age, or maiden, mother, and crone."[21] The Crone is pictured as a "wise old woman" whose "closeness to her own death gives her a distance and perspective on the problems of life."[22] The Crone is wise, a "healing hag" who is deeply in touch with nature."[23] The Crone and the broken-bodied woman both occupy a space outside the idealization of the Goddess as mother. However, the broken-bodied woman may not be close to death at all, and may identify more readily with the maiden or the mother if these are her chronological peers.

Unlike an aged Crone, the young infertile woman does not have a lifetime of experience behind her, and neither is she an expert at healing roots and herbs. Similarly, the middle-aged broken-bodied woman may be grieving infertility, experiencing the heartache of invasive medical procedures attempting to "repair" her broken body. Maidens and mothers with broken bodies may still be thwarting "natural" processes through the therapeutic use of birth control pills or hormonal treatments, with the hope of diminishing physical pain. For such women, Crone-like identity is a complex matter, since the celebration of womanly wisdom is welcome, but the grief of being unable to choose fertility can be immense.

Daly offers comfort here. A woman becomes a Crone not "merely by chronological age," but "as a result of Surviving early stages of the Otherworld Journey and therefore having dis-covered depths of courage, strength, and wisdom in her Self."[24] Embracing Crone-hood can be a profound mark of self-empowerment. A Crone has learned to "govern" and to "steer" her life, to pilot "the vehicles of our voyage" which may consist of "any creative enterprises that further women's process."[25] Daly calls every woman to be a "stunning, beauteous Crone, one who inspires revulsion from phallic institutions and morality," and embraces her own intrinsic glory.[26] Donna Wilshire tells us that Crones are "famous for their laughter." They are "experienced, confident, full of secret knowledge, with nothing to lose." Crones "get away with being raucous, brazen, bold" and "do not always feel bound by manners or tradition." Crones "thumb their noses" at others' opinions of them and "spin their own ways" as they "cackle" with joy.[27] The Crone's self confidence can be claimed anytime by any woman of any age, including the "broken-bodied" woman.

Daly calls on women—whatever kind of body they are in—to recover "Elemental reality" by "[b]reaking out of tame/tracked modes of thinking and feeling."[28] Daly reminds us that "courage" is derived from the Latin *cor*, for heart. Courage, then, "signifies a heartfelt, passionate strength."[29] The broken-bodied woman who embraces Crone-dom can be "fiery" and "Volcanic," a kind of "Nemesis" that is "built up by inspired acts of Righteous Fury."[30] "Righteous Rage" allows a Crone to "drink deeply of Wild elements and thrive, grow."[31] Daly invites us to celebrate "Quintessence," "the unifying Living Presence that is at the core of the Integrity and Elemental connectedness of the Universe."[32] This fierce celebration can be healing for the broken-bodied woman, who can find in Crone-dom an appreciation of female embodiment that does not rely on physical fertility.

Womanism. Womanists of the past three decades have repeatedly and powerfully exposed that white patriarchy has not made sufficient room for black female suffering, or acknowledged black women's strengths. Responding to a history of slavery and oppression, womanists refuse to be broken by a painful past. As Alice Walker asserts, to act womanish is to exhibit "outrageous, audacious, courageous, or willful behavior." It is "wanting to know more and in greater depth than is considered 'good' for one." To be "womanish" is also to love other women "sexually and/or nonsexually" with an appreciation for "women's culture, women's emotional flexibility . . . and women's strength."[33] It may also involve defying the heterosexual stereotypes of earlier modes of feminism, the same stereotypes that assume that motherhood is the ideal expression of femininity. The broken-bodied woman may find in womanism the courage to think differently, to love herself fully, and to define belonging in community in ways that allow acceptance and love of the body she has been given.

Emilie Townes asks us to remember, "everything we do is mediated by our bodies."[34] This means that health "is not simply the absence of disease—it comprises a wide range of activities that foster healing and wholeness."[35] Townes proposes that we need a communal "ethic of care" that heals the "fracturings of the body" caused by racism, sexism, heterosexism, homophobia, and classism.[36] Townes describes "the everydayness of moral acts" that heal, including things like real, focused attention to what others are saying; being loyal and reliable; and taking leadership responsibilities seriously. All of these together comprise "the everydayness of getting up and trying one more time to get our living right"[37] The broken-bodied woman is similarly invited to reject the "fracturings" of patriarchal labels associated with her body, and to enact belonging within a lived community focused on health and nurture.

Monica Coleman uses Christian language to argue that salvation is "participation in a community that 'makes a way out of no way.'"[38] Salvation "fits into a unified view of the world, and yet it is also gritty, localized, and contextual," discovered "in the concrete experiences of this world." Not a transcendent otherworldly thing, instead salvation "must always look, feel, and taste like something."[39] For the broken-bodied woman, salvation may look like the "gritty" acceptance of a fully lived body, allowing the concreteness of real experience to take form within a loving space of progress and hope.

Kelly Brown Douglas, writing about the deep damage caused by racist portrayals of black sexuality, also finds hope in embodied humanity. For Douglas, black sexuality is affirmed through the theological embodiment of God in human form. Bodies are essential for the fulfillment of God's love in human history. To "be like Jesus" requires that we enact relationships "that are liberating, healing, empowering, and life-sustaining."[40] The broken-bodied woman, no matter her heritage, may find comfort in the argument that even her body is affirmed as a sign of God's ongoing love. For Delores Williams, the Exodus metaphor of the wilderness suggests that human initiative is "essential" for the work of liberation in "structuring a positive quality of life for family and community."[41] In the wilderness story, "consciousness and struggle" were associated with "maintaining freedom" after leaving Egypt.[42] The broken-bodied woman will find here an incarnational insistence that the human community can offer healing and hope by acting as agents of God's love in the world. As bell hooks puts it, we should "take woman to the self as the starting point for politicization" and "to think only me—my body—I constitute a universe—all that truly matters."[43] In such a universe, even the broken-bodied woman belongs, a status that paradoxically heals her by dismissing with the very notion of brokenness.

Drawing on womanism to develop her own womanist eco-spiritual epistemology, Pu Xiumei emphasizes womanist values of connectedness but extends these to the world at large, acknowledging a deep "oneness between humankind and nature." Xiumei proposes, "We need a new way of relating to nature" that calls attention to our shared purpose. For Xiumei, we "have to realize that we are part of nature and each corporeal body is natural."[44] For the broken-bodied woman, this symbolic return to connectedness is in some ways purer than earlier manifestations of Goddess religion. Instead of requiring each human body to mimic the divine, the divine *itself* is viewed as the association of *all* human bodies—as they *are*. The universe should be viewed as "a network" in which every single thing "has its own purpose."[45]

Women who are not themselves womanists must be conscientious not to negate the uniqueness of each womanist's personal suffering. Williams asserts that womanist theology "branches off in its own direction, introducing new issues and constructing new analytical categories," but that it is also "non-separatist and dialogical." Womanist theology "opposes all oppression based on race, sex, class, sexual preference, physical disability and caste."[46] The purpose of womanism is "to exchange ideas, enlarge definitions and concepts and plan political strategies."[47] The broken-bodied woman, then, may find solidarity with womanist objections to *all* modes of subjugation, and enjoy womanist celebration of embodied self in community.

Hybridity

We lift up four modes of hybridity here as analogs for the broken-bodied woman: gender as performance, lesbianism, cyborgianism, and the monstrous. Some of the modes of feminist hybridity we consider here call attention to the particularized body, but others celebrate nonmateriality. All of these modes of hybridity consider the ways that identity can inhabit in-between spaces, manifesting itself in particularized performances of fluidity.

Gender as Performance

Judith Butler notes in *Gender Trouble* that like other modes of identity, gender is "constructed" and performed—and as such, we should ask if it could be "constructed differently."[48] Those elements of feminist practice that depend on celebration of the female body, then, may be threatened by gender performativity: "Contemporary feminist debates over the meanings of gender lead time and time again to a certain sense of trouble, as if the interdeterminacy of gender might eventually culminate in the failure of feminism."[49] The term *woman*, says Butler, "fails to be exhaustive," since "gender intersects with racial, class, ethnic, sexual, and regional modalities of discursively constituted identities"[50] The broken-bodied woman, then, performs gender in her own particularized, and particularly valuable, way.

Gender is one of the ways that we impose order: "Gender is the repeated stylization of the body, a set of repeated acts within a highly rigid regulatory frame that congeal over time to produce the appearance of substance, of a natural sort of being."[51] Butler's work on gender performance includes a critique of "the binary frame," the "compulsory and naturalized heterosexuality" accomplished "through the practices of heterosexual desire."[52] Using the example of hermaphrodite Herculine Barbin as described in the journals of Foucault, Butler argues that identity is sometimes erased by the requirement of binary gender performance, just as Herculine "occasions a convergence and disorganization of the rules that govern sex/gender/desire."[53] Gender "is always a doing."[54] If gender is performance, then any woman—whether she can have children or not—has the right to be a woman if she chooses so. Transsexual women, women who don't have sex, women with no ovaries, women with hysterectomies—all have the right to define themselves as they see fit.

Lesbianism

Adrienne Rich criticizes the "bias of compulsory heterosexuality, through which lesbian experience is perceived on a scale ranging from deviant to abhorrent, or simply rendered invisible."[55] Lesbian existence has been "written out of history or catalogued under disease; partly because it has been treated as exceptional rather than intrinsic."[56] Calling for greater awareness of many modes of self-chosen identity, Rich draws on Audre Lorde to argue that "as we deepen and broaden the range of what we define as lesbian existence . . . we begin to discover the erotic in female terms as that which is unconfined to any single part of the body or solely to the body itself."[57]

Lesbianism can be seen as a source of joy. However, Butler suggests that the too-easy assumption by some in the 1980s that lesbianism was the perfect expression of feminism is misinformed. For Butler, lesbianism "does not represent a return to what is most important about being a woman," nor does it "consecrate femininity or signal a gynocentric world."[58] But in every case, lesbianism is an enactment of self-identity with a self-negotiated relationship to the feminine. In a similar vein, then, women of *all* sexual orientations who do not conform to idealized models of the feminine can argue for a renewed sense of the erotic that borrows from Rich's celebration of self.

Cyborgianism

Whereas the optimism in cyberfeminism of the 1990s hasn't exactly panned out, the notion itself still inspires some feminists. Braidotti embraces a technologically informed feminism that makes room for more forms of embodiment when she notes that "what . . . we go on calling, quite nostalgically 'our bodies, ourselves,' are abstract technological constructs fully immersed in advanced psycho-pharmacological industry, bio-science and the new media."[59] The flipside of caution about commodified, technologized bodies are those bodies that are appreciated *even though* they are dependent on commodified pharmaceuticals for managing pain, bodies subjected to surgeries for life-saving purposes, bodies transformed through self-elected transsexual processes to become more authentic. It is with this need for materialized bodily recognition that Braidotti urges that in cyberspace, "Transcendence as disembodiment would just repeat the classical patriarchal model, which consolidated masculinity as [an] abstraction, thereby essentializing social categories of 'embodied others.'" [60] We should intentionally remain aware of our physical bodies, even when online, celebrating embodied womanhood as a distinctive experience, since "the last thing we need at this point in Western history is a renewal of the old myth of transcendence as flight from the body . . . a little less abstraction would be welcome."[61]

Evoking qualities associated elsewhere with the Crone, Volkart imagines the cyborg as "an ageless, naughty and unruled girl."[62] She uses the German term *widerspenstig* for the cyberfeminist cyborg, identifying her as "unruly," "untamed" and "stubborn," refusing to be "straightened out."[63] The *widerspenstig* reclaims "hysteria in all its manifestations" as an expression of self-determination.[64] The "wild" nature of Internet fluidity can be transferred into an audacious or womanish response *offline* as well.

The Monstrous

The 16th-century French surgeon Ambrose Pare so identified the female with the monstrous that sexuality itself was rendered a very dangerous activity: "All sexual practices other than those leading to healthy reproduction are suspected to be conducive to monstrous events."[65] The association between the feminine and the monstrous has not abated, with endless popular cultural allusions in film and other media to monstrous feminine figures, such as the femme fatale, the vamp, the Medusa, and witch.

A troubling contemporary portrait of the monstrous feminine shows up in Kanye West's 2001 music video, "Monster," in which we see vampiric, cloying women milling in the background, grasping hungrily at Kanye, draining him of money and energy as he forcefully deflects them.[66] Midway through the video, black female singer Niki Minaj appears, announcing: "First things first, I'll eat your brains; then Imma start rocking gold teeth and fangs, cause that's what a motherfuckin monster do."[67] Kanye himself remains physically unchanged, masculine and powerful, lying in bed with dead white women in a necrophiliac fantasy. One of the last lines in the song is the admission: "I crossed the line." In this violent patriarchal fantasy, he certainly did.

Braidotti observes with interest the "contemporary trend for borderline figures, especially replicants, zombies and vampires, including lesbian vampires and other queer mutants, who seem to enjoy special favor in these post-AIDS days."[68] Monsters represent our fear of the in-between, the non-binary, the fluid. The word "monster" is drawn from the Greek root *teras*, which means "both horrible and wonderful, object of aberration and adoration."[69] The "monstrous," then, like the Crone, is associated with liminality.[70]

The pop star known as Lady Gaga epitomizes the rejuvenation of the woman as "monstrous." Lady Gaga has cultivated a public practice of extravagance, flirting with homoeroticism and transsexualism, and lavished devotion on her fans, who she lovingly calls "Little Monsters." In her video "Born This Way" (2011), Gaga tells her own creation story. Identifying herself symbolically with the goddess who breeds "monsters" in the Mediterranean creation myth called the *Epic of Gilgamesh*, Gaga has also borne "monsters" in the form of her fans. But whereas Gaga exhibits the same kind of audacity as the womanists, she refuses to situate herself or her body neatly within the "womanly" mode. Gaga seems to be saying that to be a "monster" is to be adored—that even those who don't belong, belong. Celebration of feminine sexuality alone isn't enough. Instead, liberation consists of the refusal to be externally defined. Acceptance of sexual ambiguity, of choice, of gender or sexual performance, is more natural than any fixed paradigm of gender identity. By making such an argument, however, Gaga condemns herself to permanent, and somewhat paradoxical, performance of subversion of expectations. Fluidity requires maintenance.

Eroticism

When most people think of the "erotic," they think first of heterosexual passion. But as Starhawk points out, to celebrate the erotic only in heterosexual forms is to "relegat[e] other sorts of attraction and desire to the position of deviant" and "makes invisible the realities of lesbians, gay men, and bisexual people."[71] Starhawk argues that such a view "cuts us off, whatever our sexual preference, from the intricate dance of energy and attraction we might share with trees, flowers, stones, oceans, a good book or a painting, a sonnet or sonata, a close friend or a faraway star."[72] Starhawk's model of the erotic makes room for all women to celebrate their own bodies and their own innate energy of life.

bell hooks similarly argues that one of the most crucial aspects of contemporary feminism is "its demand that women revolt against standards of beauty that require females to embrace life-threatening habits of being."[73]

Lisa Isherwood makes explicit room for the erotic within traditions of celibacy, thus also making room for the broken-bodied woman for whom sex is too painful to experience. Calling for the "queering of heteropatriarchy," Isherwood argues that celibacy can be an "erotic" mode of resistance if it is reconceived as love of self and of sister, free of patriarchal control. Eros, says Isherwood, can offer women "a way of loving themselves and other women in a world which demands otherwise."[74] This activity is an example of what Jenny Marketou calls "cultural hacking," as "a syntax for resistance and critical discourse."[75] The erotic, as a mode of self-expressed productivity, a celebration of self-as-self, is a mode of cultural hacking that is the culmination of these analogs for the "broken" woman, since it nullifies the label of "broken" altogether.

Conclusion

The gestures made by Goddess feminists and cyberfeminists were, to be sure, a celebration of the feminine. But both, at root, rest on an idealization of the feminine in different modes. Goddess religion idealizes the feminine through its celebration of the functional physicality of female fertility. Cyberfeminism idealizes the feminine with its placement of imagined virtual bodies in place of real, inhabited bodies. Consequently, both Goddess religion and cyberfeminism exile the "broken-bodied" woman.

But perhaps there *could* be room for the broken-bodied woman in cyberfeminism and in traditional Goddess religions if we re-imagine them both just a bit, drawing on the wisdom produced by the analogs we have explored here. The cyberfeminist move into virtual reality itself is a utopian move—one with gritty, earthy intentions—utopian in its perfect realization of purposeful self *only* within virtual space and *only* with a wired body. If the fluid, deliberate expression of selfhood could be expanded to include *offline* reality as well, then it could make new space for non-wired, non-cyborgian, yet still audacious, erotic, and hybridized expressions of gender.

This new vision may also borrow Goddess religion's celebration of earthy, embodied womanhood, but expand it to include new audacious, hybridized, and erotic bodies: bodies without ovaries, transgendered bodies, bodies with painful or sterile wombs. Cyberfeminism's idealism about a post-dualistic world and Goddess religion's celebration of the physical female body *should* both allow embodied difference as a longstanding ideal of feminist proclamation. Braidotti alludes to this when she argues with Gilles Deleuze and Luce Irigaray that "we need to think the deep, dense materiality of bodies-in-time, so as to disengage them from the liberal bourgeois definition of the self" that is "enfleshed," "sustainable," and "limited, while having firmly departed from any reference to the 'natural' order."[76] This means, of course, that for cyberfeminism to embrace the "broken" body, it must be able to also unplug. And for Goddess religions to embrace the non-birthing broken-bodied woman, it must bring the Goddess back to Earth, but this time without a womb.

Notes

1. Aristotle, *Generation of Animals,* trans. A. L. Peck (Cambridge, MA: Harvard University Press, 1963), 465–467.
2. Rosi Braidotti, "Mothers, Monsters, and Machines," in *Writing on the Body: Female Embodiment and Feminist Theory,* ed. Katie Conboy and Nadia Medina (New York: Columbia University Press, 1997), 63.
3. Yvonne Volkart, "The Cyberfeminist Fantasy of the Pleasure of the Cyborg," in *Cyberfeminism: Next Protocols*, ed. Claudia Reiche and Verena Kuni (New York: Automedia. 2004), 99.
4. Marianne Ferguson, *Women and Religion* (Upper Saddle River, NJ: Prentice Hall, 1995), 21.
5. Monica Sjoo, *The Great Cosmic Mother* (San Francisco, CA: HarperOne, 1987), 2.
6. Merlin Stone, *When God Was a Woman* (New York: Harcourt Brace Jovanovich, 1978), 13.
7. Carol P. Christ, "Why Women Need the Goddess," in *Womanspirit Rising: A Feminist Reader on Religion* (San Francisco, CA: Harper & Row, 1979), 281.
8. Ibid., 282.
9. Ibid., 278–279.
10. See "Bitch Mutant Manifesto," www.obn.org/reading_room/manifestos/html/bitch.html.
11. Donna Haraway, "A Cyborg Manifesto: Science, Technology, and Socialist-Feminism in the Late Twentieth Century," in *Simians, Cyborgs, and Women: The Reinvention of Nature* (New York: Routledge, 1991), 181.
12. Yvonne Volkart, "The Cyberfeminist Fantasy of the Pleasure of the Cyborg," in *Cyberfeminism: Next Protocols*, ed. Claudia Reiche and Verena Kuni (New York: Autonomedia, York, 2004), 99.
13. Alla Mitrofanova, interview by Josephine Bosma April 1997, www.josephinebosma.com/web/node/55.
14. See "Cyberfeminist Manifesto for the 21st Century," www.obn.org/reading_room/manifestos/html/cyberfeminist.html.
15. Jane Caputi, "Diana Revisited," in *Goddesses and Monsters: Women, Myth, Power, and Popular Culture* (Madison, WI: University of Wisconsin/Popular, 2004), 347.
16. Ibid., 20.
17. Ibid., 356.
18. Ibid., 361.
19. Ibid., 357.
20. Ibid., 358.
21. Christ, 281.
22. Donna Wilshire, *Virgin Mother Crone: Myths and Mysteries of the Triple Goddess* (Rochester, VT: Inner Traditions, 1993), 281.
23. Ibid., 212.
24. Mary Daly, *Gyn/Ecology: The Metaethics of Radical Feminism* (Boston, MA: Beacon Press, 1990), 16.
25. Ibid., 15.
26. Mary Daly with Jane Caputi, *Webster's First New Intergalactic Wickedary of the English Language* (San Francisco, CA: HarperSanFrancisco, 1994), 156.
27. Wilshire, 212.
28. Daly, 12.

29. Mary Daly, *Pure Lust: Elemental Feminist Philosophy* (Boston, MA: Beacon Press, 1984), 280.
30. Ibid., 277, 265.
31. Ibid., 257.
32. Mary Daly, *Quintessence: Realizing the Archaic Future* (Boston, MA: Beacon Press, 1998), 11.
33. Alice Walker, *In Search of Our Mothers' Gardens: Womanist Prose* (New York: Marian Books, 2003), xi.
34. Emilie Townes, *Breaking the Fine Rain of Death: African American Health Issues and a Womanist Ethic of Care* (Eugene, OR: Wipf & Stock, 1998), 172.
35. Ibid., 2
36. Ibid., 174.
37. Emilie Townes, *Womanist Ethics and the Cultural Production of Evil* (Gordonsville, VA: Palgrave Macmillan, 2006), 164.
38. Monica Coleman, *Making a Way Out of No Way: A Womanist Theology* (Minneapolis, MN: Fortress Press, 2008), 170.
39. Ibid., 169.
40. Kelly Brown Douglas, *Sexuality and the Black Church: A Womanist Perspective* (Maryknoll, NY: Orbis Books, 1999), 118.
41. Delores Williams, *Sisters in the Wilderness: The Challenge of Womanist God-Talk* (Maryknoll, NY: Orbis Books, 1993), 160.
42. Ibid., 161.
43. bell hooks, "Reply to Cheryl J. Sanders," Part of the "Roundtable Discussion on Christian Ethics and Theology in a Womanist Perspective," *Journal of Feminist Studies in Religion.* September 1, 1989, 105.
44. Pu Xiumei, "A Womanist Reading of Di Mu (Earth Mother) and Di Mu Jing (Songs of Earth Mother) in China," in *Ain't I a Womanist Too?: Third Wave Womanist Religious Thought*, ed. Monica Coleman (Minneapolis, MN: Fortress Press, 2013), 67.
45. Ibid., 65.
46. Williams, xiv.
47. Ibid., 186.
48. Judith Butler, *Gender Trouble: Feminism and the Subversion of Identity* (New York: Routledge, 1990), 7.
49. Ibid., vii.
50. Ibid., 3.
51. Ibid., 33.
52. Butler, 31–32.
53. Ibid., 31.
54. Ibid., 33.
55. Adrienne Rich, "Compulsory Heterosexuality and Lesbian Existence" in *Feminism and Sexuality*, ed. Stevi Jackson and Sue Scott (New York: Columbia University Press, 1996), 130.
56. Ibid., 135.
57. Ibid., 136.
58. Butler., x.
59. Rosi Braidotti, "Teratologies," www.medienkunstnetz.de/quellentext/135/
60. Rosi Braidotti, "Cyberfeminism with a Difference," in *Futures of Critical Theory: Dreams of Difference* (New York: Rowman & Littlefield, 2003), 256.
61. Ibid.
62. Volkart, 100.
63. Ibid., 100–101.
64. Ibid., 101.
65. Rosi Braidotti, "Mothers, Monsters, and Machines," in *Nomadic Subjects* (New York: Columbia University Press, 1994), 85–86.

66. Kanye West, "Monster," *Late Registration* (New York: Roc-a-fella, 2005).
67. Ibid.
68. Braidiotti, "Teratologies."
69. Braidotti, "Mothers, Monsters, and Machines," 62
70. Wilshire, 212–213.
71. Starhawk, *The Spiral Dance: A Rebirth of the Ancient Religion of the Great Goddess* (San Francisco, CA: Harper Collins, 1999), 202.
72. Ibid., 20.
73. bell hooks, *Talking Back: Thinking Feminist, Thinking Black* (New York: South End Press, 1989), 108.
74. Lisa Isherwood, *The Power of Erotic Celibacy: Queering Heteropatriarchy* (London: T & T Clark. 2006), 107.
75. Jenny Marketrou, "Hacking Seductions as Art," interview by Cornelia Sollfrank. Hamburg, Germany, on July 25, 2000, www.obn.org/reading_room/interviews/down/.
76. Braidotti, "Teratologies."

Contributors

Xochitl Alvizo is a PhD candidate in Practical Theology at Boston University and is co-founder and daily project weaver of *Feminism and Religion*.

C. Yvonne Augustine is a doctoral student in Religion at Claremont Lincoln University and co-founder of the blog Feminist Philosopher.

Kristina Benson is a PhD candidate in Islamic Studies at UCLA and Visiting Instructor at Pitzer College.

Carol P. Christ is Director of Ariadne Institute in Greece. She blogs regularly at *Feminism and Religion* and is author of *Rebirth of the Goddess* (1997) and the *She Who Changes* (2003).

Monica A. Coleman is Associate Professor of Constructive Theology and African American Religions and Co-Director for Process Studies at Claremont School of Theology and Claremont Lincoln University. She is the author of multiple articles and books, including *Not Alone* (2012) and *Making a Way Out of No Way* (2008).

Elise M. Edwards is Lecturer in Christian Ethics at Baylor University and she regularly blogs at *Feminism and Religion*.

Michele Stopera Freyhauf is a PhD candidate in Theology and Religion at Durham University. She regularly blogs at *Feminism and Religion* and teaches at John Carroll University.

Sara M. Frykenberg is visiting professor at Mount Saint Mary's College and she regularly blogs at *Feminism and Religion*.

Brett C. Hoover is Assistant Professor in the Department of Theological Studies at Loyola Marymount University. He is the author of *The Shared Parish: Latinos, Anglos, and the Future of U.S. Catholicism* (2014), and co-founder of BustedHalo.com.

Mary E. Hunt is co-founder and co-director of the Women's Alliance for Theology, Ethics and Ritual (WATER). She is the editor of *A Guide for Women in Religion: Making Your Way from A to Z* (2004), and co-editor of *New Feminist Christianity: Many Voices, Many Views* (2010).

Grace Yia-Hei Kao is Associate Professor of Ethics at Claremont School of Theology and the Co-Director of its Center for Sexuality, Gender, and Religion. She is the author of *Grounding Human Rights in a Pluralist World* (2011).

Caroline Kline is completing her PhD in Religion at Claremont Graduate University. She is co-editor of *Mormon Women Have Their Say: Essays from the Claremont Oral History Collection* (2013), and co-founder of the Mormon feminist blog *The Exponent*.

Gina Messina-Dysert is Dean of the School of Graduate and Professional Studies at Ursuline College and Co-Founder of *Feminism and Religion*. She is author of *Rape Culture and Spiritual Violence* (2014), and co-editor of *Feminism and Religion in the 21st Century: Technology, Diaologue, and Expanding Borders* (2014).

Kate M. Ott is Assistant Professor of Christian Social Ethics at Drew University Theological School. She is author of *Sex + Faith: A Progressive Christian Parent's Guide from Toddlerhood through the Teenage Years* (2013), and co-editor of *Faith, Feminism, and Scholarship: The Next Generation* (2011).

Rosemary Radford Ruether is Professor of Feminist Theology at Claremont Graduate University and Claremont School of Theology. She is author of multiple books, including *Sexism and God-Talk* (1993), *Women and Redemption: A Theological History, 2nd ed* (2011), and *My Quests for Hope and Meaning: An Autobiography* (2013).

Sarah Scott is an MA student of Philosophy and Religion at California Institute of Integral Studies.

Margaret M. Toscano is an Associate Professor of Classics and Comparative Literary and Cultural Studies at the University of Utah. She is author of *Strangers in Paradox: Essays in Mormon Theology* (1990), and co-editor of *Hell and Its Afterlife: Historical and Contemporary Perspectives* (2010).

Rachel Wagner is Associate Professor of Religion and Culture at Ithaca College, and author of *Godwired: Religion, Ritual and Virtual Reality* (2011).

Bracha Yael completed an MA in Women's Studies in Religion at Claremont Graduate University. She leads the "Telephone Minyan" at her Los Angeles synagogue Beth Chayim Chadashim (BCC).

Index